AF746857

Donated by
Ian Thomson

Not for loan

WITHDRAWN

EDC

Basic Info S

CORE COLLECTION

28 APR 2005

Monetary Union in Europe

djøf FORLAG
JURIST- OG ØKONOMFORBUNDETS FORLAG
LYNGBYVEJ 17, POSTBOKS 2702
2100 KØBENHAVN Ø - TLF 39 13 55 00

Peter Birch Sørensen (ed.)

Monetary Union in Europe

Historical perspectives and prospects for the future

Essays in honour of Niels Thygesen

DJØF Publishing Copenhagen
2004

Monetary Union in Europe
Historical perspectives and prospects for the future
Essays in honour of Niels Thygensen
First edition 2004

© 2004 by Jurist- og Økonomforbundets Forlag
DJØF Publishing Copenhagen

DJØF Publishing is a company of the
Association of Danish Lawyers and Economists

All rights reserved.
No part of this publication may be reproduced,
stored in a retrieval system, or transmitted in
any form or by any means – electronic, mechanical,
photocopying, recording or otherwise – without
the prior written permission of the publisher.

Photo: Rigmor Mydtskov
Cover Design: Morten Højmark
Print: Narayana Press, Gylling
Binding: Jysk Bogbind, Holstebro

Printed in Denmark 2004
ISBN 87-574-1117-4

DJØF Publishing
17 Lyngbyvej
P.O.B. 2702
DK-2100 Copenhagen Ø
Denmark

Telephone: +45 3913 5500
Telefax: +45 3913 5555
E-mail: fl@djoef.dk
Internet: www.djoef-forlag.dk

Table of Contents

Acknowledgements

The present book, based on contributions to a conference held in honour of Niels Thygesen at the University of Copenhagen on December 10, 2004, is published with financial support from the Institute of Economics, University of Copenhagen, Danmarks Nationalbank, and the Danish Economic Association (Nationaløkonomisk Forening). The support from these institutions is gratefully acknowledged.

The author, the editor and the publisher are indebted to Blackwell Publishing Ltd. for granting permission to use, in chapter 16, the article by Tommaso Padoa-Schioppa, previously published in *International Finance*, July 2004.

List of contributors

Edmond Alphandéry
Professor Emeritus and former Minister of Economic Affairs for France

Gunter Baer,
Secretary General, Bank for International Settlements

Giorgio Basevi
Professor of Economics, University of Bologna

Lorenzo Bini Smaghi
Director, Italian Ministry of the Economy and Finances

Roman Frydman
Professor of Economics, New York University

Michael Goldberg
Professor of Economics, University of New Hampshire

Charles A. E. Goodhart
Professor of Economics, London School of Economics and Political Science

Paul De Grauwe
Professor of Economics, Leuven University

Daniel Gros
Director, Centre for European Policy Research, Brussels

Boris Hofmann
Senior Fellow, ZEI, University of Bonn

Alexandre Lamfalussy
Professor Emeritus and former President of the European Monetary Institute

Francesco Paolo Mongelli
Adviser, DG Economics, European Central Bank and Visiting Professor, University of Frankfurt

Mario Monti
Professor of Economics, Bocconi University, and former Member of the European Commission

Tommaso Padoa-Schioppa
Member of the Executive Board, European Central Bank

Lorenzo Pecchi
Lecturer at the University of Rome – Tor Vergata

Gustavo Piga
Professor of Economics, University of Rome – Tor Vergata

Luigi Spaventa
Professor of Economics, University of Rome – Tor Vergata

Guido Tabellini
Professor of Economics, Bocconi University, Milan

Charles Wyplosz
Professor of Economics, Graduate Institute of International Economics, Geneva, and CEPR

INTRODUCTION

Niels Thygesen and European Monetary Integration

*Peter Birch Sørensen**

December 13, 2004 marks the 70th birthday of Niels Thygesen. By the end of the year he will therefore retire from his Chair as Professor of Economics at the University of Copenhagen. On that occasion a number of Niels' international friends and colleagues gathered in Copenhagen on December 10, 2004 for a conference to pay tribute to Niels and to discuss a topic close to his heart: *Monetary Union in Europe – Historical Perspectives and Prospects for the Future*. The conference was organized by the Institute of Economics, University of Copenhagen, in collaboration with Danmarks Nationalbank and with the Danish Economic Association. This book volume contains the proceedings from the conference.

The present introduction is not the appropriate place to offer a complete overview of Niels Thygesen's writings and career, for the simple reason that his career is not over yet. Reflecting his physical and intellectual vitality, Niels will fortunately continue many of his current activities. However, given the theme of this book, Niels' 70th birthday is a natural occasion to take stock of some of his many contributions to the process of European monetary cooperation, as an academic and policy economist. Below I shall try to do so, although I will undoubtedly be unable to do

* Without implicating them in any remaining errors or shortcomings, I wish to thank Daniel Gros, Peter Erling Nielsen and Jens Thomsen for comments on an earlier draft of this paper.

full justice to Niels' achievements, given my limited knowledge and the limited space available.

Niels Thygesen's Early Career

A hallmark of Niels Thygesen's work has been his continued emphasis on the application of economic research to the solution of real world policy problems, and his strong dedication to the promotion of European and international economic cooperation.

Graduating from the University of Copenhagen with an M.Sc. in Economics in 1960, Niels spent the following academic year at Harvard University from which he obtained a master degree in Public Administration in 1961. He then served for a few years as Staff Economist in the Danish Ministry of Economic Affairs, but in 1964 his academic interests led him back to an Associate Professorship at the University of Copenhagen. There he spent the following years working on his treatise on *The Sources and the Impact of Monetary Changes* which earned him the degree of State Doctorate in Economics (Dr. polit.) and enabled him to obtain a chair as Professor of Economics in 1971.

However, Niels' interest in policy advice and policy making remained strong. In the period 1969-71 he served for two years as an Economic Advisor to the Treasury of Malaysia, sponsored by the Harvard Development Advisory Service, and already in 1971 he obtained a two-year leave from his professorship to act as Head of the Monetary Division of the OECD until 1973.

In the following years, while maintaining the University of Copenhagen as his base, Niels participated in numerous international committees and study groups offering (often highly influential) policy advice. I shall return to some of these activities below, but before then it is worthwhile to briefly describe the intellectual ballast which Niels carried with him.

Intellectual Ballast

Niels' formative years coincided with the great Keynesian-monetarist debate from the late 1950s to the mid-1970s. During my own years as a student of Economics in the second half of the 1970s, Niels was regarded by most of his colleagues and students as a prototype monetarist. However, during his year of postgraduate study in the United States, Niels had actually taken classes from prominent Keynesians like James Duesenberry, Franco Modigliani and Albert Ando, and in the preface to his treatise (Thygesen, 1971) he acknowledges an important intellectual debt to these scholars. Although he became increasingly influenced by monetarist thought, he was never a dogmatist in the often heated Keynesian-monetarist controversy.

It is testimony to Niels' high international standing as a monetary economist that, when Milton Friedman was granted the Nobel Prize in Economics, the Nobel Foundation asked Niels to write an overview and evaluation of Friedman's scientific contributions (see Thygesen, 1977). Apart from giving an excellent review of Friedman's work, this well-written article also suggests which parts of the monetarist heritage that Niels considered to be most valuable. Niels clearly shared Friedman's scepticism regarding the possibility of fine tuning aggregate demand through activist policies, the preference for simple and transparent policy rules over discretion, and the emphasis on the benefits of price stability. Niels also accepted Friedman's proposition that there is no long run trade-off between inflation and unemployment.

However, Niels did not endorse Friedman's methodological proposition that theories should never be assessed on the basis of the realism of their assumptions, but only on the basis of the usefulness of their predictions. As Niels pointed out: "The possibilities of verifying either the assumptions or the implications of economic theory are limited. In such circumstances one should be reluctant to discard any possibilities of assessing a theory even in the indirect form of subjecting the assumptions to the test of 'realism'" (Thygesen, 1977, p. 58).

Furthermore, Niels never shared Friedman's optimistic view of a flexible exchange rate system where currency speculation is stabilizing and where endogenous nominal exchange rate adjustment works as a powerful shock absorber (see Friedman, 1953). On the contrary, Niels has always been sceptical of flexible exchange rates, for reasons to which I shall return later.

The Marjolin Report

In 1970 a group of high officials delivered the so-called Werner report containing a plan for a transition to Economic and Monetary Union in the European Community, with the final stage to be reached by 1980. The growing divergence of national inflation rates following the breakdown of the Bretton Woods system and the first oil price shock of 1973 quickly made the Werner plan seem highly unrealistic.

Against this background the European Commission decided in the winter of 1973-74 to have a group of independent experts study whether introducing EMU by 1980 was still possible. The group was headed by Robert Marjolin, former Secretary General of the OEEC and the Vice-President for Economic Affairs of the first European Commission established in 1958. The group included, among others, economists such as Herbert Giersch from Germany and Sir Donald McDougall from Great Britain. Niels Thygesen was also asked to join the Marjolin Group.

It is somewhat ironic that Niels, always a strong believer in the ultimate goal of a European monetary union, actually started his work on this issue as a member of the Marjolin Group which published a very sceptical report in April 1975, dismissing the possibility of realizing EMU by 1980. It is clear from Thygesen (2000, p. 29) that Niels himself actually held a more optimistic view. However, the group was dominated by scepticists, including Robert Marjolin himself who, although a dedicated European, apparently believed that a durable monetary union could not be established until some sort of political union had been achieved. The Marjolin Group therefore recommended that European governments should concentrate on solving the immediate problems of inflation, balance of payments deficits and unemployment.

The All Saints' Day Manifesto

Soon after having signed up to the Marjolin Report, Niels put his name under a rather different and radical plan for a transition to a common European currency. In the famous *All Saints' Day Manifesto* (Basevi et al., 1975), published in *The Economist* on November 1, 1975, a group of nine liberal academic economists, including Giorgio Basevi, Michele Fratianni,

Herbert Giersch and Michael Parkin, among others, proposed that the EEC central banks should issue a European currency of constant purchasing power in parallel to their own national currencies. Specifically, this new parallel currency, the Europa, would be allowed to appreciate against the national currencies in such a way that its purchasing power measured in terms of a weighted average of national consumer price indices would remain constant. Moreover, households and firms would be free to use either the Europa or the national currencies in their transactions.

The proposal was based on the Hayekian idea that, because of its superior quality as a store of value, the Europa would gradually drive the inflation-prone national currencies out of the market. In this way the European public would be induced to voluntarily adopt a common currency. As the signatories to the Manifesto put it: "Our emphasis on the use of market forces stems from our conviction that it is difficult to bring about a monetary union by official edict or by the establishment of grandiose institutions, no matter how well intentioned." One wonders whether Niels was really in full agreement with this statement; it is certainly a fact that he soon came to believe much more in the usefulness of institution-building on the road to EMU. But perhaps he felt that, in the unfavourable economic and political climate of the mid-1970s, a market-based parallel currency approach was the only realistic way of making progress towards monetary unification.

From today's perspective it is interesting to note the strong emphasis in the Manifesto on the need for central bank independence: "To preserve the benefits of the monetary reform, i.e., the benefits which derive from a stable-valued money, monetary authorities should be given the same independence from political power and the same responsibilities to the rule of law we have accorded the judicial system." This idea of the value of central bank independence is one that Niels carried with him during the following years.

A quarter-century after the publication of the *All Saints' Day Manifesto* Niels wrote: "The proposal was arguably naïve and excessively brutal. It seems unlikely that European governments could ever have agreed to the joint issue of a completely stable currency in competition with their own much weaker ones; that would no doubt have been perceived as too risky" (Thygesen, 2000, p. 40). On the same occasion Niels also acknowledged a major weakness of the scheme: once the new Europa had fully replaced the national currencies, its purchasing power could no longer automatically be held constant via the technical rule for its appreciation against the national monies. At that stage the maintenance of constant purchasing power would require careful management of the supply of the Europa, and the need to build common European monetary institutions for this purpose would reassert itself.

Despite this weakness, the liberal idea of introducing a parallel currency remained popular in many circles for many years, particularly in Great Britain.

The OPTICA Reports

The period following the first oil price shock of the 1970s was marked by clear tendencies towards monetary disintegration and even a tendency towards increasing trade barriers in Europe. The two floating currencies of Britain and Italy were highly unstable and tended to fluctuate a lot more than what seemed justified by fundamentals. Further, in 1976 France withdrew from the 'currency snake', established in 1972 as a modest attempt to preserve some exchange rate stability in Europe in the aftermath of the breakdown of the Bretton Woods system. On top of all this, several currency realignments within the snake had to be improvised at short notice as national inflation rates continued to diverge, and high rates of unemployment tempted deficit countries to try to escape from the external constraint on expansionary policies by introducing protectionist measures such as national regulations favouring domestic over imported products.

In this environment the prospect of monetary union seemed as remote as ever, but policy makers in the European Commission struggled to create at least some momentum towards enhanced monetary and exchange rate cooperation. For this purpose the Commission established two groups of independent experts who were given the mandate to propose new approaches to European monetary unification. The work of the experts led to the two so-called OPTICA – OPTImum Currency Area – reports of 1976-77 (Commission, 1976, 1977). Niels Thygesen and Giorgio Basevi were members of both OPTICA groups; the second group also included Paul De Grauwe, among others.

The final OPTICA report of 1977 is well summarized in Thygesen (1978). As an echo of the *All Saints' Day Manifesto,* the last chapter of the report restated the case for introducing a European Parallel Currency as a way of harmonizing inflation rates at a low level and moving towards a common currency. However, the authors of the report also recognized that governments would hardly be prepared in the foreseeable future to run the risk of allowing the role of their national monies to shrink significantly as a result of competition with a parallel currency of superior quality. Hence much of the report focused on developing a new strategy for the management of the exchange rates between the existing national currencies.

As a background for its policy recommendations, the final OPTICA report included empirical studies of the historical relationship between inflation differentials and exchange rate changes (essentially a study of the validity of the theory of relative purchasing power parity) and the potential role of devaluation in short run macroeconomic adjustment. The report found that in the long run nominal exchange rate changes closely reflected inflation differentials when prices are measured in terms of the wholesale price index. In other words, in the long run devaluations are approximately neutral. Today this proposition is widely accepted, but in the 1970s where many (perhaps most) policy makers believed that the inflationary pressure following a devaluation could somehow be contained through "incomes policies", this neutrality proposition was a lot more controversial.

Importantly, the OPTICA report also concluded on the basis of econometric model simulations that devaluations were not a very effective instrument for current account adjustment. Given the high degree of trade integration in Europe, the increases in import prices induced by a devaluation would be rather quickly transmitted to the domestic price level, so the effect of nominal exchange rate adjustment on the real exchange rate would soon be neutralized. This finding that nominal exchange rate flexibility seems of little help in ensuring real macroeconomic adjustment in the Western European context undoubtedly helps to explain why Niels has always been in favour of moving towards a European system of fully fixed exchange rates, i.e. monetary union.

Against the background of these empirical studies the OPTICA report recommended that, as long as harmonization of national inflation rates at a low level could not be achieved through closer policy coordination, the necessary periodic adjustments of nominal exchange rates within the EC should be based on a PPP rule according to which exchange rate realignments should aim only at neutralizing the effects of inflation differentials on the competitiveness of individual member countries. In other words, "aggressive" realignments aimed at engineering real exchange rate changes should be avoided. By following a PPP rule, policy makers would have an objective indicator and guideline for exchange rate management, paving the way for greater predictability and stability of Europe's monetary affairs.

Seen in retrospect, the OPTICA report is interesting for its emphasis on the benefits of a simple fixed rule for exchange rate management. Today it is widely (although not universally) accepted that policy rules can play a useful role by imposing policy discipline and increasing the predictability of economic policy, thereby limiting welfare-reducing expectational errors in the private sector. But back in the 1970s, discretionary policies improvised at short notice was the typical pattern of reaction to the need for macroeconomic adjustment.

The European Monetary System

Although the PPP rule proposed by the OPTICA group was never formally adopted, in some respects events did start to move in the direction suggested by the group. The group had emphasized the need for recurrent nominal exchange rate adjustments as long as governments were not willing to engage in tighter macroeconomic policy coordination. It had also stressed the need for more regular consultations on and a more systematic analytical basis for exchange rate management, as a way of escaping from some of the drama and ad hocery associated with the necessary realignments. From the summer of 1977 the Commission did in fact begin to submit to the EC Monetary Committee at regular intervals analytical papers on recent trends and prospects in exchange markets and balance of payments, and in 1977 and 1978 a number of realignments within the snake were implemented in a fairly smooth and harmonious way.

Furthermore, the idea that focus on some objective indicator (such as deviations from relative PPP) was necessary to trigger automatically discussions of policy coordination remained in the air. This became clear when the European Monetary System (EMS) was launched on January 1, 1979.

In Thygesen (1979) Niels describes the formation of the EMS as a "quantum jump in ambitions" which took most observers by surprise. Apparently the EMS was very much a creation emerging from private consultations between French President Valéry Giscard D'Estaing and German Chancellor Helmut Schmidt, and according to Niels it was only after the Bremen meeting of the European Council in July 1978 that officialdom in the Community discovered the willingness of the key political players to take a large step forward in monetary cooperation.

Apart from adding France, Italy and Ireland to the fixed exchange rate system, the EMS established a role for the ECU as an indicator of divergence in intra-EC currency relationships. Divergence beyond a certain limit would automatically trigger consultations among the EMS countries aimed either at reducing divergence through intervention or policy coordination or at adjusting the central exchange rate parities. Clearly this reliance on the ECU was different from a PPP rule, but it did represent a response to the call for an objective indicator serving to initiate policy coordination.

The history of the EMS has been excellently described in Gros and Thygesen (1998) and will not be summarized here. Let me just note that Niels seems to have greeted the launching of the EMS with enthusiasm, even though it was based on the kind of institution-building of which the *All Saints' Day Manifesto* had expressed great scepticism. Most of Niels' co-signatories to the Manifesto were critical of the EMS emphasis on enhanced central bank cooperation which they tended to label a central bank cartel, unlikely to have the same anti-inflationary effect as unfettered competition between national currencies and a parallel European currency. Indeed, these liberals feared that the members of the "central bank cartel" would have an incentive to inflate together (Thygesen, 2000, p. 40). In retrospect we know that this fear was unfounded: after 1982-83 inflation convergence towards the low German level was put high on the agenda of the EMS.

The Delors Report

As the EMS firmed up and exchange rate realignments became ever less frequent during the 1980s, the prospect of a full scale monetary union began to seem less unrealistic than perceived in the 1970s and early 1980s. In 1986 Niels joined a self-established Committee for Monetary Union – the so-called Giscard-Schmidt Committee – which advocated moving towards full monetary unification in Europe. To the surprise of many observers, European top decision makers responded positively, and in 1988 the European Council nominated a committee led by Commission President Jacques Delors to prepare a first outline of how an Economic and Monetary Union should work. Apart from Jacques Delors, the committee included the 12 governors of central banks in the then Member States, plus Frans Andriessen, Miguel Bayer, Alexandre Lamfalussy, and Niels Thygesen.

Among the many high points in Niels' career, his appointment to the Delors Committee – as the only academic member – was probably his finest hour as a policy economist. It certainly demonstrated the high status he had achieved as an expert on European and international monetary affairs. As we all know, the report by the Delors Committee (Committee for the Study of EMU, 1989) became immensely influential as a basis for the negotiations leading to the Maastricht Treaty of 1992 which laid out the institutional framework for the EMU. All the essential features of the EMU designed in Maastricht were inherited from the Delors Report: the transition to monetary union in three stages, the reliance on convergence criteria during the transition, the transfer of monetary policy authority in Stage III to an independent European Central Bank committed to the prime goal of price stability, the need to go all the way to a common currency and not just to complete locking of exchange rates, and the need for fiscal rules to prevent excessive public budget deficits and debt.

The Delors Report itself was rather brief, but it was supplemented by a number of background papers written partly by some of the committee members, and partly by outside experts, including Gunter Baer, Willem Duisenberg, and Tommaso Padoa-Schioppa, among others. Niels was the author of a background paper on "A European central banking system – Some analytical and operational considerations" (Thygesen, 1988). Among other things, this paper identifies price stability as the prime ultimate goal of a common European monetary policy and suggests that "price stability" be defined as a rate of inflation in the range between 0 and 2 percent. Niels' paper also suggests that keeping the growth rate of a monetary aggregate within a targeted interval should be an important intermediate objective for the European Central Bank.

A paper on the EMS and the road to monetary union written by Niels and his long time friend and collaborator Daniel Gros (Gros and Thygesen, 1988), coming out of a CEPS Working Group chaired by Niels, also appears to have had significant influence on the deliberations of the Delors Committee. The final part of this paper discusses the design of monetary institutions in a future monetary union, recommending central bank independence, and advocating a federal structure for a future European system of central banks. These views were very much reflected in the Delors report.

Thus Niels has clearly left his mark on European monetary institutions. Even abstracting from all his other contributions to international economic cooperation, his membership of the Delors Committee alone suffices to make him the most influential policy economist Denmark has ever produced.

The Robert Marjolin Lecture

In 1998 Niels Thygesen was invited to give the Robert Marjolin Lecture at the Frankfurt Colloquium of the Société Universitaire Européenne de Recherches Financières (SUERF). This lecture, later published in Thygesen (2000), draws in large part on Niels' authoritative book with Daniel Gros on European monetary integration (Gros and Thygesen, 1998). It provides a nice overview of the road to monetary union in Europe as well as a succinct statement on Niels' own views on the rationale for monetary union and the specific design given to it in Maastricht. It is therefore worthwhile to briefly summarize the main points of Niels' Marjolin Lecture.

The lecture identifies five evolving ambitions in Europe's monetary unification: 1) reducing, then eliminating nominal exchange-rate fluctuations, 2) reducing, then eliminating inflation, 3) developing rules for non-monetary national policies, then scope for coordinating them without undermining the rules, 4) developing a potential role for the EMU institutions in the international monetary system, and 5) developing a European profile in financial regulation.

With the advent of the euro, the first ambition has already been achieved. With some regret, Niels notes that many academic economists, drawing on optimum currency area theory, have found it hard to accept this ambition as reasonable in economic terms. Not surprisingly, Niels argues that this scepticism is misplaced, reflecting an overoptimistic view of the alternatives to EMU and an exaggeration of the importance of asymmetric shocks. The alternatives to EMU would be either a system of fixed exchange rates á la EMS or floating exchange rates possibly combined with national inflation targets. As for the first alternative, Niels points to the well-known vulnerability of a fixed exchange rate system to speculative attacks in a world of high capital mobility. With regard to the second alternative, Niels acknowledges that several countries with floating exchange rates have managed to keep inflation low in recent years through a regime of inflation targeting, but they have also tended to experience significant exchange rate volatility. According to Niels, the academic literature has tended to underestimate the real economic costs of such volatility as well as the gains (in terms of increased economic integration) from introducing a common currency. As for asymmetric shocks, Niels' empirical work with Daniel Gros suggests that asymmetric export shocks have had little impact on changes in employment in the EU countries. Moreover, given the low short run price elasticities in foreign trade, it would take dramatic changes in real exchange rates to achieve a noticeable short run effect on unemployment in the typical EU country (Gros and Thygesen, 1998). On this basis Niels argues that giving up the exchange rate instrument makes only a modest difference to the macroeconomic performance of the EU economies.

Niels proceeds to note that the second ambition of eliminating inflation has also largely been achieved as a result of the transition to EMU, and with the establishment of a European Central Bank committed to price stability. Citing work by Feldstein (1996), Niels argues that even reducing inflation from a low level to zero would bring non-trivial welfare gains, e.g., by eliminating the distortionary effects of a nominal tax system (he does not address the concern that by reducing inflation all the way down to zero, monetary policy makers face a greater risk of being constrained by the zero bound on the nominal interest rate in case of a large negative shock).

Turning to the third ambition, that of developing rules for non-monetary policies and subsequently coordinating them, Niels reports that the discussions in the Delors Committee convinced him of the need for upper limits to budget deficits in a monetary union, and he is a staunch supporter of the Maastricht criteria for sound fiscal policy. He also argues that apart from monitoring adherence to such upper limits, the ECOFIN Council should also try to coordinate national budgetary policies with the purpose of attaining an appropriate aggregate policy stance and policy mix for the euro area as a whole. With the current crisis of the Stability and Growth Pact in mind, the EU is obviously still far from having achieved this ambition.

The same thing may be said about the ambition to develop a role for the euro and the EMU institutions in the international monetary system. Niels argues that in order to reinforce the international monetary system, Europe should cooperate more efficiently with the United States to contain international financial instability and to improve the international financial architecture. In part the EMU can contribute to this goal by pursuing stability-oriented macro policies characterized by an appropriate overall policy stance and policy mix. But Niels also argues that to strengthen its bargaining position and facilitate coordination, Europe needs to appoint a "State Secretary for International Economic Affairs" who could represent the EU in international fora such as the G8 and the Executive Board and the Interim Committee of the IMF.

As for the need to develop a European profile in financial supervision, Niels acknowledges that this is not a universally agreed ambition for the EMU, but according to him it *should* be an ambition. At the moment, responsibility for financial stability in the EMU remains in the hands of national authorities. This creates a need for coordination across Member States and between supervisors and the European system of central banks. In particular, Niels argues for a clarification of the allocation of responsibilities for lender-of-last-resort operations in crisis situations.

The themes discussed in Niels' Marjolin lecture are of obvious importance and they are further developed in many of the contributions to this book volume.

The Outward-Looking European

Although most of Niels' work has been devoted to the analysis and promotion of European monetary integration, he has always taken a strong interest in international economic affairs reaching beyond Europe: he is a prime example of an outward-looking European. I have already mentioned his early activities as an Economic Advisor to the government of Malaysia and his work at the OECD in the early 1970s where he provided an overview of the experience with monetary policy in six major industrial countries (see Thygesen and Shigehara, 1975). Since 1981 Niels has also been a member of the Executive Committee of the Trilateral Commission, dedicated to the promotion of cooperation between the United States, Europe and Japan.

As a Senior Research Fellow of the Brussels-based Centre for European Policy Studies (CEPS), Niels contributed to the activities of the Quadrangular Forum, a group of governmental and non-governmental leaders from Canada, Japan, the United States, and Western Europe, which was formed in 1982-83 to promote understanding and cooperation between the countries participating in the world economic summits. In Thygesen (1984) Niels proposed an agenda for the 1984 World Economic Summit in London, against the background of widely divergent fiscal policies in Europe and the United States. This paper is characteristic of the type of policy problems which Niels has repeatedly addressed over the years. Specifically, Niels' paper proposed four items for the agenda of the London Summit. The first was a two-stage strategy for joint management of the (then) prospective decline of the dollar and of the more stable exchange rate system which would subsequently emerge. This is a clear reflection of Niels' long-standing scepticism towards freely floating exchange rates: in the absence of some sort of exchange rate management, floating exchange rates may often become seriously misaligned relative to any reasonable measure of a long run equilibrium rate. The second item on Niels' proposed agenda was the constellation of US and European monetary policies that would move exchange rates in the right direction. The third was a more systematic approach to the international debt problem (rather acute in the early 1980s), and the fourth was a shift in the European monetary-fiscal policy mix intended to reduce international macroeconomic imbalances. Niels promoted this as a program for "damage limitation", while in fact it seems to have been a call for a much more serious approach to international (or, rather, cross-Atlantic) policy coordination than the one existing at the time (and, sad to say, existing today).

In 1998-99 Niels was appointed as one out of three independent experts to prepare a critical review of the experience of twelve IMF member countries with IMF advice and to make proposals for enhanced surveillance. The review was solicited against the backdrop of the East Asian financial crisis of 1997-98 and gave Niels some interesting insights into the background for as well as the handling of the crisis. According to the IMF about 20 of the 29 recommendations made in the report by Niels and his two co-examiners of IMF surveillance have now been implemented.

Since July 2000 Niels has served as Chairman of the OECD Economic Development and Review Committee (EDRC) which conducts surveillance of economic performance and policies in OECD member countries, leading to the publication of the well-known OECD country surveys. This task involves chairing 2-3 one-day meetings a month in Paris, where it falls upon Niels to summarize the proceedings with a view to sharpening the policy conclusions. For those of us who have experienced Niels' eminent ability to extract and elegantly summarize the essence of a discussion, there is no doubt that he does an excellent job as Chair of the EDRC, a function in which he will continue to serve after his retirement from the University of Copenhagen.

Services to Danish Society

One might think that, given all his international activities, Niels has hardly had any time to tend to his home front in Copenhagen. This conjecture is wrong. Reflecting Niels' immense capacity for work, he has done numerous services to his home institution. From 1973 to 1977 he was Chairman of the Institute of Economics, and he has regularly taught highly popular graduate courses in Monetary Theory and Policy and International Monetary Economics.

Moreover, for more than a quarter century he supervised about 20 Master's theses and 2-3 Ph.D. theses per year. Indeed, during all these years Niels personally accounted for a major fraction of all the supervision of Master's students carried out at the Institute of Economics. Yet all of this work never became mere routine for him. He has always been ready and eager to encourage and support young talents, and he still chairs numerous committees and foundations allocating scholarships to students and young scholars. He has a remarkable ability to remember details about each individual student, and he has followed the careers of his most talented students with great interest. Literally speaking he must have written hundreds of letters of recommendation in support of his students.

I have personally benefited from Niels' positive attitude towards younger scholars. When a group of younger colleagues and I approached Niels in the early 1990s, inviting him to become a co-founder of the Economic Policy Research Unit (EPRU), he immediately gave strong support to the project. There is no doubt that his high standing helped to attract the important grant which EPRU obtained from the Danish National Research Foundation.

Niels has also made several public service contributions to Danish society. From 1972 to 1983 he served as Advisor to the Danish Central Bank and its Governor, and he has served on three Danish government committees over the years. In particular, he chaired an important committeeI on the regulation of bank profits in 1977-78. In addition, he was Co-chairman of the Danish Economic Council in 1983-85, where he helped to prepare an extensive report on Danish monetary policy, and he was President of the Danish Economic Association 1974-79. On top of all this, Niels found time to serve as President of the National Olympic Committee of Denmark between 1984 and 1988 and to sit on the board of several Danish companies.

This may sound like a description of a true workaholic, but in fact Niels always seems very relaxed and at ease with himself. For many years he never travelled abroad without bringing his golf clubs. But golf was not always pure relaxation for him; he actually won the Danish golf championship several times. The story goes that when he was advising the Malaysian government, he had no trouble getting quick access to the top decision makers: he just published his golf handicap in the local golf club, thereby immediately attracting the interest of the local elite!

A Man of His Time, and often Ahead of His Time

Although Niels is in many respects a gentleman of the old school, it seems to me that he has always been very much a man of his time. For him European monetary unification is not just an interesting topic for academic research; it is also a project which he has actively tried to promote for more than three decades, deeply convinced of its beneficial economic and political effects. Even those colleagues who have not shared his enthusiasm for EMU have always respected the consistency and clarity with which he has argued the case for monetary union. When the EMU became a reality on January 1, 1999, it must have been immensely gratifying to Niels. He is a rare example of an idealist whose dream has come true. If his own country, Denmark, ever decides to join the EMU, his triumph will be complete.

But Niels is not only a man of his time; he has often been ahead of his time. As a policy-oriented economist, Niels has focused on applied economic research, but with his strong intuition it appears that he has sometimes anticipated important results or approaches which were subsequently given a stronger theoretical rationale by other scholars. For example, in his doctoral treatise (essentially finished in 1968) Niels experimented with the estimation of reaction functions for Danish monetary policy to see if a systematic policy pattern could be uncovered. Of course, nowadays the estimation of policy reaction functions is standard practice, but this was not the case back in the 1960s.

Much of Niels' later work also reveals a strong interest in policy rules, not just as a description of actual policy, but also as a normative prescription intended to improve macroeconomic performance. Some of this work, such as the analysis carried out in the OPTICA groups, precedes the theoretical rationale for rules rather than discretion offered by Kydland and Prescott (1977) and others.

Closely related to his interest in policy rules, Niels was always preoccupied with the design of monetary policy institutions. As far as I can see, he had an intuitive grasp of the problem of establishing the credibility of an announced anti-inflationary policy long before Barro and Gordon (1982) offered a coherent theoretical explanation for the inflation bias in monetary policy. For example, I have mentioned the emphasis in the *All Saints' Day Manifesto* on the importance of central bank independence.

This suggests that a decade before Rogoff (1985) provided the theoretical foundation for the delegation of monetary policy, Niels and his collaborators had an intuitive understanding of the value of delegation. It should be added that while Niels was an early defender of central bank independence, there was never any doubt in his mind that monetary policy makers should be held democratically accountable for their actions. In Thygesen (1979) he sketches a procedure whereby the Monetary Committee of the EC would report at regular intervals on monetary and exchange rate developments to the new directly elected European Parliament. In other words, long before "accountability" became a buzzword, Niels made very concrete proposals to promote it.

As far as the European integration process is concerned, Niels also anticipated trends that went unnoticed by most others. I have personally attended several meetings and conferences in the 1980s and in the early 1990s where the prospect of a European monetary union was dismissed as a mere hallucination. On some of these occasions Niels was also present, and he repeatedly warned against underestimating the political will among key European decision makers to move towards monetary unification. In the end it turned out that Niels was right. Again, a rare example of a social scientist whose predictions were correct!

Outline of This Book

The papers in this book deal with issues with which Niels has long been preoccupied. The chapters in Part I discuss the rationale for limiting exchange rate fluctuations and provide an overview and interpretation of the experience with the European Monetary System. Part II contains a series of chapters describing and evaluating the experience with the first five years of the Eurosystem. Parts III and IV address the "unfinished business" of the EMU. The contributions in Part III discuss the fiscal framework of the EMU against the background of the current crisis for the Stability and Growth Pact, while Part IV focuses on the framework needed to secure financial stability. The final Part V discusses the implications of Europe's experience with monetary unification for other regions, specifically East Asia.

The authors of the papers in this book are colleagues and friends of Niels Thygesen who have all made important contributions to European or international monetary cooperation, either through the insights gained via their academic research, or as key policy makers. On the occasion of Niels' 70th birthday I say on behalf of all the contributors: Hail Niels Thygesen, a great colleague and a great European!

References

Barro, Robert J. and David B. Gordon (1983), "A Positive Theory of Monetary Policy in a Natural Rate Model", Journal of Political Economy 91, pp. 589-610.
Basevi, Giorgio et al. (1975), The All Saints Day Manifesto, The Economist, November 1, 1975.
Commission of the European Communities (1975), *Report of the Study Group 'Economic and Monetary Union 1980'* (Marjolin report).
Commission of the European Communities (1976), *Towards Economic Equilibrium and Monetary Unification in Europe* (OPTICA report I).
Commission of the European Communities (1977), *Inflation and Exchange Rates: Evidence and Policy Guidelines for the European Communities* (OPTICA report II).
Committee for the Study of EMU (1989), *Report on Economic and Monetary Union* (Delors report).
Feldstein, Martin (1996), "The Costs and Benefits of Going from Low Inflation to Price Stability", NBER Working Paper no. 5469, National Bureau of Economic Research, Cambridge, Massachusetts.
Friedman, Milton (1953), "The Case for Flexible Exchange Rates, in *Essays in Positive Economics*, Chicago: University of Chicago Press.
Gros, Daniel and N. Thygesen (1988), "The EMS: Achievements, Current Issues and Directions for the Future". *CEPS Papers No. 35*, Centre for European Policy Studies, pp. 198-203.
Gros, Daniel and Niels Thygesen (1998), *European Monetary Integration – From the EMS to EMU*, London and New York: Addison-Wesley Longman.
Kydland, Finn E. and Edward C. Prescott (1977), "Rules rather than Discretion", Journal of Political Economy 88, pp. 867-896.
Rogoff, Kenneth (1985), "The Optimal Degree of Commitment to an Intermediate Monetary Target", Quarterly Journal of Economics 100, pp. 1169-1189.
Thygesen, Niels (1971), *The Sources and the Impact of Monetary Changes*, Copenhagen: Gads Forlag.
Thygesen, Niels (1977), "The Scientific Contributions of Milton Friedman", Scandinavian Journal of Economics 79, pp. 56-98.
Thygesen, Niels (1978), "Inflation and Exchange Rates – Evidence and Policy Guidelines for the European Community", Journal of International Economics 8, pp. 301-317.
Thygesen, Niels (1979), "Community Decision-Making on Exchange Rates and Money – Some reflections on the Launching of the European Monetary System" and the first direct elections to the European Parliament", Journal of Common Market Studies 17, pp. 313-331.
Thygesen, Niels (1984), "An Agenda for the London Economic Summit: Policy Convergence, Exchange Rates and International Liquidity", CEPS Papers No. 10, Centre for European Policy Studies.
Thygesen, Niels (1988), "A European Central Banking System – Some Analytical and Operational Considerations", Background Paper to the Delors report.
Thygesen, Niels (2000), "Evolving Ambitions in Europe's Monetary Unification (the Robert Marjolin Lecture)", in Artis, M., A. Weber and E. Hennessey (eds.),

The Euro – A Challenge and Opportunity for Financial Markets, London: Routledge.

Thygesen, Niels and K. Shigehara (1975), *The Role of Monetary Policy in Demand Management: The Experience of Six Major Countries*, OECD Monetary Studies Series, Paris.

Part I

Limiting Exchange Rate Swings – The Precarious Road to EMU

CHAPTER 1

Limiting Exchange Rate Swings in a World of Imperfect Knowledge

Roman Frydman and Michael Goldberg[1]

In this short chapter, we sketch our recent research on modeling prices and risk in financial markets. This is a topic that Niels Thygesen has thought deeply about for many decades. Both of us have had the great fortune of spending time in Copenhagen which gave us the opportunity of learning about these issues from Niels. Niels has always stressed that combining pure theory with the knowledge of history and institutions is important for understanding exchange rate movements and the effects of policy. He has steadfastly held to this view even though the development of the literature has increasingly left little room for such considerations. It is a great honor and pleasure for us to outline how our research illuminates and supports this life-long focus of Niels's work.

It is clear from the last three decades of floating that exchange rates have a tendency to experience large and persistent swings away from historical benchmark levels such as those based on purchasing power parity (PPP). Figure 1, for example, which plots the German mark-U.S. dollar nominal and PPP exchange rates since 1973, shows large and per-

1. The authors are grateful to the Nathan Cummings Foundation, the Alfred P. Sloan Foundation and the CV Starr Center for Applied Economics at New York University for support of this research. Responsibility for the ideas and opinions presented in this paper remains, of course, solely with the authors.

sistent swings in every decade of floating.[2] According to Rudi Dornbusch and Jeffrey Frankel, "exchange rates have turned out to be more volatile than they were expected to be, than they should be, and perhaps than they need be (Dornbusch and Frankel, 1988)."

Figure 1. The German Mark – US Dollar Nominal and PPP Exchange Rates

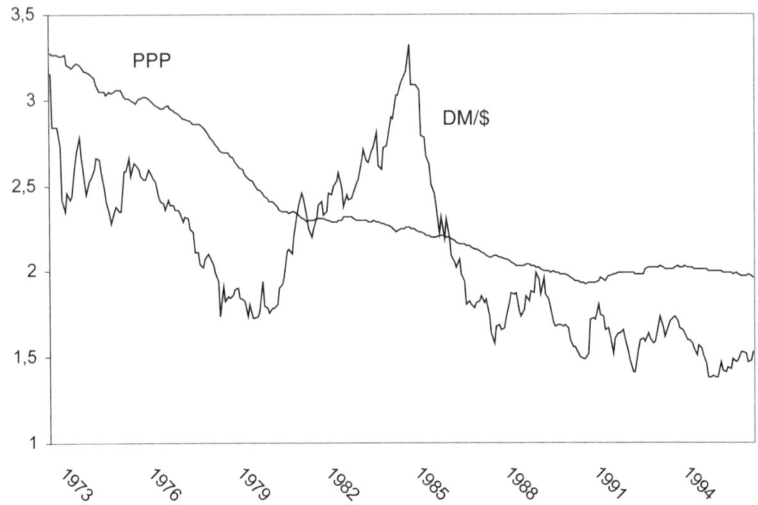

Policy officials and academic economists have long been interested in the question of whether some intermediate regime between a pure float and a firmly fixed rate, such as a target zone, might help to limit the long-swings behavior of floating exchange rates. Current exchange rate theory, however, provides weak support for the efficacy of such intermediate regimes. This weak support has led many to embrace the bipolar view of exchange rate arrangements: a country should either fix its exchange rate

2. The PPP exchange rate in figure 1 is based on the Big Mac PPP exchange rate reported in the April 1993 edition of the Economist (which is 2.02) and CPI inflation differentials from the IFS data bank.

irrevocably with a genuine currency board or monetary union, or allow its exchanges rate to float freely.

The weak support for target zones and other intermediate exchange rate regimes stems from the current view of what drives long swings in exchange rates. Standard exchange rate theory based on the rational expectations hypothesis (REH) implies that one-time deviations from PPP can occur, but exchange rates and goods prices should always move, albeit slowly, back toward benchmark levels.[3] The empirical failure of this theory has led to the view that long swings represent bubble movements which are unrelated to macroeconomic fundamentals. To model bubble movements, researchers have used the unstable trajectories of REH models (e.g., Meese, 1986) and the presence of noise traders (e.g., Frankel and Froot, 1986).

According to the bubble view, the only way for target zones and other intermediate regimes to limit departures from benchmark levels is for these policies to break the market psychology that drives bandwagon movements. But it is unclear how such policy interventions would influence market psychology. Moreover, it is understood that the ability of policy officials to defend an intermediate exchange rate regime is limited. After the inability of developing countries such as Brazil, Russia and Indonesia to defend their crawling bands led to severe crises in the 1990's, most enthusiasm for intermediate exchange rate regimes evaporated.

Our research provides a new rationale for policy intervention aimed at limiting exchange rate swings away from benchmark levels. There are two distinctive features of this research. First, we develop an alternative framework for modeling forecasting behavior that recognizes that market participants possess only imperfect knowledge about the relationships driving asset prices. Second, we replace expected-utility theory with the prospect theory of Kahneman and Tversky (1979). We build on prospect theory to model an idea due to Keynes (1936) that risk in financial markets is connected to departures of asset prices from historical benchmark levels.

Our research leads to two major conclusions concerning exchange rate behavior and the efficacy of policy intervention. First, swings away from parity can be based solely on macroeconomic fundamentals. In contrast to

3. The seminal article here is Dornbusch (1976).

the bubble view, this result rationalizes policy intervention designed to alter the course of macroeconomic fundamentals. Second, our new model of risk in financial markets implies that target zones and other intermediate exchange rate regimes may be effective even in situations in which policy officials are unable to credibly defend the boundaries of any particular zone around a parity. More importantly, even if policy officials do not commit to any specific target zone, the central banks' announcement that it is prepared to intervene to limit the amplitude of swings away from parity is likely to be effective. This analysis leads us to advocate a *reference-rate proposal* for the foreign exchange market.

1. Fundamentals and Long Swings

The central problem facing speculators in financial markets is that they must decide how to form forecasts of future prices at each point in time. A speculator may choose from a myriad of existing strategies, including strategies based on formal economic models as well as informal technical rules. Or, a speculator may decide to devise a new model. On account of skill or luck, she may find a strategy that delivers profits initially. But financial markets are always in flux. Relationships that initially hold are sooner or later replaced by new relationships. Strategies that initially generate profits lose their ability to produce profits with the passage of time.[4] Eventually, then, a speculator must decide when and how to revise her forecasting strategy. The dominant REH approach ignores this creative forecasting process in modeling individual behavior.

Irrespective of whether an economist adheres to REH, she has to model agents' forecasts in order to model speculative behavior and its implications. In general, we can think of an agent's forecasting strategy at time t as a way to transform an information set, X_t, into a forecast of the future value of some payoff-relevant variable, z_{t+1}. To fix ideas, we repre-

4. The widely publicized troubles of Long Term Capital Management reveal that no strategy, including those based on the most sophisticated finance theory, can be relied on to deliver profits from speculation indefinitely.

sent an agent's forecasting strategy by the function $F_t(X_t \mid \theta_t)$, which maps X_t into a forecast, $\hat{z}_{t+1}$, that is:

$$\hat{z}^i_{t+1} = F^i_t\left(X^i_t \mid \theta_t\right) \tag{1}$$

where θ_t is a set of parameters. Modeling individual forecasting behavior amounts to imposing restrictions on (1).

REH imposes a particularly restrictive set of such conditions. It assumes that the parametric structure of (1) is given by the quantitative structure of an economist's model. In doing so, REH assumes that all market participants have no need to search among the plurality of existing forecasting strategies, let alone invent new ones. Under REH, agents are assumed to use the one model written down by the economist in perpetuity.[5] Thus, an REH theorist assumes away, completely, the creative process of model discovery and revision. It is unsurprising, then, given the centrality of the creative forecasting process for market outcomes, that REH models have performed so poorly.

The main premise of our recent research on modeling asset markets is that the creative process of model discovery and revision is the key factor driving outcomes in all real-world financial markets. To represent this creative forecasting process, an economist needs to impose restrictions on (1) in a way that can account for the myriad of forecasting models and revision strategies agents might use. Our approach, developed in Frydman and Goldberg (2003, 2004a,c) and dubbed the *Imperfect Knowledge Forecasting* (IKF) framework, accomplishes this goal by imposing only *qualitative* restrictions on (1). The qualitative restrictions of an IKF model represent formalizations of behavioral and empirical regularities uncovered by economists, psychologists and other social scientists. These formalizations of behavioral and empirical regularities – because they are qualitative – do not pertain to just one forecasting model or revision strategy. In sharp contrast to REH, IKF restrictions represent the qualitative properties that *diverse* forecasting procedures and their revisions have *in common*.

5. This one REH model may involve switches among prespecified forecasting strategies according to a fixed rule as in Engel and Hamilton (1990).

In our recent research, we have constructed a number of IKF models of the exchange rate and equilibrium premium on foreign exchange (see Frydman and Goldberg, 2004a). An early class of IKF models imposes qualitative restrictions on (1) that come from extant economic models.[6]

In Goldberg and Frydman (1996a), we base qualitative restrictions in (1) on the monetary class of exchange rate models.[7] In particular, we assume that an agent's information set, X_t^i, includes only those macroeconomic variables implied by one or more of the monetary models and that the algebraic signs of the parameters agents attach to these variables (those in θ_t) are consistent with the predictions of models in this class. We note that these qualitative restrictions allow an agent to alter the fundamental variables in her information set and/or revise the weights she attaches to different variables from one time period to the next.[8]

We show that swings away from PPP arise in the monetary class of models even though all market participants are assumed to use only economic models and, therefore, to form their exchange rate forecasts solely on the basis of macroeconomic fundamentals.[9] The intuition behind this long-swings result is straightforward. With imperfect knowledge, the weights market participants attach to the fundamentals differ from the weights they would have used if they formed their forecasts according to REH. In general, then, the aggregate forecast of the change in the exchange rate, $\hat{z}_{t+1} - z_t$, can imply a movement away from or towards PPP. Moreover, new realizations of the fundamentals in the market's information set will cause the market's $\hat{z}_{t+1}$ to move and, with imperfect knowl-

6. The idea of imposing qualitative restrictions based on economists' models, dubbed theories consistent expectations (TCE), was proposed in Frydman and Phelps (1990).
7. This class of models includes the flexible-price models of Frenkel (1976) and Bilson (1978) and the sticky-price models of Dornbusch (1976), Frankel (1979) and Hooper and Morton (1982).
8. For regression analysis indicating that different sets of macroeconomic variabels matter for exchange rate movements during different time periods see Goldberg and Frydman (1996a,b,2001). For survey evidence on this phenomenon, see Cheung, Chinn and Marsh (1999) and Cheung and Chinn (2001).
9. In Frydman and Goldberg (2003) we allow for nonfundamental factors to enter individual forecast functions, such as technical trading rules. We show that long swings are not a consequence of technical trading per se, but arise because of the more general phenomenon of imperfect knowledge.

edge, this movement can be away from or towards PPP. But as $\hat{z}_{t+1}$ moves either towards or away from PPP, the current exchange rate follows suit. And, if the directions of movement of the fundamentals on which the market has focused remain unchanged, then the persistent movements of $\hat{z}_{t+1}$ and the exchange rate will continue.[10]

On one level, the logic behind long swings under IKF is the same as the logic behind bubbles, whether based on the unstable trajectories of REH models (e.g., Meese, 1986) or on the presence of noise traders (e.g., Frankel and Froot, 1986). Under all of these setups, swings away from PPP occur because the market's forecast, $\hat{z}_{t+1}$, moves persistently away from PPP, causing the current exchange rate to follow suit. But under the rational-bubble and noise-trader views, macroeconomic fundamentals are unimportant in driving exchange rates. Consequently, these views imply little difference in the efficacy of unsterilized and sterilized intervention. The only way for both types of intervention, as well as target zones, to dampen an exchange rate swing is for these actions to somehow break the psychology driving the market.

In contrast, our research on modeling exchange rates under imperfect knowledge suggests that macroeconomic fundamentals are much more important than commonly believed among academic economists. Even if market participants are rational, eschew chartism and avoid bandwagon movements based on market psychology, we would still expect long swings away from benchmark levels.

But if macroeconomic fundamentals do play a role in exchange rate swings, then policy officials would be able to dampen an exchange rate swing through their ability to influence movements in macroeconomic fundamentals. In such a world, we would expect the efficacy of unsteril-

10. We note that in Goldberg and Frydman (1996a), we derive the long-swings result under the assumption that the set of individual F_t^i 's remains unchanged. In Frydman and Goldberg (2003, 2004c), we show that the assumption of unchanging F_t^i 's can be relaxed. To relax this assumption, we impose a qualitative restriction on (1) that is motivated by one of the key findings in psychology called conservatism. Psychologists have found that agents are slow to change their models in uncertain situations. We formalize such conservative behavior as corresponding to continuous revisions in the individual F_t^i 's. We show that persistent movements either away or towards PPP occur during those time periods in which forecast revisions are conservative.

ized intervention to be greater than sterilized intervention. Moreover, the ability to defend a target zone would become easier if policy officials could influence the market by influencing the time paths of macroeconomic fundamentals.

Finally, the fundamentals view of long swings suggests that if policy officials want to limit swings away from benchmark levels, then they need to be concerned about the course of macroeconomic variables. If, however, swings are driven only by non-fundamental factors, then such concerns are misplaced.

2. Risk in Financial Markets and Policy Interventions

As we noted above, policy interventions designed to limit departures of the exchange rate from some parity are intended to break "market psychology". The standard model of risk in economics implies that risk in asset markets depends on the variances and covariances of asset returns. Thus, policy interventions are not usually thought to influence the risk faced by rational speculators in financial markets. However, standard risk-premium models have had great difficulties in explaining the empirical record on excess returns.[11] Indeed, this poor performance is often viewed as the clearest evidence that "irrationalities" of one kind or another drive behavior in financial markets.

We now sketch some of our research that develops a new model for risk in asset markets. Our model presumes that individual agents are rational, in the sense that they do not pass up profit opportunities. But agents are assumed to have only imperfect knowledge concerning the relationships driving the future payoffs from their decisions.

To build our new model of risk, we follow Kahneman and Tversky (1979) and assume that speculators are loss averse. Moreover, we augment prospect theory and assume that an agent's degree of loss aversion increases with the size of her speculative position. The resulting *endogenous prospect theory* leads to a key result: all agents require a minimum

11. For excellent review articles in the context of foreign exchange, see Lewis (1995) and Engel (1996).

premium before they are willing to commit any capital to speculating in the foreign exchange market.[12]

We show that this premium, which we call an *individual uncertainty premium* and denote by $\widetilde{up}^i_{t+1}$, depends positively on an agent's assessment of the likelihoods and magnitudes of the potential losses.

In Frydman and Goldberg (2004b,c), we rely on a behavioral insight of Keynes (1936) and relate the risk of potential losses not to volatility, but to the divergence of an agent's forecast of an asset price, $\hat{z}^i_{t+1}$, from its perceived historical benchmark level, $\hat{z}^{HB_i}_{t+1}$. According to Keynes, if an agent is a bull (i.e., holds a long position), then a rising gap – $\widetilde{gap}^i_{t+1} = \hat{z}^i_{t+1} - \hat{z}^{HB_i}_{t+1}$ – creates more "fear" of an eventual countermovement.[13] This greater fear leads her to simultaneously revise up her assessment of the likelihoods and/or magnitudes of the potential losses from speculation. If, on the other hand, an agent is a bear (i.e., holds a short position), then a rising gap enhances her confidence that a countermovement is likely to occur. This greater confidence leads her to revise down her assessment of the likelihoods and/or magnitudes of the potential losses from speculation.

The implications of Keynes's insight follow in a straightforward way. If agents' assessments of the potential losses from speculation depend on their $\widetilde{gap}^i_{t+1}$'s, then as they raise these forecasts, they simultaneously raise their uncertainty premia if they are bulls and lower their uncertainty premia if they are bears.

In the aggregate, the market's premium on foreign exchange, which we denote by $\widetilde{pr}_t$, is equal to the uncertainty premium of the group of bulls *minus* the uncertainty premium of the group of bears.[14] Thus, as

12. Endogenous prospect theory augments the original formulation of prospect theory not only with the assumption of endogenous loss aversion, but also with an assumption we call endogenous sensitivity. Endogenous sensitivity implies that the marginal (negative) value of a loss eventually increases as the loss becomes large. We argue in Frydman and Goldberg (2004b) that this assumption is consistent with Kahneman and Tversky (1979).
13. A long (short) position in an asset is defined as a position that delivers a profit when the asset price rises (falls).
14. The market's $\widetilde{pr}_t$ depends negatively on the bear's uncertainty premium because profits for bears occur when the return on holding foreign exchange is negative. This market premium also depends on the net foreign asset position of the domestic country vis-a-vis the foreign country. We omit this term because it plays no role in our long swings result.

agents' forecasts of the gap rise, leading the bulls to increase their uncertainty premium and the bears to decrease their uncertainty premium, the market premium on foreign exchange also rises. Under reasonable aggregation conditions, we are able to write the equilibrium $\widetilde{pr}_t$ as a positive function of the aggregate forecast of the gap, $\widetilde{gap}_{t+1} = \hat{z}_{t+1} - \hat{z}^{HB}_{t+1}$.

This analysis forms the basis for a new momentary equilibrium condition for the foreign exchange market:

$$\hat{z}_{t+1} - z_t + i^*_t - i_t = \widetilde{pr}_t(\widetilde{gap}_{t+1}) \qquad (2)$$

where z_t denotes the log level of the current spot rate and i_t and i^*_t denote the domestic and foreign nominal interest rate, respectively. Consequently, $\hat{z}_{t+1} - z_t$ is the market's forecast of the rate of change of the exchange rate from *t* to *t+1* and the left-hand side of (2) is the market's forecast of the one-period ahead excess return on foreign exchange. The condition in (2), which we call uncertainty adjusted uncovered interest rate parity (UAUIP), says that momentary equilibrium in the foreign exchange market occurs when the aggregate, uncertainty-adjusted, forecasted returns on foreign and domestic assets are equal.

In figure 2, we provide some evidence that the equilibrium premium on foreign exchange depends positively on the market's forecast of the gap. The figure plots the excess return on foreign exchange, which we denote by $\tilde{r}_{t+1}$, and $\widetilde{gap}_{t+1}$ based on survey data from Money Market Services International (MMSI). These data, which have been used extensively in the literature, are the median responses from weekly surveys of market participants on their four-week-ahead forecasts of the German mark-U.S. dollar exchange rate.[15] We use the same PPP estimate of $\hat{z}^{HB}_{t+1}$ as before in figure 1. The data set spans the period from January 1983 through mid 1995.[16] The time plots in figure 2 bear out the prediction of our model of

15. We used end-of-month observations in constructing monthly data from the weekly observations of $\tilde{s}_{t+1}$ To obtain our measure of $\tilde{r}_{t+1}$ we used one-month forward rates from DRI. For the seminal study that first used survey data on exchange rate forecasts, see Frankel and Froot (1987).
16. MMSI began surveying participants in the foreign exchange market in January 1983.

$\widetilde{pr}_t$: there is a strong tendency for the equilibrium premium to move positively with the market's forecast of the gap.[17]

Figure 2. The Excess Return on Foreign Exchange and the "Gap"

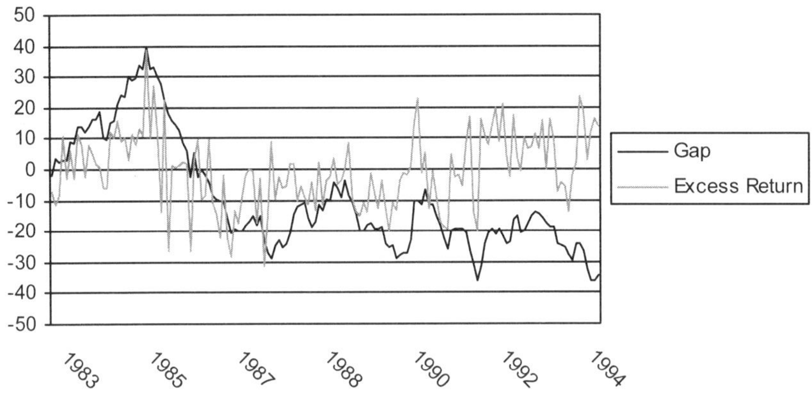

This positive relationship between the equilibrium $\widetilde{pr}_t$ and $\widetilde{gap}_{t+1}$ plays an important role in limiting the exchange rate effects of a swing in the market's forecast, $\hat{z}_{t+1}$. This implication can be seen by differentiating UAUIP in (2) with respect to $\hat{z}_{t+1}$ and z_t, yielding

$$\frac{dz_t}{d\hat{z}_{t+1}} = 1 - x, \qquad x = \frac{\partial \widetilde{pr}_t}{\partial \widetilde{gap}_{t+1}} \tag{3}$$

Eqation (3) reveals that a given change in $\hat{z}_{t+1}$ will have a smaller effect on the exchange rate as agents attach more weight to their forecasts of the gap in assessing the potential losses, i.e., as the derivative x in (3) increases.

The intuition behind this result is straightforward. As bulls, for example, increase their forecasts of the future exchange rate, they push up $\hat{z}_{t+1}$.

17. The time plots in figure 2 also bear out another prediction of our model: sign reversals in $\widetilde{pr}_t$ should be more frequent when the forecasted gap is closer to zero. See Frydman and Goldberg (2004b,c).

These higher forecasts lead them to increase their long positions in foreign exchange. But the rise in $\hat{z}_{t+1}$ also implies a higher $\widetilde{gap}_{t+1}$ and a higher assessment of the potential losses. The resulting increase in $\widetilde{pr}_t$ works to temper the willingness of the loss-averse bulls to increase their long positions. A larger value of the derivative x implies a larger increase in $\widetilde{pr}_t$ and, therefore, a larger tempering effect on the bulls' desire to risk more capital. Less buying on the part of the bulls, in turn, implies a smaller movement in the exchange rate.

Thus, a swing in $\hat{z}_{t+1}$ would lead to a more limited swing in the exchange rate if market participants were to attach a greater weight to their $\widetilde{gap}_{t+1}$'s in assessing the risk of potential losses from speculation. This result rationalizes a new channel for policy intervention in the foreign exchange market. Policy officials should announce at regular intervals, say monthly, an official estimate of some parity, with a detailed commentary as to how this official estimate was computed.[18] In 1922, Keynes recommended that this parity should be based on PPP, but other considerations, such as productivity differentials, may be important.[19] The central bank should also announce their willingness to intervene at any moment to push the exchange rate back to parity.

This reference-rate proposal is reminiscent of the proposal of Ethier and Bloomfield (1975), which was used in drafting the temporary guidelines for floating adopted by the IMF in 1974. At that time, there was no clear theoretical rationale for such a proposal. The reference-rate proposal was ultimately abandoned when the IMF amended its articles in 1978 (see Williamson, 2002).

The effectiveness of our reference-rate proposal hinges on the ability of this policy to heighten the sensitivity of individual risk premia with respect to the gap.[20] Moreover, such policy does not require an official

18. This policy parallels the current practice of many central banks of announcing inflation targets and the rationale behind them.
19. For Keynes' recommendation, see Moggridge (1980). For a thorough analysis of alternative models of the benchmark in the foreign exchange market, see Lorenzen and Thygesen (2000).
20. The research of Fratzscher (2004) shows that oral interventions, akin to the one we propose here, appear to have a significant impact on exchange rate movements.

commitment to any specific band around parity. In fact, the announced possibility of intervention is likely to be more effective if the authorities do not commit to any boundaries around parity at which they will intervene. As long as the speculators are concerned that intervention can occur at any time, the sensitivity of the premia with respect to the divergence from parity is likely to increase.

We hope this short note makes clear that once we recognize that market participants and policy officials must cope with imperfect knowledge, new ways of thinking about asset market behavior, the role of institutions and policy interventions emerge. Indeed, as we argue in our forthcoming book (Frydman and Goldberg, 2004c), once we accord a central role to imperfect knowledge in our models of asset markets, we do not need to appeal to irrationalities, "market psychology," market imperfections or informational asymmetries to rationalize policy interventions in these markets.

References

Bilson, J. F. O. (1978), "The Deutsche Mark/Dollar Rate A Monetary Analysis," in K. Brunner and A. H. Meltzer (eds.), *Policies for Employment, Prices and Exchange Rates,* Carnegie-Rochester Conference 11, Amsterdam: North-Holland.

Cheung, Y. and M. Chinn (2001), "Currency Traders and Exchange Rate Dynamics: A Survey of the U.S. Market," Journal of International Money and Finance, 20, 439-471.

Cheung, Y., M. Chinn and I. Marsh (1999), "How Do UK-Based Foreign Exchange Dealers Think Their Market Operates?," CEPR Discussion Paper 2230, London, Center for Economic Policy Research.

Dornbusch, R. (1976), "Expectations and Exchange Rate Dynamics," Journal of Political Economy, December, 1161-1174.

Dornbusch, R. and J.A. Frankel (1988), "The Flexible Exchange Rate System: Experience and Alternatives," in S. Borner (ed.), *International Finance and Trade,* London: Macmillan.

Engel, C.A. (1996), "The Forward Discount Anomaly and the Risk Premium: A Survey of Recent Evidence," Journal of Empirical Finance, 3, 123-191.

Ethier, W. and A. Bloomfield (1975), *Managing the Managed Float,* Princeton Essays in International Finance no. 112, Princeton, NJ: Princeton University Press.

Fratzscher, M. (2004), "Communication and Exchange Rate Policy," ECB Working Paper No. 363, May.

Frankel, J.A. (1979), "On the Mark: A Theory of Floating Exchange Rate Based On Real Interest Differentials," American Economic Review, September, 610-622.

Frankel J. A. and K. A. Froot (1987), "Using Survey Data to Test Standard Propositions Regarding Exchange Rate Expectations," American Economic Review, June, 133-153.

Frankel J. A. and K. A. Froot (1986), "Understanding the U.S. Dollar in the Eighties: The Expectations of Chartists and Fundamentalists," Economic Record, December, 24-38, and reprinted in J.A. Frankel (ed.), On Exchange Rates, The MIT Press: Cambridge, Mass., 1995, chapter 14, 295-316.

Frenkel, J. A. (1976), "A Monetary Approach to the Exchange Rate: Doctrinal Aspects and Empirical Evidence," Scandinavian Journal of Economics, 78, 200-224.

Frydman, R. and M. Goldberg (2003), "Imperfect Knowledge Expectations, Uncertainty Adjusted UIP and Exchange Rate Dynamics," in Aghion, P., Frydman, R., Stiglitz, J. and M. Woodford (eds.), *Knowledge, Information and Expectations in Modern Macroeconomics: In Honor of Edmund S. Phelps,* Princeton, NJ: Princeton University Press.

Frydman, R. and M. Goldberg (2004a), "A New Approach to Modeling Forecasting Behavior: Imperfect Knowledge and Premia on Foreign Exchange," mimeo.

Frydman, R. and M. Goldberg (2004b), "Heterogeneity of Forecasts, Endogenous Prospect Theory and Equilibrium in the Foreign Exchange Market," mimeo.

Frydman, R. and M. Goldberg (2004c), *Exchange Rates and Risk in a World of Imperfect Knowledge: A New Approach to Modeling Asset Markets,* under contract, Princeton, NJ: Princeton University Press.

Frydman, R. and E. S. Phelps (1990), "Pluralism of Theories Problems in Post-Rational-Expectations Modeling," paper presented at the 1990 Siena Summer Workshop on "Expectations and Learning", June.

Goldberg, M. D. and R. Frydman (2001), "Macroeconomic Fundamentals and the DM/$ Exchange Rate: Temporal Instability and the Monetary Model," International Journal of Finance and Economics, October, 421-435.

Goldberg, M. D. and R. Frydman (1996a),"Imperfect Knowledge and Behavior in the Foreign Exchange Market," Economic Journal, July, 869-893.

Goldberg, M. D. and R. Frydman (1996b), "Empirical Exchange Rate Models and Shifts in the Cointegrating Vector", Journal of Structural Change and Economic Dynamics, 7, 55-78.

Hooper , P. and J. Morton (1982), "Fluctuations in the Dollar: A Model of Nominal and Real Exchange Rate Determination," Journal of International Money and Finance, April, pp. 39-56.

Kahneman, D. and A. Tversky (1979), "Prospect Theory: An Analysis of Decision Under Risk," Econometrica, 47, 263-291.

Keynes, J.M. (1936), *The General Theory of Employment, Interest and Money,* New York: Harcourt, Brace and World.

Lewis, K. (1995), "Puzzles in International Financial Markets," in G. Grossman and K. Rogoff (eds.), *Handbook of International Economics,* Vol. III, Amsterdam: North-Holland, 1913-1917.

Lorenzen, H. P. and Niels Thygesen (2000), "The Relation Between the Euro and the Dollar," paper prepared for an EPRU conference on "Perspectives on Danish and European Economic Policy," Copenhagen, November 9-10.

Meese, R. (1986), "Testing for Bubbles in Exchange Markets: A Case of Sparkling Rates?," Journal of Political Economy, 94, No. 2, 345-373.

Moggridge, Donald, ed. 1980, *The Collected Writings of John Maynard Keynes,* London: Macmillan, vol. 18.

Williamson, J. (2000), "The Evolution of Thought on Intermediate Exchange Rate Regimes," Annals, AAPSS, 579, 73-86.

CHAPTER 2

The EMS 1979-1993: A Lesson of Limits to Policy Coordination

Gunter D. Baer

When in August 1993 it was decided to widen the fluctuation margins of the European Monetary System (EMS) to ±15%, the constraints imposed by the exchange rate commitment became inoperative. Even though Europe succeeded subsequently in realising Economic and Monetary Union (EMU), the enlargement of margins and the transformation of the EMS into a quasi-flexible exchange rate arrangement was a defeat for European monetary cooperation.

With the benefit of hindsight, but also drawing on insights gained during several years of involvement in European monetary affairs and on Niels' extensive contributions on European monetary cooperation, this review attempts to trace and assess the efforts made to cooperate and, in particular, to coordinate monetary policies in the framework of the EMS. As Niels (see Thygesen (1992)) noted, coordination is a strong form of cooperation. It goes beyond the systematic exchange of views and information, and implies modification of national policies in recognition of international economic interdependence, usually supported by an agreement – such as the EMS – which constrains the use of some policy instruments.

* The views expressed are the author's own and do not necessarily reflect those of the Bank for International Settlements.

The analysis presented here is inevitably broad-brush and cannot do justice to the complex interrelationships between exogenous events and policy responses which determined fourteen years of EMS developments. Monetary cooperation and policy coordination are considered primarily in the context of the exchange rate mechanism. No reference is made to cooperation with respect to the financing and settlement arrangements and to the promotion of the ECU, which frequently helped to find political compromises on operational issues, but otherwise had only limited significance for the functioning of the system.

After briefly discussing in the following section some basic models for organising monetary policy under a fixed exchange rate arrangement, the next two sections look at the practical experience within the EMS, first between 1979 and 1987 and then during the following years until 1993. The final section presents some concluding remarks.

1. Monetary Policy Coordination in a Fixed Exchange Rate Arrangement

A fixed exchange rate system imposes in principle a uniform interest rate level and, therefore, the necessity of a common monetary policy, but it does not automatically determine the direction of monetary policy.

As fixed rates are compatible with different policy stances, the participants in the system must share a common view on the objective of monetary policy and on how to implement it. In essence, what is needed is the designation of someone as central banker (Krugman (1990)). This issue is central to any fixed exchange rate system. It reflects the well-known fact that with n participants there are only n-1 exchange rates. When n-1 members of the system ensure the maintenance of fixed rates the n-th central bank is free to set its monetary policy independently. There are, however, different options in terms of how the decision on the stance of monetary policy can be taken.

One option would be that all participants accept the leadership of the n-th central bank because they share the underlying inflation objective and expect to benefit from the credibility the n-th central bank may enjoy on the basis of its long-term performance. A second option could be to assign the n-th currency status to a central bank outside of the exchange rate arrangement, i.e. all participants would peg to a third currency and generally follow the non-participating central bank's monetary policy. This would ensure intra-system exchange rate cohesion but, depending on the strictness of pegging, would also allow a certain leeway to differentiate the participants' common monetary policy from that of the outside central bank. Finally, the n-th central bank's monetary policy could be agreed upon jointly by all participants for the entire currency area, whereby the n-th central bank would pursue the agreed policy while the other participants would target the exchange rate.

Any of these approaches requires a conscious decision on the direction and implementation of a common monetary policy and should not, in the event of exchange rate pressures, give rise to discussions about symmetry of corrective action or about the sharing of the adjustment burden. The allocation of operational responsibilities is straightforward: the n-th central bank is committed to keep the agreed monetary policy on track, the other central banks are committed to defend the exchange rates. Consequently, there exists a firm benchmark against which to assess divergences and determine the responsibility for taking the necessary adjustment measures.

Why then are there recurrent discussions about the adjustment burden and symmetry in fixed exchange rate arrangements? The basic reason is that there is no agreement on the common stance of monetary policy. For at least two reasons it is not easy to reach such an agreement. Firstly, the interrelationships between exchange rates, interest rates and inflation are tenuous and, in practice, leave considerable scope for judgement on what should be the appropriate response to exchange rate tensions. Secondly, exchange rate arrangements are normally not entered into in an equilibrium situation where exchange rate expectations are stable and interest rates are roughly the same across all participating countries. On the contrary: the initial conditions typically vary strongly at the time a fixed exchange rate arrangement is launched, reflecting differences in cyclical positions, economic structures and policy preferences. In these circumstances it is hazardous to peg the exchange rate rigidly (Thygesen (1983)); it is also virtually impossible to agree on a common monetary policy stance or to avoid conflicts in organising the response to exchange rate tensions. For this reason it is not surprising that no attempt was made at the start of the EMS to define more precisely what was meant by gradually realising a zone of monetary stability; nor were any specific rules laid down for coordinating monetary policies.

During the preparatory phase for the EMS an alternative approach was considered which, without an explicit decision, would have resulted in a common overall stance reflecting the weighted average of all participants' national monetary policies. The basic idea was to define central rates in terms of a standard basket of EEC currencies – the ECU – with fluctuation margins on either side of the basket central rate. Owing to the properties of a standard basket (Baer (1979)), such a system implies that intervention limits are normally reached by only one currency, deviating towards strength or weakness vis-à-vis the average as measured by the standard basket. The responsibility for corrective measures would fall on the divergent currency and, in this way, establish symmetry. But the proposal raised a number of practical and complex issues. If, for instance, interventions were to be conducted in participants' currencies, it was unclear which intervention currency to choose and which obligations the issuer of that currency would incur. Moreover, given the currencies' different weights in the basket, the scope for fluctuation would differ for individual currencies and, on the assumption of uniform intervention margins, would allow more heavily weighted currencies more room for manoeuvre. In addition, there were problems as regards neutralising the impact of movements of currencies represented in the basket which were outside the exchange rate system. Technical solutions would have been possible, although at the expense of great complexity and lack of transparency of the system. But more importantly, acceptance of the proposal would have implied agreement with an overall monetary policy stance geared towards an average inflation objective, which, in fact, would have changed with each adjustment in any participant's monetary policy.

2. Cooperation During the Period 1979-1987

When the EMS entered into operation in March 1979, the participants did not have a common strategy or common tactics (Szasz (1999)). The operating procedures laid down in the appendix to the Resolution of the European Council of December 1978 were a mix of tested and new rules, which largely reflected compromises found after lengthy negotiations.

The ECU was formally placed in the centre of the system, but the definition of central rates in terms of ECUs and the introduction of the ECU as a means of settlement had no practical relevance for the functioning of the system. The use of the ECU as divergence indicator – to measure a currency's divergence from its ECU central rate and establish a presumption for taking corrective measures – suffered from the same deficiencies as a basket-based exchange rate arrangement and therefore never assumed any practical importance. The operations of the EMS thus continued to rely essentially on the same ground rules as its predecessor, the narrow margins arrangement ("snake") of 1972 – with one significant exception: adjustments of bilateral parities were no longer left to the discretion of an individual country, but were now subject to mutual agreement in a common procedure. This novel provision introduced for the first time an element of joint decision-making into a European exchange rate arrangement.

There was ample opportunity to apply the common procedure for adjusting central rates, especially during the first four years of the system's existence, when a number of central rate realignments took place in quick succession (for an excellent description and analysis of the EMS developments between 1979 and 1993 see Gros and Thygesen (1998)). By March 1983 the cumulative revaluation of the Deutsche Mark (leaving aside the Dutch Guilder) ranged between 23% against the Irish Pound and 37% against the Lira. But even thereafter, when parity adjustments became less regular, realignments remained a prominent feature – sometimes involving only one or two currencies, but often leading to a comprehensive rearrangement of the pattern of central rates.

The frequent realignments during the early years owed much to the rather unfavourable starting conditions. Marked divergences in economic performance among the EMS members, exacerbated by sharply rising US interest rates and the repercussions from the second oil price shock as well as different national policy preferences, left little choice but to resort repeatedly to changes in central rates. The EMS did not impose much discipline and when conflicts arose between internal objectives and the exchange rate commitment, it was the exchange rate that usually had to give. By and large, while there were some differences from country to country, changes in parities accommodated inflation differentials. As changes in competitive positions were corrected, there was little nominal convergence. After the first four years of operation, average inflation in the participating countries had declined only very moderately. The annual increase in the average private consumption deflator in 1983 was still close to that of 1979, although considerably below the 1981 peak. However, the situation began to change gradually after France in 1983 shifted the emphasis of domestic policies to give priority to price stability. Realignments were thereafter less frequent and the cumulative revaluation of the Deutsche Mark between 1983 and 1987 amounted only to 3% against the Belgian franc and 19.5% against the Lira. At the same time the participating countries achieved a remarkable downward convergence of inflation, with the annual rise in the average private consumption deflator declining from close to 8% in 1983 to around 2.5% in 1986-87. However, as divergences in price performance diminished, it also became more difficult to ascertain whether exchange rate tensions stemmed from fundamental imbalances, or were caused by speculative market behaviour which should be resisted without a parity change. When, towards the end of 1986, currency unrest flared up, notwithstanding the major realignment of nine months earlier and the maintenance of moderate inflation differentials, the realignment of January 1987 was widely considered to be a concession to speculation pressures and not to have been justified by fundamental factors (Szasz (1999)). This was indeed the first time that the EMS experienced one of the two dangers which, as Niels has emphasised on many occasions, are inherent in a fixed but adjustable exchange rate system. One is to defend misaligned exchange rates, the other is to give in to speculative behaviour when rates are in line with fundamentals (Thygesen (1994), (2001)).

Greater exchange rate cohesion and the accompanying nominal convergence went hand in hand with progressively closer cooperation among the EMS participants, meeting in the international structure of the ECOFIN Council, the Monetary Committee and the Committee of Governors. While the decisions on parity changes were the prerogative of the political authorities, the operation of the system was in the hands of the central banks. The situation in the exchange market, monetary policy developments and the use of the ECU by the private sector were monitored by the Committee of Governors (Baer (1994)). The regular exchanges of views fostered a convergence of opinions on the role of central banks and the objectives of monetary policy, as well as concrete measures to better manage the exchange rate system.

With the turnaround in French official thinking in early 1983 the primacy of price stability gained wider acceptance and there was now a growing willingness to manage bilateral rates vis-à-vis the Deutsche Mark more tightly (Gros and Thygesen (1998)). This was an implicit recognition of the Deutsche Mark's role as the nominal anchor of the system. The question of the Bundesbank's dominance in monetary policy setting has been the subject of extensive academic analysis and empirical research. Various studies have been conducted to evaluate the degree of monetary policy independence that Germany and the other countries may have enjoyed (see eg Monticelli (1996)). The timing of interest rate changes, the volume of interventions and the extent to which they were sterilised all suggest that Germany's "monetary hegemony" was not complete and that at times there was scope for autonomous monetary management in other countries. However, all the studies also recognise that Germany played a special role in the system. This was also apparent in the regular monitoring, where the Committee of Governors always gave special attention to the Bundesbank's policy stance. For all practical purposes, in the second half of the 1980s Germany was the system's central banker, determining the direction of overall monetary policy in line with its objective of price stability, mirroring the model (mentioned in Section 2 above) where the leadership of the n-th central bank is voluntarily accepted. However, while Germany's monetary policy was pivotal, each of the participating central banks made its decision on national interest rates separately and there was no attempt at coordinating directly monetary policies.

By contrast, cooperation in the management of exchange rates and efforts to stabilise market expectations produced concrete measures, such as changes in parity adjustment techniques and more sophisticated intervention policies. During the first few years changes in bilateral parities were often large, exceeding the width of the fluctuation band, and thus resulted in a jump in market rates after realignments. In order to reduce the expectations of sizable speculative gains, realignments, especially after March 1983 when imbalances were building up more slowly, kept changes in bilateral parities small enough to fall within the new fluctuation bands (de Grauwe (2000)). Moreover, realignments no longer fully offset inflation differentials in order to let international competition exert a dampening effect on domestic prices.

Much attention was also devoted to the question as to whether intervention should be conducted in participants' currencies and/or dollars. The Bremen Communiqué of 1978 had called for a coordinated approach vis-à-vis third currencies. While occasionally the idea of common dollar intervention was floated – so, for example, after the 1987 realignment to fight speculation (Szasz (1999)) – in practice interventions in the dollar market were restricted to smoothing erratic fluctuations in the dollar rate and to safeguarding the cohesion of EMS exchange rates. Nonetheless, dollar interventions were substantial, especially in the early years. But when tensions began to abate somewhat after March 1983, the dollar was increasingly replaced by participants' currencies, with intervention conducted within the margins in order to steer exchange rates close to the centre of the fluctuations. After the 1987 realignment, rigid exchange rate management was identified as one of the sources of speculative expectations and a more flexible employment of all available instruments was advocated in the Basel/Nyborg agreement of autumn 1987. Apart from some technical changes in the financing and settlement of intervention, the agreement established a set of rules for a more active use of exchange rate movements within the fluctuation bands, interest rates and interventions. These rules of conduct became in the following years the benchmark for assessing the appropriateness of policy responses to exchange rate pressures.

3. Cooperation Between 1987 and 1993

The outstanding features of EMS developments between 1987 and 1993 were the remarkable stability of exchange rates and an unprecedented experiment to explicitly coordinate the participating countries' domestic monetary policies. The two developments were closely linked to the political drive towards Economic and Monetary Union which gained strong momentum towards the end of the 1980s.

Leaving aside the technical adjustment of the Lira's central rate in January 1990 in connection with the narrowing of the fluctuation margins, no realignment took place between January 1987 and September 1992.

The EMS appeared to have turned into a fixed rate system, a "new" EMS (de Grauwe and Papademos (1990)). The Bundesbank seemed to have lost its anchor role (Collignon (1993)) and the Commission concluded in its 1991 report to the ECOFIN Council that realignments were a thing of the past. As we now know, these conclusions proved premature. In fact, it was the very stability exhibited by the system which was at the origin of the crisis of 1992-93 and the end of the EMS with narrow margins.

The reasons for the crisis have been widely discussed and analysed (eg Committee of Governors (1993), Portes (1993)). In summary, there was first of all the surprising move towards EMU, which stabilised exchange rate expectations. In quick succession the Delors Report was endorsed, a political consensus emerged to implement its recommendations, the necessary Treaty amendments were quickly negotiated and Stage One of the EMU process began on 1 January 1990. The political will and determination behind the process clearly impressed the markets and the prevailing pattern of central rates began to look more credible.

Secondly, the liberalisation of capital movements in the late 1980s, in combination with markets' confidence in central rates, created a novel environment for EMS operations. Contrary to the expectations of the proponents of capital liberalisation, capital flows did not exert disciplinary effects on weak currencies. With nominal interest rate differentials in their favour, countries with traditionally weak currencies attracted capital inflows and, by pushing their currencies to the upper part of the fluctuation band, generated a false sense of strength and markets' endorsement of domestic policies. When temporary exchange rate tensions occurred, the use of the Basel/Nyborg instruments proved effective in quickly restoring stability.

Thirdly, capital inflows into countries with traditionally weak currencies also enlarged their room for manoeuvre in monetary policy and eased adjustment pressures. Interest differentials narrowed and weakened the overall anti-inflationary stance of policy in the EMS. Real interest rates and real exchange rates diverged and little progress was made in reducing existing imbalances.

As long as exchange rate expectations were firmly anchored the situation remained manageable, even when cyclical positions became desynchronised after reunification boosted demand in Germany, while some other countries moved into recession. However, once market confidence was shaken by political uncertainties surrounding the ratification of the Maastricht Treaty, the crisis began to unfold. Strong downward pressures were felt by currencies of countries with unfavourable domestic conditions, but soon tensions spread to other currencies and the exchange market exhibited features of a speculative run, with short-term unwarranted exchange rate expectations feeding on themselves (Committee of Governors (1993)). At that point deep-seated policy dilemmas surfaced and massive interventions, interest rate changes and devaluations proved inadequate to contain the crisis of autumn 1992, or to deal with the unprecedented turbulence that led the authorities on 1 August 1993 to abandon the system's exchange rate constraint of 2.25% margins.

What is perhaps most surprising is that all this happened in a period when immense efforts were being made to assess jointly the sustainability and need for timely adjustment of exchange rates and the direction and consistency of national monetary policies. These efforts were undertaken by the Committee of Governors in response to their revised mandate of 12 March 1990, which defined the Committee's task as: "to promote the co-ordination of monetary policies .... with the aim of achieving price stability as a necessary condition for the proper functioning of the EMS". To fulfil this mandate and, in particular, to achieve price stability, the Committee developed an anti-inflationary strategy with a view to enhancing the effectiveness of adjustment mechanisms other than parity changes. The strategy focused on the compatibility of monetary policies and was implemented through regular examinations of national monetary policies in the form of a forward looking exercise and an ex-post evaluation to compare actual developments with earlier projections. As it was recognised that widely divergent inflation rates made it impossible to achieve price stability in all countries in a short period of time, national monetary policies were considered compatible if they were seen to be consistent with downward convergence in inflation rates without generating major exchange rate tensions. The assessment took place in autumn in the framework of ex-ante consultations where each central bank presented its monetary policy intentions. This left the possibility for adjustments before final decisions on next year's policy course were taken, if national monetary policy intentions were found to be incompatible. The approach allowed a joint assessment without impinging on the prerogative of autonomous national decision-making. The projected results were compared with actual developments six months later in the ex-post exercise in order to identify the reasons for divergences and examine the need for policy corrections.

Why did this enormous cooperative effort, combining an elaborate coordination framework, thorough analysis and regular intensive exchanges of views among experts and decision-makers, fail to prevent the 1992-93 crisis?

There were, firstly, some technical issues which limited the usefulness of the analytical framework. Differences in the measurement of inflation, definitions of monetary targets and indicators, operating procedures, financial structures and transmission processes all posed serious technical challenges. Much progress was made over time by harmonising statistics, making key variables comparable and setting national monetary targets according to similar procedures. Moreover, projections of economic developments in each country were based on the same external conditions. Nonetheless, the uncertainties regarding the short-term interrelationships between money, prices and exchange rates meant that the assessment of compatibility was ultimately qualitative and left much room for interpretation. It is therefore not surprising that, apart from some minor adjustments to policy intentions, the ex-ante consultations regularly confirmed the appropriateness of the envisaged national monetary policies.

The forward looking exercise did, however, always identify vulnerabilities and potential risks. Why was there so little action to mitigate the risks and why, when they materialised, were the central banks not better prepared to deal with the crisis?

It is inherently difficult to address potential risks. For example, there was always agreement that divergent competitive positions necessitated a realignment. But when the risks arising from accumulated and projected cost and price differentials were identified in the early 1990s, the authorities concerned were not prepared to take preventive action as sufficiently attractive interest differentials produced capital inflows which masked the build-up of imbalances. Other potential risks, recognised in the ex-ante exercise, were considered to be outside of the control of the central banks. There were, for instance, repeated warnings that a lack of fiscal consolidation or excessive wage claims would overburden monetary policy. Likewise, the threat of conflicts between domestic and external policy objectives was highlighted long before the markets began to take note of policy dilemmas in mid-1992. The voice of the central banks, many of them not yet independent, was clearly not strong enough to influence the relevant authorities.

At the same time, the ex-ante and ex-post framework did provide guidance on what to do in the event some of the identified risks materialised. For example, in the review of monetary policies which took place shortly before exchange rate pressures developed in mid-1992, it was confirmed that price stability needed to be restored in Germany and that this would be consistent with the appropriate overall monetary stance. However, the implicit recommendation on how to address the emerging crisis shortly thereafter was not heeded. Instead, an acrimonious discussion about symmetrical action and burden-sharing re-erupted.

With hindsight there is even a question whether the ex-ante and ex-post exercises did not facilitate to some extent the developments in 1992-93. While it was agreed that monetary policies would have to be reviewed and, if necessary revised, if identified risks materialised (Committee of Governors (1992)), in practice this did not happen. Rather, as mentioned above, monetary policy intentions were usually judged to be appropriate and attention was drawn to the risk of excessive budget deficits and the responsibility of the fiscal authorities. The question of what contingency measure should be considered if budgetary consolidation did not occur was never openly addressed. This became particularly evident in its last Annual Report, where the Committee offered only a very short, cautious assessment of monetary policy orientations, but argued extensively in favour of adequate support from fiscal policies and wage developments (Committee of Governors (1993)).

4. Conclusions

This broad-brush review of EMS developments was not intended to be a detailed analysis of the various episodes of exchange rate unrest and realignments in the EMS. Its focus was simply to identify and describe the main efforts at cooperating in the management of the exchange rate mechanism and coordinating monetary policies with a view to ensuring exchange rate cohesion. There is no doubt that all participants seriously endeavoured to cooperate closely, even though earlier and more decisive action by central banks and more support from non-monetary policies might have helped to avoid one or other realignment. Nonetheless, the experience with the EMS leaves considerable doubt as to whether an arrangement of fixed but adjustable exchange rates is sustainable in the longer run in an environment of decentralised and autonomous decision-making. The EMS was exceptional in many respects: it enjoyed an extraordinary political backing; it was underpinned by a solid institutional structure; it developed over time an increasingly refined set of ground rules; it was subject to continuous monitoring and analysis; and it was supported by an unprecedented framework to coordinate underlying monetary policies. All these features involved different aspects of cooperation and they became more important over time, especially when views converged on the need to achieve price stability. Decisions on central rates were taken jointly in a common procedure and there were short moments of closely coordinated interventions and simultaneous interest rate changes. But the decisive step, ie to bring monetary policies into line to approach a common and consistent policy for all participants, proved impossible, even when there was a shift after 1987 from German leadership in the setting of monetary policy to an approach based on mutual consultation. As a result, when faced with the choice between domestic and external objectives, the authorities ultimately abandoned their exchange rate commitment. The EMS, in spite of its unique support, shared this experience with the Bretton-Woods system and other arrangements of exchange rate pegging, all of which demonstrated that there are limits to coordinating policies under decentralised decision-making and that systems of fixed but adjustable exchange rates are arrangements of limited duration. Economists have therefore advocated "corner solutions" – and the European Union has made its choice in favour of centralised decision-making and a single monetary policy conducted by the European Central Bank.

References

Baer, Gunter D (1979): "Some Technical Implications of Pegging Exchange Rates against a Basket of Currencies", in The Economist 127, Nr 3, pp 371-398.

Baer, Gunter D (1994): "The Committee of Governors as a Forum for European Central Bank Cooperation" in Bakker, Age et al. (eds): *Monetary Stability through International Cooperation*. Essays in honour of André Szasz, Kluwer Academic Publishers, Dordrecht.

Collignon, Stefan (1993): "The EMS in Transition", A Study prepared at the request of the European Parliament, Association pour l'union monétaire de l'Europe, Paris.

Committee of Governors of the Central Banks of the Member States of the European Economic Community (1992, 1993): Annual Reports, April 1992 and 1993, Basel.

De Grauwe, Paul and Papademos, Lucas (1990): Introduction to "The European Monetary System in the 1990s", edited by the authors, Centre for European Policy Studies and Bank of Greece, Longman, New York.

De Grauwe, Paul (2000): *Economics of Monetary Union*, Oxford University Press, Oxford.

Gros, Daniel and Thygesen, Niels (1998): *European Monetary Integration*, 2nd edition, Longman, Harlow.

Krugman, Paul (1990): "Policy Problems of a Monetary Union", in: De Grauwe, Paul and Papademos, Lucas (eds), *The European Monetary System in the 1990s*, Centre for European Policy Studies and Bank of Greece, Longman, London and New York.

Monticelli, Carlo and Papi, Luca (1996): *European Integration, Monetary Coordination and the Demand for Money*, Clarendon Press, Oxford.

Portes, Richard (1993): "EMS and EMU after the Fall", in The World Economy, January 1993, volume 16, no 1, pp 1-15.

Szasz, André (1999): "The Road to European Monetary Union", Macmillan, London and New York.

Thygesen, Niels (1983): Comment on de Grauwe, Paul "What are the Scope and the Limits of Fruitful International Monetary Cooperation in the 1980s?" in von Furstenberg, George M (ed) "International Money and Credit: The Policy Roles",. International Monetary Fund, Washington, DC, pp 419-428.

Thygesen, Niels (1992): "Coordination of National Economic Policies", in Newman, Peter (ed), *The New Palgrave Dictionary of Money and Finance*, Macmillan, London, pp 458-461.

Thygesen, Niels (1994): "Towards Monetary Union in Europe – Reforms of the EMS in the Perspective of Monetary Union" in Johansson, Christopher and Collignon, Stefan (eds). *The Monetary Economics of Europe*, Pinter Publishers, London, pp 141-165.

Thygesen, Niels (2001): "Inflation and/or Exchange Rate Targets for Monetary Policy" in Leijonhufvud, Axel (ed) *Monetary Theory and Policy Experience*, Palgrave, UK, pp 97-113.

CHAPTER 3

The Exchange Rate Mechanism ERM as a Prelude to EMU

Charles Wyplosz

"One should not judge the EMS by its end, but rather by the years during which it proved useful."

D. Gros and N. Thygesen (1998), p.179.

The adoption of a common currency is a unique event and its success is often attributed to the long transition period spent within the Exchange Rate Mechanism (ERM) of the European Monetary System. This is not an obvious assertion. For a while, it was believed that monetary union could be achieved fast, as envisioned in 1971 by the Werner Plan. Back then, the ebate pitted "economists" against "monetarists", two misleading labels that opposed those in favor of a gradual approach and those who thought that a regime change did not require any transition. Niels Thygesen has been a key contributor to these debates in many ways. He contributed to the influential OPTICA report (Basevi et al., 1976), a call for the fast adoption of the common currency, which used to be required reading in my student years. His membership on the Delors Committee – he was the sole academic in a group of policy-makers – made him a role model for many of us who thought that economists have a role to play in crafting Europe's economic integration.

In spite of its ignominious end, the ERM has been a great success. Yet, it may be worthwhile to note at the outset that exchange rate pegs are generally considered as temporary arrangements.[1] A consequence is that they should include an exit strategy, even if that strategy remains implicit. A peculiarity of the ERM is that the exit strategy was adopted many years after its creation, in 1991 when it was decided to establish a single currency by January 1999 at the latest. This commitment may have been instrumental in the aftermath of the 1992-3 crisis. Even though the ERM then ceased to exist formally – the ±15% fluctuation band made it look like a managed float – *de facto* it survived until the exit strategy was implemented as planned in Maastricht. This suggests two important lessons. First, causality between ERM and EMU is likely to run both ways. Second, it shows how crucial institutions are; once the ERM became embedded in the convergence process with a high pay-off at the end, it became more stable than before, even though capital was freely mobile by then. Markets sustained the ERM because they believed – well, just about – that the monetary union would occur on time.

The present paper discusses the many ways in which the ERM made the adoption of a common currency possible. It challenges the commonly held view that the main merit of the ERM was to instill the kind of macroeconomic discipline that is required for monetary union membership. This is a revisionist view. Macroeconomic discipline was not high in the minds of the founding fathers of the EMS, who were chiefly concerned with international financial volatility after the end of the Bretton Woods system and the disappointing performance of the European Snake. Macroeconomic discipline became a key concern much later on, when inflation had grown to double-digit rates and public debts seemed out of control. The view that the ERM brought about discipline was developed later on by those who wanted to make it a pre-condition of monetary union membership, as eventually codified in the Maastricht Treaty.

If macroeconomic discipline was not the main contribution of the ERM to EMU, what was its contribution, then? The present paper argues that the ERM's role was more subtle. Its perceived success made the idea of a common currency less radical than it once seemed. Its operation gradually eroded monetary policy independence in all countries but Germany, making the loss of this instrument more formal than practical. It pro-

1. For a lucid statement of this point, see Eichengreen (1994).

moted the development of monetary cooperation. Its failures – recurrent speculative crises – illustrated the dangers of soft pegs and made the ultimate hard peg, a single currency, look like a lasting solution.

1. Did the Exchange Rate Mechanism Deliver Fiscal Policy Discipline?

One way the ERM is deemed to have prepared the launch of the euro is to instill a "culture of monetary stability" in most countries that had not shared Germany's declared priority to keep inflation in check. Indeed, looking at Figure 1, inflation declined to very low levels. But much the same happened elsewhere in the OECD area. This has led astute observers, including Gros and Thygesen (1998), to reject the inflation discipline view.[2]

Figure 1. Inflation Rates in Western Europe

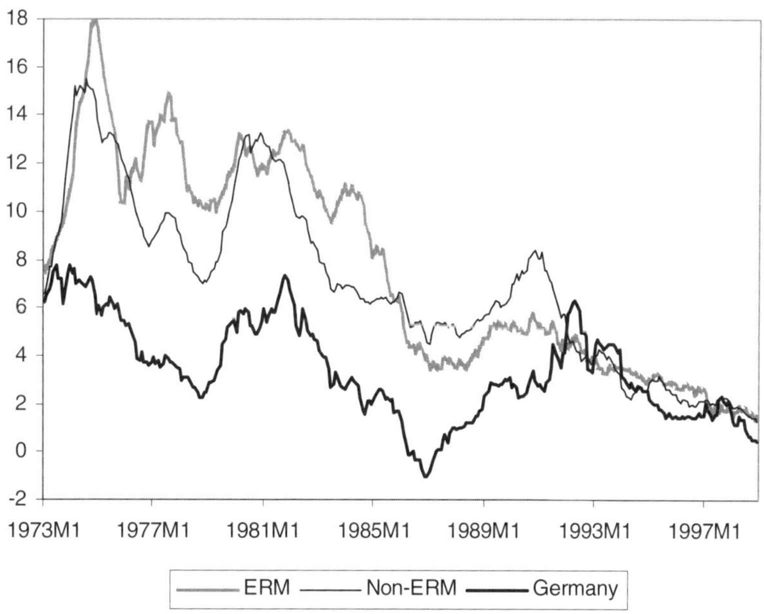

2. Burda and Wyplosz (2001) take the same position.

This is an important issue of more than historical interest. Very broadly, exchange rate pegs are often seen as providing monetary policy with an anchor; the claim is that, by fixing its exchange rate, a country will eventually drive domestic inflation to the rate achieved in the country whose currency serves as a peg. This is indeed the impression left by Figure 1.

It is worthwhile to go beyond naked eye evidence. The anchor argument, when carefully set, is that a peg constrains the monetary authorities. The underlying logic is the impossible trinity, which establishes that monetary policy independence is lost when the exchange rate is fixed, provided that capital is fully mobile. Thus, the constraint imposed by the ERM on member countries depends on the degree of fixity of the exchange rate and on the capital mobility regime. But ERM exchange rates were adjustable and, in many member countries, capital movements were not fully freed until the late 1980s. As a consequence, the constraint may have been less than tight. The crucial test, therefore, is not whether inflation rates converged – they converged to the German level in all OECD countries, as Figure 1 shows – but whether ERM significantly affected the conduct of monetary policy.

One way of formally revisiting this issue, therefore, is to directly investigate whether the monetary authorities changed their behavior once they had joined the ERM? The natural approach is to estimate Taylor rules for the ERM member countries, allowing for both the intercept and the slope coefficients to change during the period of ERM membership. The standard specification of the Taylor rule is:

$$(1) \quad i_t = (1-\alpha)(\beta E_t \pi_{t+n} + \gamma y_t) + \alpha i_{t-1} + \varepsilon_t$$

where i_t is the short-term interest rate, $E_t \pi_{t+n}$ is expected inflation and y_t is the output gap. A question is how to measure expected inflation. Recent evidence, see Gerdesmaier and Roffia (2003), is that it makes little practical difference whether one uses current or future inflation rates. For the sake of simplicity, I use the current inflation rate and instrument both the inflation rate and the output gap using a GMM estimator. For each country for which data is available, (1) is estimated as:

$$(2) \quad i_t = (1-\alpha)(\beta E_t \pi_{t+n} + \gamma y_t) + \alpha i_{t-1} + D^{ERM}\left[(1-\alpha')(\beta' \pi_t + \gamma' y_t) + \alpha' i_{t-1}\right] + \varepsilon_t$$

where D^{ERM} is a dummy variable that takes the value one during the period of the country's ERM membership. The data is monthly and the sample period runs from January 1973 to December 1998. The results are shown in Table 1; the upper part reports the coefficients for the whole sample, the lower part corresponds to the variables interacted with D^{ERM}.

Table 1. Taylor Rules for ERM Member Countries (1977:3-1998:12)

		Austria	Belgium	Denmark	France	Germany	Italy	Netherlands	Spain	UK
All sample	constant	-2.736	3.305	15.500	1.639	-0.261	0.719	-0.036	-6.548	-3.102
		0.044	0.000	0.000	0.000	0.369	0.005	0.955	0.000	0.000
	i(t-1)	0.620	0.345	0.095	0.945	0.634	0.886	0.703	0.814	0.774
		0.000	0.000	0.392	0.000	0.000	0.000	0.000	0.000	0.000
	inflation	1.470	0.149	-0.285	-1.964	1.259	0.304	0.994	1.658	1.010
		0.000	0.000	0.250	0.320	0.000	0.066	0.002	0.000	0.000
	gap	0.044	0.619	-0.028	0.922	0.529	0.755	-0.426	-2.737	0.468
		0.792	0.000	0.884	0.051	0.000	0.000	0.267	0.004	0.026
ERM	constant	3.681	-3.039	-15.334	-1.545	0.549	0.053	0.060	6.325	4.119
		0.008	0.000	0.000	0.000	0.089	0.832	0.924	0.000	0.000
	i(t-1)	0.078	0.593	0.849	0.029	0.273	0.021	0.285	0.187	0.076
		0.359	0.000	0.000	0.466	0.000	0.098	0.000	0.000	0.002
	inflation	-0.553	-0.178	2.332	0.134	-0.497	0.027	-0.421	-0.344	-0.107
		0.031	0.029	0.362	0.001	0.013	0.224	0.000	0.001	0.012
	gap	0.001	-0.995	0.218	0.010	-0.182	-0.034	0.231	0.706	0.703
		0.991	0.000	0.844	0.705	0.037	0.335	0.098	0.000	0.000
	R2 adj.	0.751	0.818	0.581	0.973	0.917	0.967	0.778	0.613	0.819
	SER	1.119	1.148	2.821	0.526	0.732	0.723	1.310	3.372	1.641
	J-statistic (p-value)	0.989	0.285	0.516	0.399	n.a	0.399	0.676	0.676	0.946

Notes: GMM estimator with pre-whitening. p-values are reported under each estimate. The ouput gap is calculated as deviation of the log of the industrial production index from its Hodrick-Prescott trend. The instruments include D^{ERM}, six lags of i, π and y, as such and interacted with D^{ERM}, and six lags of German inflation and output gap. For Germany, the instruments include six lags of the US interest rate. In the case of Germany, the J-statistic rejects the overidentifying restrictions, so the reported result is obtained with two-stage least squares.

For monetary policy to be directed at stabilizing inflation we need $\beta > 1$; for the whole sample, four countries (Austria, Germany, Spain and the UK) satisfy this condition. For monetary policy to be output stabilizing we need $\gamma > 0$; this is generally the case for the whole sample, with three exceptions (Denmark, the Netherlands and Spain). Thus there is limited evidence that the behavior of ERM central banks is fully described by Taylor rules (Denmark is not well described at all). Germany, on the other hand, did follow a Taylor rule, actually almost adopting Taylor's postulated coefficients $\beta = 1.5$ and $\gamma = 0.5$.

The most interesting part of Table 1 is its lower panel, which shows the difference that ERM membership has made. A reinforcement of monetary discipline geared at price stability would be captured by a higher weight on inflation or a lower weight on the output gap, or both. For all countries, the coefficient on inflation is either negative or non significant. This suggests that the implicit weight on inflation has either declined or not changed. On the other hand, the change in the implicit weight on output is not uniform; it increases in three cases (the Netherlands, Spain and the UK), declines in two cases (Belgium and Germany) and is not significant in the remaining four cases (Austria, Denmark, France and Italy). Finally, a general change is an increase in the degree of interest smoothing as measured by coefficient α in (2), which, interestingly, also concerns Germany.

Many students of the ERM, including Giavazzi and Giovannini (1989), Gros and Thygesen (1998) and Baldwin and Wyplosz (2003), have noted that the ERM evolved from a loose symmetric system to a tighter arrangement centered on the Deutschemark. After the French franc crisis and France's adoption of the competitive disinflation strategy, a period of frequent realignments was followed by a period when national monetary authorities publicly committed themselves to keep their DM parities unchanged, an explicit effort to use the ERM to achieve monetary discipline. In order to explore the idea that the use of the ERM as a monetary anchor only started with this second phase, the ERM dummy is changed to $D^{ERM\prime}$, which is zero until 1983:5 and then equal to D^{ERM}. The cut-off date is chosen to follow the early 1983 crisis.[3] It matches the start of disinflation observed in Figure 1.

The results are shown in Table 2, which excludes the countries that joined the ERM after the cut-off date. The results do not differ much from those presented in Table 1, and are often much less satisfactory. In par-

3. One might ask how the 1992-3 crisis and the subsequent adoption of the wide fluctuation margins are treated. The view taken here is that the crisis was treated as an accident affecting the new, tight ERM and that the wider bands were not utilized once speculation abated. It is possible to test the validity of this view but this would require adding more dummies, rapidly expanding the number of right-hand side variables.

ticular, there is no evidence that the weight on inflation has risen. Note, however, that the weight on the output gap significantly declines in four countries (Austria, France, Germany and the Netherlands).

Table 2. Taylor Rules for Second-Phase ERM Member Countries (1977:3-1998:12)

		Austria	Belgium	Denmark	France	Germany	Italy	Netherlands
All sample	constant	0.325	1.772	0.469	1.444	-0.125	0.139	0.544
		0.000	0.000	0.828	0.000	0.440	0.293	0.244
	i(t-1)	0.958	0.871	0.526	0.900	0.954	0.971	0.867
		0.000	0.000	0.000	0.000	0.000	0.000	0.000
	inflation	-0.129	-0.537	1.353	-0.390	1.444	0.525	0.809
		0.668	0.008	0.002	0.277	0.034	0.027	0.056
	gap	2.257	0.588	-0.745	1.082	1.922	2.518	1.193
		0.000	0.000	0.008	0.000	0.002	0.061	0.023
ERM'	constant	-0.183	-1.733	-0.499	-1.528	0.113	-0.278	-0.555
		0.011	0.000	0.821	0.000	0.531	0.080	0.224
	i(t-1)	-0.007	0.107	0.442	0.105	0.047	0.040	0.110
		0.069	0.000	0.000	0.000	0.009	0.039	0.013
	inflation	0.023	0.085	-0.990	0.050	-0.077	-0.024	-0.094
		0.113	0.009	0.079	0.164	0.122	0.311	0.035
	gap	-0.090	0.036	0.638	-0.068	-0.062	-0.032	-0.149
		0.000	0.200	0.002	0.018	0.000	0.337	0.036
	R2 adj.	0.949	0.823	0.628	0.970	0.910	0.966	0.791
	SER	0.501	1.132	2.658	0.561	0.763	0.734	1.270
	J-statistic (p-value)	0.982	0.105	0.499	0.477	0.135	0.623	0.087

Notes: GMM estimator with pre-whitening. p-values are reported under each estimate. The ouput gap is calculated as deviation of the log of the industrial production index from its Hodrick-Prescott trend. The instruments include $D^{ERM'}$ (which is zero until 1983:5), six lags of i, π and y, as such and interacted with $D^{ERM'}$, and six lags of German inflation and output gap. For Germany, the instruments include six lags of the US interest rate.

Taken together, the results confirm the visual impression from Figure 1,, that the ERM did not act as a monetary policy discipline device. The reason is quite clear. As long as realignments remain a frequently utilized escape clause, an exchange rate anchor is unable to constrain the monetary authorities. If the post-1983 attempt to dispense with realignments was meant to strengthen the constraint, it failed. Indeed, inflation differentials remained large and eventually led to an exchange rate correction during the 1992-3 crisis. What may be surprising is that some ERM countries – Belgium, Denmark and France – did not devalue during the crisis.

By then, they had achieved a lower inflation rate than Germany, not because of home-made discipline but because inflation rose in Germany in the wake of its unification with the former East-Germany.

2. Did the Exchange Rate Mechanism Deliver Fiscal Policy Discipline?

A similar question can be raised regarding fiscal policy. There is no direct link from the exchange rate regime to fiscal policy discipline. The indirect link assumes fiscal dominance, the view that fiscal indiscipline eventually forces debt monetization and a monetary policy relaxation that is incompatible with a peg. This indirect link is important and ought to be taken seriously, but not literally. It only calls for debt sustainability, a mild and long-term requirement that most ERM member countries have fulfilled, even if a few countries, primarily Belgium and Italy, failed to achieve debt sustainability in the mid-1980s. Italy was indeed forced out of the ERM in 1992.

Figure 2 displays the primary budget balances of the current Eurozone members, the US and the whole OECD area. Formal testing of the fiscal discipline hypothesis is not possible given the limited number of relevant observations.[4] We are reluctantly left to rely on visual inspection. The figure shows that, between 1979 and 1997, the EU12 evolution is virtually identical to that of the whole OECD area. It is only after 1997 that fiscal discipline appears to be higher in the Eurozone, which undoubtedly reflects the Maastricht entry criteria and the effect of the Stability and Growth Pact. This observation suggests that the ERM did not generally foster fiscal discipline, although it is impossible to reject the hypothesis that it may have played a role in Belgium and Italy.

4. Budget data are only meaningful at the annual frequency so any estimation of a fiscal policy reaction function would have to be carried out with too small a sample. A solution would be resort to panel data but a proper specification requires some dynamics, including the lagged dependent variable (e.g. smoothing the primary budget balance) which raises a fairly intractable problem of inconsistent estimates. Such an attempt, anyway, fails to identify an ERM effect.

Figure 2. Primary Budget Surplus (% of GDP) in the OECD Countries (1970-2003)

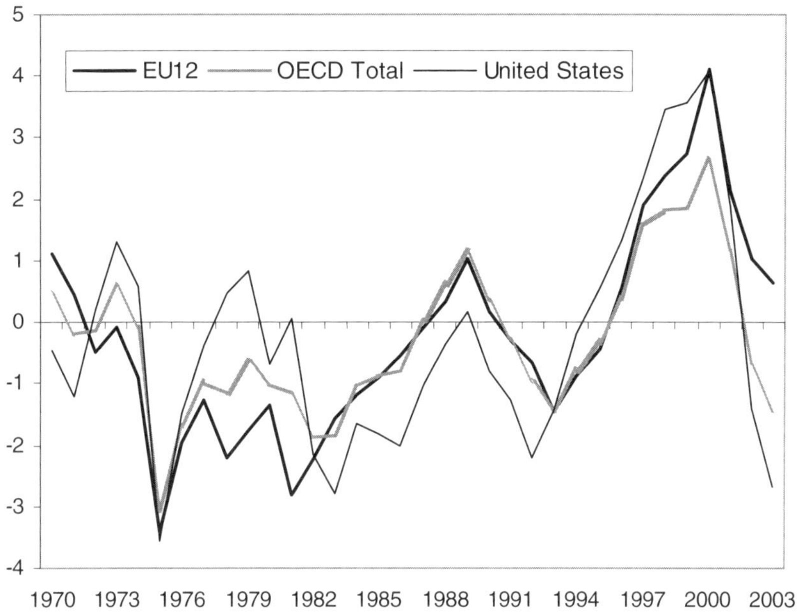

Source: Economic Outlook, OECD, 2004-09-27
Note: EU 12 includes all Eurozone members.

3. What Role for the ERM?

The evidence presented here should dispel the notion that fixed and adjustable exchange rates work as a disciplinary macroeconomic policy device. This conclusion raises two interesting questions. First, what made the launch of the euro so successful? Second, why is the ERM widely seen as a useful step on the way to monetary union?

Many authors accept the view, initially formulated by the Delors Committee, that nominal convergence is a necessary condition for joining a common currency area. This is the rationale behind the adoption of convergence criteria. That these criteria were satisfied in 1997-8 might be seen as vindication of this view. Yet, some doubts remain. The experience of high-inflation countries that have adopted a hard peg, for instance Argentina or Ecuador, is that the period of adjustment to the new regime is short, even when the initial situation is pathological. In Europe, nominal

nal convergence made the process seamless. Nominal convergence, therefore, is desirable if it comes at no cost. If it requires prior disinflation, the balance of costs and benefits ought to be carefully assessed.[5] Moderate inflation differentials are unlikely to be costly to handle while disinflation is generally more efficient through a policy regime change, see Sargent (1982). At any rate, if nominal convergence has been achieved, it is likely to be the consequence of the imposition of convergence conditions, not through ERM membership. Maintaining a pegged regime with full capital mobility only exposed European economies to potential speculative attacks, as the 1992-3 crisis showed. In that sense, the ERM was counterproductive.

Yet, the ERM has been crucial in two main respects. To start with, the ability to successfully operate a fairly elaborate arrangement has emboldened policymakers. Monetary union has long been seen as Europe's Holy Grail; ten years of relative exchange rate stability created the impression that a common currency was not as far-fetched a project as it was previously thought. More importantly, perhaps, the ERM promoted new institutions and practices. In particular, the realignment rules – especially the need for consensus decision-making – represented a significant limitation on what was hitherto seen as a crucial component of national sovereignty. The ECOFIN meetings have become increasingly important as all countries, save Germany, started to operate within the law of the impossible trinity. The establishment of formal Maastricht-style central bank independence in the early 1990s – a step that was not promoted within the ERM – further represented for most countries a radical departure from a long tradition of subservience to the Finance Ministry, in effect finally removing monetary policy from the arsenal of political tools.

Thus, the ERM served as a prelude to EMU in the sense that it showed member countries that monetary policy independence can be given up without serious consequences. The 1992-3 crisis further established that, once capital mobility is accepted, monetary policy independence is, in effect, lost. Along the way, monetary cooperation developed. Both inter-

5. Debt stabilization is also part of the convergence process. The link between debt stabilization and monetary union raises too many issues to be considered here.

governmental fora and the Commission started to operate as institutions entrusted with significant powers. Institution and confidence building was more important than economic prowess. The much-publicized establishment of a culture of price stability, assuming that it is a done deal, was not the result of learning by doing but of the adoption of institutions that provide policymakers with adequate incentives at a time when the view that macroeconomic policies should be restrained prevailed. Anyway, this view came to be widely shared, not just in Europe, in response to the excesses of the 1970s and 1980s. Attributing this evolution to the ERM is one more instance of confusion between simultaneity and causality.

4. Conclusions

Would EMU have occurred without the previous ERM experience? Technically, from a purely economic viewpoint, the ERM was not necessary and may have made things more difficult once full capital mobility was established. Taking a wider view, however, the ERM prepared the ground for the difficult political and institutional decisions that were required. In this concluding section, looking forward, I draw two lessons from this experience that seem to have been forgotten.

First, today's ERM is different from its previous incarnation. Not only is it a euro-centered arrangement with limited commitments from the Eurosystem, but the institutions are in place and the political will of the new EU members to adopt the euro is clear. The decision to maintain ERM membership as a precondition to EMU admission therefore lacks any justification and carries significant dangers. As a number of authors – including Thygesen (2002) and Begg et al. (2003) – argue, the case for achieving nominal convergence prior to adopting the euro is weak and operating within the ERM with full capital mobility exposes the new members to potentially damaging speculative attacks.

Second, other regions – chiefly East Asia and Latin America – are looking at the European process of monetary integration as a blueprint. If they are mostly interested in stabilizing their bilateral real exchange rates, they must wonder whether it is enough to stabilize their effective nominal exchange rates vis a vis the dollar or the euro under the assumption that inflation rates will automatically converge. As long as the arrangements include the possibility of realignments, the probability that inflation rates converge is low. If, as seems the case, they are interested in moving towards a common currency, an ERM-style arrangement should be used to build up adequate institutions, which are currently lacking in these regions. Focusing only on fixed exchange rates may end up being a distraction rather than a prelude.

References

Baldwin, Richard and Charles Wyplosz (2003) *European Economic Integration*, McGraw-Hill.

Basevi, Giorgio, Emil-Maria Claassen, Pascal Salin and Niels Thygesen (1976) "Towards Economic Equilibrium and Monetary Unification in Europe" (OPTICA Report), Commission of the European Communities.

Bayoumi, Tamim and Barry Eichengreen (1998) "Exchange Rate Volatility and Intervention: Implications of the Theory of Optimum Currency Areas", Journal of International Economics 45(2): 191-209.

Begg, David, Barry Eichengreen, Lászlo Halpern, Jürgen von Hagen and Charles Wyplosz (2003) "Sustainable Regimes of Capital Movements in Accession Countries", Policy Paper 10, CEPR, London, March 2003.

Burda, Michael and Charles Wyplosz (2001) *Macroeconomics, A European Text*, 3rd Edition, Oxford University Press.

Eichengreen, Barry and Charles Wyplosz (1993) "Unstable EMS", Brookings Papers on Economic Activity 1: 51-144.

Eichengreen, Barry (1994) *International Monetary Arrangements for the 21st Century*, The Brookings Institution.

Gerdesmaier, Dieter and Barbara Roffia (2003) "Empirical Estimates of Reaction Functions in the Euro Area", Working Paper 206, ECB.

Giavazzi, Francesco and Alberto Giovannini (1989) *Limiting Exchange Rate Flexibility, The European Monetary System*, MIT Press.

Gros, Daniel and Niels Thygesen (1998) *European Monetary Integration*, Second Edition, Longman.

Sargent, Thomas (1982) "The End of Four Big Inflations", in R. Hall (ed.), *Inflation*, University of Chicago Press: 41-98.

Thygesen, Niels (2002) "The Path to the Euro for Enlargement Countries", Special Notes for the Economic and Monetary Affairs Committee, 2nd quarter 2002, European Parliament, http://www.europarl.eu.int/comparl/econ/emu/default_en.htm

Part II

How Has EMU Worked?

CHAPTER 4

Was It Worth It?

Guido Tabellini

Much of Niels Thygesen's professional life was devoted to the analysis of how to design and implement EMU. Now we have it, and it works well. But was it worth it? Of course, it is too early to tell. Even with time we will never know the true answer, since we cannot observe the counterfactual (what Europe would have been like without the Euro). Nevertheless, we can still compare Europe before and after the Euro and ask whether some of the expected benefits of EMU have materialized. This is what I do in this paper.

EMU was widely expected to bring about significant economic improvements for Europe. This is how Niels Thygesen viewed the prospect of a single currency in 1994: "Only a common currency can assure that all the benefits expected from goods market integration will be attained. It is not easy to put a figure to these benefits, but it would appear that some of the very substantial expected gains from creating the Internal Market estimated in the late 1990s could only materialize within a common currency area" – Thygesen (2004). This optimism stemmed from the premise that lower transaction costs and reduced exchange rate uncertainty would lead to a complete integration of product and financial markets in Europe. A fully integrated product market would have several benefits: gains from trade could be more fully exploited; increased price transparency would strengthen competition; reduced exchange rate uncertainty would increase cross border investment. Other benefits were expected to stem from the integration of European financial markets: deeper and more liquid market would entail a lower cost of capital and more risk sharing opportunities;

the new European currency could acquire an international role, perhaps reaping some seignorage revenues, giving a further boost to liquidity and improving Europe's resilience in the face of economic shocks.[6]

In contrast with those optimistic expectations, macroeconomic performance in the Euro area has been disappointing since the launch of the new currency, both in comparison to earlier years and to other industrial countries. The disappointment is particularly stark when we look at the growth of labor productivity – the ultimate measure of economic efficiency. Not only it failed to improve, it actually slowed down! As shown in Table 1, output per hour worked fell in all the large countries of the Euro area with the exception of France, while it rose in the US and it remained about constant in the three European countries that did not adopt the Euro.

Table 1: GDP per Hour Worked (Average Yearly Growth Rate)

	France	*Germany*	*Italy*	*Netherlands*	*Spain*	*Denmark*	*Sweden*	*U.K.*	*U.S.A*
1994-98	1,16	2,47	1,91	1,69	0,57	1,73	2,31	1,91	1,31
1999-03	2,75	1,95	0,57	0,02	-0,31	2,19	2,21	2,09	1,93

Source: OECD, Groningen Growth and Development Center

Why this disappointing performance? Can it be blamed on the Euro? In particular, have the expected benefits of the new currency failed to materialize? Almost six years after the launch of the Euro, a few empirical papers have started to assess its effects, looking at a variety of indicators. In the next sections I review the main results. Section 2 focuses on the single market for goods and services, while section 3 looks at financial

6. According to the European Commission (2004), an important expected benefit of EMU concerned the improvement in the framework for conducting macroeconomic policy, and the resulting enhanced macroeconomic stability. While there is no doubt that this was an important improvement for many Euro area countries, it is not really a consequence of the Single Currency itself: nothing prevented these traditionally unstable countries from reforming their domestic institutions so as to gain stability and credibility in their monetary and fiscal affairs, without adopting the Euro.

markets and banking. Section 4 reviews the role of the Euro as an international currency. Section 5 discusses the effect of the Euro on labor market reforms. Section 6 asks whether the launch of the Euro had any discernible political effects. Section 7 summarizes and concludes.

1. Product Markets after the Euro

1.1. Trade Volume

The Euro gave a significant boost to trade volumes within the Euro area, and perhaps also to trade between Euro and Non-Euro countries (i.e. the effect has been trade creation, not trade diversion). This is the conclusion reached by a number of recent empirical studies that exploited data on bilateral trade flows up to 2002, with a difference-in-difference methodology (i.e. they compared the time path of trade flows in the countries that joined the Euro with that of similar countries over the same period). The estimated effect ranges from 5% to 30% of pre-EMU trade, with the most reliable estimates in the range of 5% - 15% - see Table 2. The effect seems to be rising over time, so a further boost should be expected in the years ahead. These numbers are lower than some of the most optimistic estimates circulated before the launch of the Euro, but are economically very relevant.[7] A large empirical literature suggests that international trade is one of the main forces behind economic development. In the long run, a boost to trade due to lower transaction costs could entail a significant acceleration in economic growth.[8] Judged from this perspective, EMU has not been disappointing.

7. Rose and Van Wincoop (2001) estimated the potential impact of EMU on trade to be 50%.
8. See the references quoted in Helpman (2004).

Table 2: The Impact of EMU on International Trade

Study	Estimated effect
Micco, Stein and Ordonez (2003)	5-15%
Faruqee (2004)	10%
Barr, Breeden and Miles (2003)	30%
Bun and Klaassen (2002)	10%

1.2. Price Dispersion

In contrast with the optimistic expectations, so far the Euro has not significantly reduced price dispersion. The most careful study to date, by Engel and Rogers (2004), compares the prices of about 100 narrowly defined traded consumer goods from 18 European cities in the Eurozone over the period 1990-2003 (the source of the data are surveys conducted by the Economist Intelligence Unit). Prices did converge during the implementation of the Single market program, in the early 1990s. But there is no evidence of further price convergence from 1997 onwards. Similar negative conclusions have been reached by other studies using aggregated price data (the European Commission 2004, Rogers 2002), or data for a smaller set of goods (Lutz 2002). Thus, the idea that the single currency would increase price transparency and through this channel strengthen competition in product markets has not been supported by the data so far.

1.3. Cross-Border Investment

Lower transaction costs and reduced exchange rate volatility were widely expected to increase the attractiveness of the Euro area countries as a destination for foreign direct investment (FDI). The evidence to date suggests that this is what happened. Comparing the periods 1996-1998 vs 1999-2001 (or 1999-2002), the European Commission (2003, 2004) finds that the share of FDI into the EU going to Euro countries increased significantly, at the expenses of non-Euro countries: the share of inward FDI going to non-Euro countries fell from 37% in 1998 to 20% in 2001, with a corresponding increase in the Euro area. The increase of inward FDI towards the Euro area is more pronounced for FDI originating from other EU countries, but it is visible also for FDI originating from outside of the EU. This evidence is only suggestive, however. Given the volatility of investment data, the time period is too short. Moreover, several other factors could have influenced investment flows over the last few years: increased globalization and the asset market bubble meant that FDI flows rose everywhere in the late 1990s and in 2000; the large exchange rate fluctuations could have influenced the location or timing decisions; deregulations, privatizations, the wave of M&A, are all confounding factors. Thus, although the Euro countries seem to have become more attractive to foreign investors, it is too early to draw firm conclusions.

2. Financial Markets after the Euro

Not surprisingly, the launch of the single currency has had a huge impact on financial market integration within the Euro area. Part of this effect is due to the removal of exchange rate risk, but an important component also reflects the removal of regulatory barriers and the creation of unified trading platforms. To a large degree, these institutional changes too can be attributed to the single currency itself, however: without the Euro, the impetus towards harmonizing financial regulation would have been much weaker.

In this section I briefly review recent changes in the money market, the bond market, the equity market and banking. I then conclude by discussing the implications for effect of the Euro on the cost of capital.[9]

2.1. The Money Market

The interbank and money market is now fully integrated in the Euro area, with the main exception of the secured segment where integration has proceeded more slowly.[10] Cross border lending in the interbank market now accounts for almost half of total interbank lending in the Euro area.

9. A large recent literature has studied the recent evolution of European financial markets. In this section I draw in particular on The European Commission (2004), Baele et al (2004), HM Treasury (2003), Adjaoutè and Danthine (2002), Dermine (2002), Cabral et al. (2002), Goodhart et al (2002), Detken and Hartmann (2002).
10. Secured lending, such as repos, commercial paper or certificates of deposits, involves the exchange of liquidity for collateral.

And interest rates prevailing in the different countries have converged almost immediately after the launch of the Euro.

2.2. The Bond Markets

The market for government bonds has also become highly integrated since the launch of the Euro. On the demand side, the home bias has shrunk and bond portfolios have become more diversified across countries. At the same time, issue size has increased and the market has become more liquid. Of course, yield differentials have not disappeared, but according to Codogno et al (2003) they mainly reflect underlying sovereign risk, not liquidity. An important question is whether these developments have led to a reduction of the risk-free component of the cost of capital. The answer is probably negative. While the nominal returns on the high yield government bonds of countries like Italy or Spain have dropped dramatically, one cannot detect a significant reduction in the return of, say, German bonds relative to those of other reliable sovereign borrowers. Thus, here the removal of exchange rate risk has benefited some countries only. As noted in footnote 1 above, this improvement cannot be attributed to the Euro per se: it could have been achieved with appropriate domestic institutional reforms in the countries with unstable macroeconomic regimes.

The Euro also spurred important changes in the market for corporate bonds. Between 1998 and 2003, corporate bonds outstanding in the Euro area increased almost by a factor of three (Baele et al. 2004). According to HM Treasury (2003), however, the increase concerned mainly bonds rated from A to BBB, and not the higher yield segment. Not all of this change can be attributed to the single currency: over this period the gross volume of corporate bonds increased rapidly also in the US; and Europe was bound to move in this direction anyway, given its almost exclusive reliance on bank credit until recently. Nevertheless, the single currency certainly played an important role. This is suggested by the fact that home bias in the portfolio of bond funds has shrunk, but only for the Euro area, by the increase in net corporate debt issues in the Euro area relative to other countries, and by the finding that traditional country risk factors only play a marginal role in explaining corporate bond yield spreads in the Euro area (Baele et al 2004, European Commission 2004).

2.3. The Equity Market

Currency movements are traditionally regarded as only a secondary component of equity returns. Yet, like other financial markets, equity markets too have become more integrated since 1999, though again part of the change also reflects a trend common to all countries and cannot be entirely attributed to the single currency. Market capitalization increased in the Euro area (from 25% of GDP in the mid 1990s to about 50% of GDP in 2003), by more than in other industrial countries over the same period. The home bias in the portfolios of households and other institutional investors significantly decreased since the launch of the Euro, again by more than for non-EMU countries. Table 3 displays data on the portfolios of equity mutual funds operating in the Euro area. Between 1997 and 2002, the proportion of assets invested at home decreased significantly, mainly to the benefit of the assets invested in other European countries.

Table 3: Allocation of Assets of Equity Mutual Funds Operating in the Euro Area

% of assets invested					
Domestically		**In other EU countries**		**In non-EU countries**	
1997	*2002*	*1997*	*2002*	*1997*	*2002*
49	28	10	26	41	46

Source: European Commission (2004)

Note that the reduction in home bias and the increased proportion invested in equity of other European countries has taken place despite the fact that the underlying convergence of the Euro area economies has reduced the diversification opportunities offered by cross-border equity holdings: as documented by many empirical studies, equity returns in the Euro area are now mainly explained by sectoral risk factors, while country risk factors seem to play a secondary role. In other words, the reduction in the home bias was taking place at the same time that international diversification was becoming less beneficial to investors. This is another symptom that the reduction in home bias was caused by the reduction in transaction costs and exchange rate risk brought about by the single currency.

Finally, and despite all these improvements, there is no credible evidence to date that the Euro also had an impact on cross-border listings (European Commission 2004).

2.4. Banking

As already noted, one of the effects of the single currency has been to achieve full integration of the interbank market. Capital-market related activities (such as underwriting and corporate bond issues) have also become very closely integrated within the Euro area. The wave of deregulations throughout the 1990s, together with the launch of the Euro, have enhanced competitive pressures and have set in motion structural changes in the banking market. The number of credit institutions in the Euro area has declined by 15% between 1997 and 2002 (European Commission 2004). The bulk of mergers and acquisitions has taken place within national borders, however, and cross-border branching did not increase. As a result, the market share of foreign branches and subsidiaries in the Euro area is rather low. This is important, because it implies that retail banking remains a segmented market. Interest rates on bank deposits and on lending to households or small firms have converged within the Euro area. But this is the result of macroeconomic convergence, more than of a fully integrated retail banking market. Cabral et al (2002) note that bank margins have converged much less than nominal interest rates and cross-border lending to non-banks within the Euro area remains very low.

2.5 The Cost of Capital

The main benefit of more efficient financial markets is to reduce the cost of capital, and through this channel to increase investment and growth. In turn, the cost of capital can be decomposed into the risk free interest rate, and a market risk premium (against liquidity risk and credit risk). As argued above, the Euro does not seem to have reduced the risk free rate: the real interest rate on government debt in Germany does not seem to be any lower (compared to other non-Euro countries) than it was before the launch of the Euro – see also HM- Treasury (2003). Thus, if the Euro has reduced the cost of capital, it is mainly through a reduction in the market risk premium. The progress described in the previous subsections certainly has had an impact: lower transaction costs, more competitive intermediaries and more diversification opportunities, are bound to have reduced both the liquidity risk premium and the credit risk premium. According to some studies, the reduction in the cost of capital is as large as 1/2 a percent – the European Commission (2004). But quantifying this reduction is very difficult and any attempt is bound to result in imprecise estimates. Moreover, the effect has been different on different debt instruments, and large corporate borrowers (who are less dependent on retail banking) have benefited more than the rest.

3. The Euro as an International Currency

One of the alleged benefits of the single currency was to provide Europe with a truly international currency, that could perhaps one day challenge the supremacy of the US $. This outcome would be important, because it would provide additional seignorage revenues, facilitate international borrowing in domestic currency, lead to invoicing of goods denominated in Euros and thus reduce exposure to shocks. According to Portes and Rey (1998), transactions costs in foreign exchange and securities markets are the key determinant of the extent and speed of internationalization of the Euro.

What has happened so far? We have already discussed how, thanks to the new currency, the Euro area now has achieved a fully integrated bond and money market. From this perspective, the Euro has clearly matched optimistic expectations. The foreign exchange market has been more disappointing, however. According to Hau et al. (2002), Goodhart et al. (2002) and Detken et al. (2002), transactions costs on foreign exchange trades have increased, not shrunk. The reason for this surprising outcome might have to do with quoting conventions and the choice of currency units (the so called "granularity hypothesis" advanced by Goodhart et al. 2002). In terms of turnover, the spot foreign exchange market seems unaffected, while the swap market is smaller than that of the previous Euro area currencies. It is too early to tell how much more important will the Euro be as an international currency, relative to its predecessors. But at least so far, the supremacy of the US $ remains unchallenged.

4. The Euro and Labor Market Reforms

EMU did not take place in a vacuum. The countries that joined it were bogged down by large supply side distortions, in particular by inefficient labor market institutions and high distorting taxes on labor. These pre-existing distortions were due to national policy decisions, not to European integration. Nevertheless, national supply side distortions interact with EMU and influence its overall effects.

Specifically, it is quite possible that the Euro has amplified the effect of these pre-existing distortions. As suggested by Bertola and Boeri (2003), for instance, increased product market integration is likely to have increased the elasticity of labor demand within each country. This in turn could amplify the unemployment effects of high taxes on labor in countries with monopolistic unions (Daveri and Tabellini 2000). Similarly, more mobile investment flows are likely to favor the more efficient Euro area countries and hurt the laggards. Over time, and if labor market distortions remain unchanged, the single currency could lead to worse economic performance in the more distorted economies (typically the large countries of continental Europe), to the benefit of the more efficient Euro area countries. It is too early to tell whether this divergence has taken place, but the relatively worse performance of Germany and Italy compared to the rest of EMU suggests that this might be happening already.

But policy induced distortions are endogenous too, and monetary unification could also influence the policymakers' incentives to reform. A priori, the effect could go either way. On the one hand, stronger competitive pressures should force governments to adopt efficiency enhancing reforms. On the other hand, the demand for protection could increase, because the inefficient sectors feel more threatened. More importantly, governments have lost the exchange rate as a signal of policy success or failure, and this could lead to further procrastination of unpopular but needed reforms.

Can the evidence to date shed any light on these opposite effects on the incentives to reform? If anything, Euro area countries seem to have intensified their effort to remove labor market distortions, compared to the rest of Europe. But this effect is visible only for marginal reforms, not for the more radical and far-reaching reforms. Specifically, using the data base collected by Boeri (2002) (http://www.frdb.org/), we can compare reform effort in the European countries that joined EMU and in those that didn't, over the period 1985 and 2002. These data cover three dimensions of welfare state reforms: pension systems, firing costs and unemployment benefits. They also distinguish between marginal and radical reforms, and between reforms that enhance economic efficiency or hurt it. Reform effort intensified throughout Europe in the late 1990s, both inside and outside of EMU. As shown in Figure 1, Euro area countries increased the number of marginal reforms (going in the right direction) compared to non-Euro countries, and the effect of EMU is statistically significant when estimated with a difference in difference regression. This is mainly due to reforms that have increased labor market flexibility (generally by creating dual structures that increase flexibility at the margin). But significant reforms are much more rare and there is no difference between the "ins" and the "outs".

Figure 1: Average Number of Marginal Welfare State Reforms (Per Country)

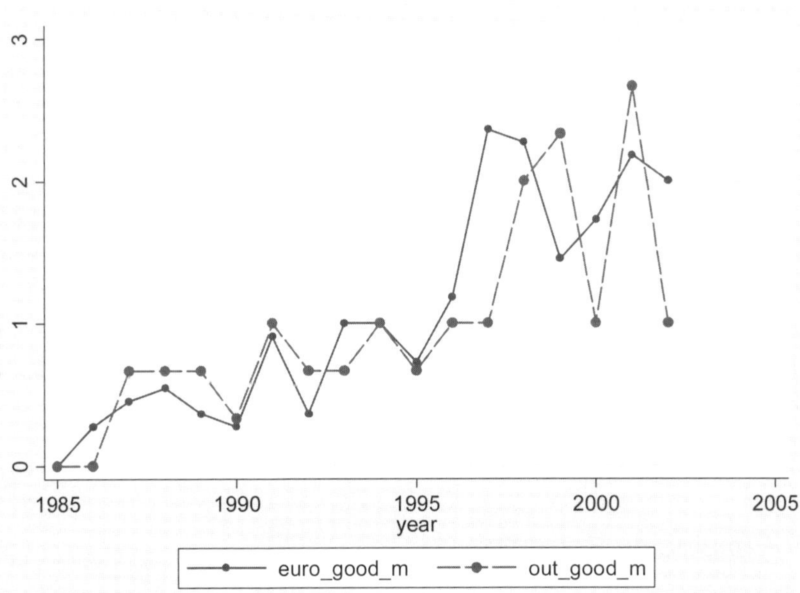

Source: Boeri (2002). *Euro_good_m* denotes the average number of marginal reforms in the countries that have now joined the Euro area. *Out_good_m* denotes the average number of marginal reforms in the UK, Sweden and Denmark. Only changes in legislation that increase labor market flexibility, reduce the generosity of pension systems, or increase the rewards from labor market participations are coded as reforms. The distinction between marginal and radical reforms is explained in http://www.frdb.org/.

5. Political Effects of the Euro

The calculus of economic costs and benefits behind EMU is only part of the story. It has always been thought that one of the effects of the single currency (whether good or bad) would be to promote further political integration in the EU. The single currency would become a new symbol of European unity, the Euro-area would now face similar policy challenges thus stimulating a Euro-wide debate, and policy coordination would have to expand into new domains. Has this happened? Again, it is too early to tell; but the data from the Eurobarometer surveys published in the spring of 2004 provide some interesting evidence.

It is indeed true that the Euro has quickly become a symbol of European unity. When asked "what does the EU mean to you personally", 50% of the EU 15 citizens answer the Euro; this is the second most common response (just behind the answer "the ability to travel, study and work anywhere in the EU").

This symbol has not made the EU or the Euro area any more popular than it was, however. Support for EU membership remains to date where it was in the mid 1990s (and below the peak reached in 1990). And even support for the single currency has not increased further compared to 1997.

Probably, this lukewarm support reflects the grim economic performance of the Euro-area. It could also be due to the mistaken perception that the introduction of the single currency has caused a substantial drop in purchasing power: the gap between perceived and actual inflation rose dramatically after the launch of the Euro. Whatever the explanation, the single currency has not increased the demand for political integration by individual citizens, at least for the time being.

6. Concluding Remarks

What do we make of these findings? Did the expected benefits of the single currency materialize? It is certainly too early to tell, but the data portray a mixed picture, and the glass can be seen as either half full or half empty. International trade and cross-border investment increased in the Euro area relative to similar countries. Particularly in the case of trade flows, the increase is quantitatively significant and can be attributed to the new currency. On the other hand, competitive pressures among Euro area producers do not seem stronger, at least judging from the lack of convergence in the prices of similar commodities produced in different countries. Money and bond markets are now fully integrated in the Euro-area, and this implies a relevant reduction in the cost of capital for large corporate borrowers. But retail banking remains segmented among national borders, meaning that households and smaller producers have not been much affected. The new currency is playing an important role throughout Europe, but it is a long distance away from challenging the supremacy of the $. And European political integration is not more likely today than it was 10 years ago.

The Euro was not expected to only have unambiguous positive economic effects. Some significant and lasting costs were also anticipated. In particular, the loss of the exchange rate as a policy tool reduces the flexibility to cope with idiosyncratic shocks. Moreover, according to some critics, the constraints imposed by the Maastricht framework went too far in the direction of imposing a rigid straightjacket on macroeconomic policy. It is too early to assess whether these costs turned out to be higher or lower than expected, but certainly they could play a role in explaining the disappointing macroeconomic performance of the Euro area.

The main reason why European growth is stalling has little to do with monetary unification, however. The problem lies with the supply side distortions (in particular the labor market distortions) induced by misguided national policies in the 1970s and 1980s. The Euro was a true revolution, and we cannot yet see all its effects. But it took place on shaky national economic foundations. The revolution only transformed the up per floors of the European economy: financial markets and the institutions that govern macroeconomic policy. It did not reach the shaky foundations. The countries that joined EMU had poor labor market institutions, bloated pension systems, inefficient service sectors in the late 1990s, and they still do now. The launch of the Euro did not change this fundamental deficiency, nor could it be expected to do so.

Overhauling these shaky foundations is the next key challenge for Europe – though this next revolution should mainly take place within each country rather than at the European level. One can only hope that it will be met with the same mix of ability, competence, and vision that went into the creation of the single currency.

References

Adjaouté K., and J. P. Danthine (2002), "European Financial Integration and Equity Returns: A theory – based assessment", conference paper, presented at the Second ECB Central Banking Conference on "The Transformation of the European Financial System", Frankfurt am Main, October 2002.

Baele L., A. Ferrando, P. Hördhal, E. Krylova and C. Monnet (2004), "Measuring Financial Intergration in the Euro Area." Mimeo, European Central Bank vol. 14, April 2004.

Barr D., F. Breedon and D. Miles (2003), "Life on the Outside: Economic Conditions and Prospects Outside Euroland." Economic Policy 37: 573-613.

Bertola, G. and T. Boeri (2003), "Product Market Integrations, Institutions and the Labor Market", mimeo, IGIER, Bocconi University

Boeri, T. (2002), "Reforming Labor and Product Markets: Some Lessons from two Decades of Experiments in Europe", mimeo, IGIER, Bocconi University

Bun M. and F. Klassen (2002), "Has the Euro Increased Trade?", Tinbergen Institute Discussion Paper No. 108/2, University of Amsterdam.

Cabral I., F. Dierik and J. Vesala (2002), "Banking Integration in the Euro Area." European Central Bank, Occasional paper No. 6, December.

Codogno L., C. Favero and A. Missale (2003), "Yield Spreads on EMU Government Bonds." Economic Policy 37 : 503-532.

Daveri, F, and G. Tabellini (2000), "Unemployment, Growth and Taxation in Industrial Countries", Economic Policy, n. 30, April

Dermine J. (2002), "European Banking: Past, Present and Future", Conference Paper, presented at the Second ECB Central Banking Conference on "The Transformation of the European Financial System", Frankfurt am Main, October 2002.

Detken C. and P. Hartmann (2002), "Features of the Euro's Role in International Financial Markets." Economic Policy 35 : 553-569.

Engel C. and J. H. Rogers (2004), "European Product Market Integration after the Euro." Economic Policy 39 : 347-384.

European Commission (2003), "The Impact of EMU on Trade and FDI." *Quarterly report on the Euro Area*, No III, September.

European Commission (2004), "EMU after 5 Years." Mimeo, Directorate-General for Economic and Financial Affairs.

Faruqee H. (2004), "Measuring the Trade Effects of EMU." IMF Working Paper.

Goodhart C., R. Love, R. Payne and D. Rime (2002), "Analysis of Spreads in the Dollar/Euro and Deutschmark/Dollar Foreign Exchange Markets." Economic Policy 35 : 535-552.

Hau H., W. Killen and M. Moore (2002), " How has the Euro Changed the Foreign Exchange Market?" Economic Policy 34 : 149-191.

Helpman E. (2004), *The Mystery of Economic Growth*. Mimeo, Harvard University.

HM Treasury (2003), "UK Membership of the Single Currency: Assessment of the Five Economic Tests." HM Treasury, London.

Lutz M. (2002), "Price Convergence under EMU? First Estimates", working paper, Institute of Economics, Washington, DC.

Micco A., E. Stein and G. Ordonez (2003), "The Currency Union Effect on Trade: Early Evidence from EMU." Economic Policy 37 : 309-356.

Portes R. and H. Rey (1998), "The Emergence of the Euro as an International Currency." Economic Policy 26 : 305-343.

Rogers J.H. (2002), "Monetary Union, Price Level Convergence, and Inflation: How close is Europe to the United States?", Board of Governors of the Federal Reserve System, International Finance Discussion Paper No. 2002-740.

Rose A.K. and E. Van Wincoop (2001), "National Money as a Barrier to International Trade: the Real Case of Currency Union." American Economic Review 91(2), 386 – 90.

Thygesen N. (1994), "Why is Economic and Monetary Union an Important Objective for Europe?" International Review of Law and Economics 14 : 133-145.

CHAPTER 5

Endogeneities of Optimum Currency Areas

Paul De Grauwe and Francesco Paolo Mongelli[*]

This paper brings together several strands of the literature on the endogenous effects of monetary integration. The start of the European Economic and Monetary Union (EMU) has spurred a new interest in this debate: i.e., whether sharing a new single currency, the euro, sets free forces that bring euro area countries closer together.[1] Much of the merit for having kick-started this debate goes to Andrew Rose and Jeffrey Frankel (see Rose (2000 and 2002 a and b) and Frankel and Rose (1997 and 2001)).

By studying the effects of several currency unions that have occurred in the past, Frankel and Rose first showed that monetary integration leads to very significant deepening of reciprocal trade. The implication for EMU is that the euro area may turn into an optimum currency area (OCA) after the launch of monetary integration even if it wasn't an OCA before, or *"countries which join EMU, no matter what their motivation may be, may satisfy OCA properties ex-post even if they do not ex-ante!"* (Frankel and Rose 1997). Consequently, the borders of new currency unions could be

* The views expressed are those of the authors and do not necessarily reflect those of the ECB.

1. On 1 January 1999 the euro was established as the single currency of eleven European countries and the European Central Bank started operating and managing their common monetary policy. Greece then joined on 1 January 2002.

drawn larger in expectation that trade integration and income correlation will augment once a currency union is created. This has been termed the "endogeneity of optimum currency area" effect.[2]

The endogeneity of OCA effect is grounded on two main insights. The first insight is that the degree of openness, i.e., reciprocal trade between the members of the currency area, is likely to increase. This insight is widely accepted although there are different views on its strength (as we shall discuss below). The second insight postulates a positive link between trade integration and income correlation. On this insight there are diverging views as not all authors would subscribe to a positive link between trade integration and income correlation (as we shall also discuss below).

This paper revisits the arguments behind these two insights and explores more systematically the notion of endogeneity of OCA that could originate from several other sources. Several authors have in fact brought forward concepts similar to the above hypothesis of "endogeneity of OCA" but in different areas than trade. Artis and Zhang (1999) and others have discussed the endogeneity of symmetry of shocks. Blanchard and Wolfers (2000), Saint Paul and Bentolila (2002), and Saint-Paul (2002) discuss the endogeneity of labour market institutions. Several authors have discussed the effects of sharing a single currency on financial markets and insurance schemes. Therefore, we address here the issue of "endogeneities of OCA." These endogeneities of OCA can be seen as a set of processes triggered by the start of a monetary union, improving the OCA-ratings of the union.

2. However, an optimum currency area needs to be judged along more dimensions than just trade openness. Optimality is also captured by the mobility of labour and other factors of production, price and wage flexibility, diversification in production and consumption, similarity in inflation rates, financial integration, fiscal integration, similarity of shocks, and political integration. Sharing of these OCA properties – among sovereign countries, forming an "area" – reduces the usefulness of nominal exchange rate adjustments among them by: fostering internal and external balance; reducing the impact of some types of shocks; or facilitating the adjustment thereafter. See Mundell (1961), McKinnon (1963), Kenen (1969), and Corden (1972). For recent surveys see Tavlas (1993), De Grauwe (2001) and Mongelli (2002).

Against this background there are four areas that we analyse:

a. the **endogeneity of economic integration**, in which we look primarily at evidence on prices and trade;
b. the **endogeneity of financial integration** or equivalently of insurance schemes provided by capital markets;
c. the **endogeneity of symmetry of shocks**; and
d. the **endogeneity of product and labour market flexibility.**

Changes in these four areas are of course inter-linked and we shall try to highlight some of the main connections and interdependences.

The paper is organised as follows. Section 2 presents a conceptual framework. Section 3 discusses the endogeneity of economic integration. Section 4 discusses the endogeneity of symmetry of shocks. Section 5 discusses the endogeneity of labour market flexibility. Section 6 presents a set of concluding observations and open issues for further analysis.

1. Some Conceptual Elements of Endogeneities of OCA

Why should European monetary integration improve the *OCA-rating* of the euro area? What drives any endogenous effect?

1.1. Market-Based Forces Fostering Endogeneity

There are diverse market-based forces at play. Some pecuniary costs disappear or fall following monetary integration. The introduction of the euro contributes, amongst others, to reducing trading costs both directly and indirectly: e.g., by removing exchange rate risks and the cost of currency hedging. Some information costs will be reduced. The euro is expected to have a catalyzing role for the Single Market Program by enhancing price transparency and discouraging price discrimination. This should contribute to reducing market segmentation and fostering competition.

A common currency among partner countries is seen as "a much more serious and durable commitment" than other monetary arrangements between countries (McCallum (1995)). It precludes future competitive devaluation, facilitates foreign direct investment and the building of long-term relationships, and is likely to encourage forms of political integration. This will promote reciprocal trade, economic and financial integration and foster even business cycle synchronisation among the countries sharing a single currency. However, there are diverging views on this link (as we shall also discuss below).

Finally, one single money is more efficient than multiple currencies in performing the roles of medium of exchange and unit of account. As a result, a common currency promotes convergence in social conventions with potentially far reaching legal, contractual and accounting implications (Garcia-Herrero et alii (2001)).

1.2. Institutional Forces Fostering Endogeneity

There are institutional forces at play, and EMU might have a catalysing role. The existence of EMU is likely to intensify ongoing institutional reforms, as for example, those fostered and monitored by the EU Commission and including the Financial Services Action Plan (FSAP), the Lamfalussy Report and its follow ups, the Giovannini Report and others (see for example the EU Commission Scoreboard). As a result, political institutions might also be endogenous to some extent (Issing (2003)).

1.3. Economic Integration and Income Correlation

In the following sections we use a simple graphical device to illustrate changes in the OCA-rating along three main dimensions: i.e., economic openness, income correlation within the currency area, and flexibility of each country participating to the currency area. A deepening of different OCA properties generates improvements in the scores of these three dimensions.

The degree of economic openness and the correlation of incomes are crucial in assessing the net benefits from currency union. We illustrate this in Figure 1. The OCA-line is the collection of combinations of symmetry and integration among groups of countries for which the cost and benefits of a monetary union just balance. It is downward sloping for the following reason. A decline in symmetry (increase in asymmetry) raises the costs of a monetary union. These costs are mainly macroeconomic in nature. They arise because the loss of a national monetary policy instrument is more costly as the degree of asymmetry increases. Integration is a source of benefits of a monetary union, i.e. the greater the degree of integration the more the member countries benefit from the efficiency gains of a monetary union. Thus, the additional (macroeconomic) costs produced by less symmetry can be compensated by the additional (microeconomic) benefits produced by more integration. Points to the right of the OCA-line represent groupings of countries for which the benefits of a monetary union exceed its costs. We have put the US states and the Euro area to the right of the OCA-line because we believe that the microeconomic benefits of these monetary unions more than compensate their macroeconomic costs.

Figure 1. Openness, Income Correlation and OCA

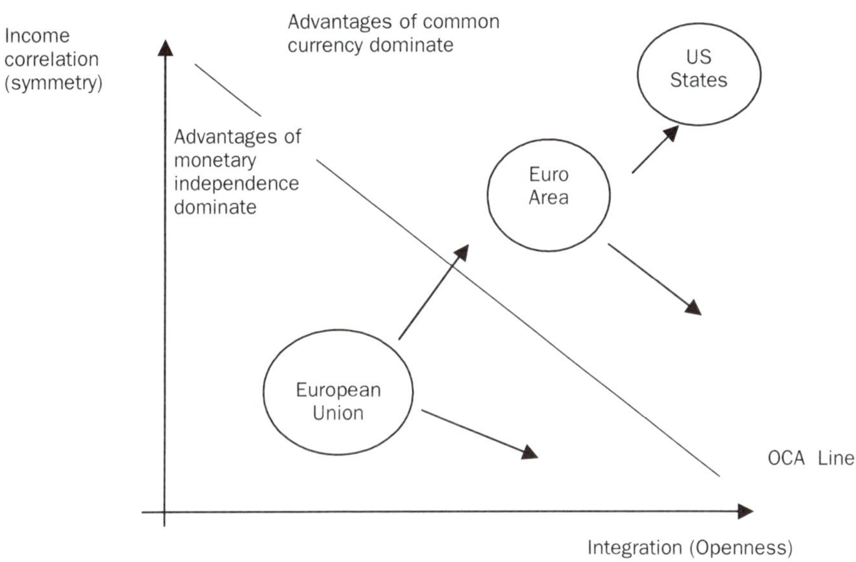

To the left of the OCA line the benefits from monetary independence dominate the efficiency gains from the union. We have put the European Union as a whole to the left of the OCA-line because we believe that these countries are not yet sufficiently integrated to generate efficiency gains that will compensate for the macroeconomic costs of the union. We realize, however, that this is a controversial issue and that not all economists may agree on this.

The degree of economic integration and income correlation evolve over time. There are different views on such evolution (as illustrated by the arrows around the EU and Euro circles in Figure 1). As is discussed in Section 3 below, most authors agree that openness is likely to increase among countries sharing a single currency. The intuition is the following: the introduction of the single currency will contribute to reducing trading costs both directly and indirectly, e.g., by removing exchange rate risks (and the cost of hedging) and diminishing information costs. The single currency will also spur transparency and competition, lessen segmentation, and reduce transportation and transaction costs.

There is disagreement concerning the extent to which income correlation might rise, or fall. In one case the increased openness raises income correlation (and reduces asymmetry of shocks). The EU then moves along the upward arrow. In another case, that we call the specialisation case, we move along the downward sloping arrows in figure 1. This then produces the opposite effect, and more flexibility for the monetary union would be required as is discussed next.

1.4. Income Correlation and Flexibility

In addition to the degree of economic openness and income correlation there is another important dimension to judge the merit of monetary integration, i.e., the degree of flexibility. The trade-off between symmetry and flexibility is illustrated by the downward sloping "OCA line" in Figure 2. Points on the OCA-line define combinations of income correlation (symmetry) and flexibility for which the costs and the benefits of a monetary union just balance. It is negatively sloped because a declining degree of symmetry (which raises the costs) necessitates an increasing flexibility (which is a source of benefits of a monetary union) To the right of the OCA-line the degree of flexibility is large given the degree of symmetry, so that the benefits of the union exceed the costs. To the left of the OCA-line there is insufficient flexibility for any given level of symmetry. Note that the OCA-line is drawn for a given level of integration (I_1).

Figure 2. Symmetry, Flexibility and OCA

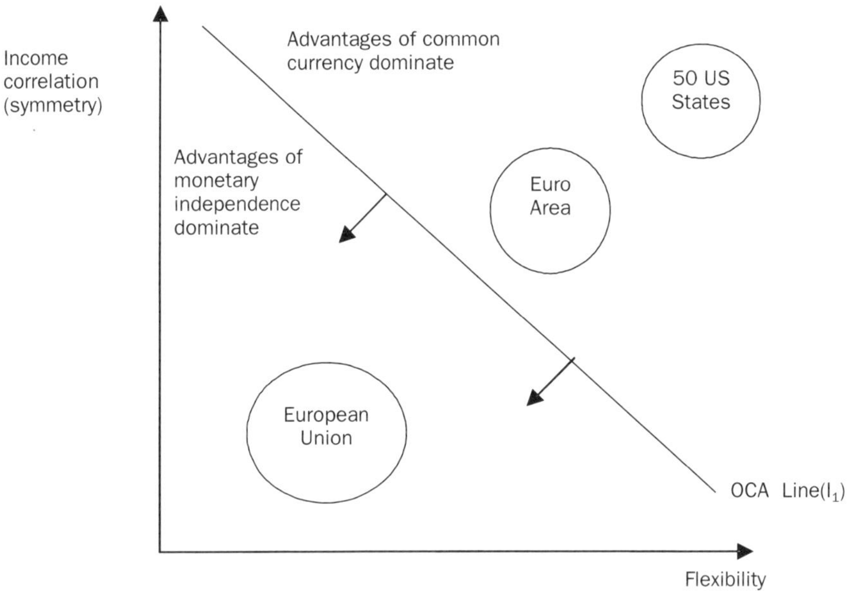

Again, the 50 US States and the current members of the euro area (*according to us*) are located to the right of the OCA line. One can have doubts that the European Union (EU) as a whole should share a single currency, and we illustrate this by placing the EU on the left of the OCA line. Assuming that the newly enlarged EU25 is not yet in the OCA zone, how does further integration affect the movement towards OCA? The OCA-line was drawn for a given level of integration (I1). Increasing integration has the effect of shifting the OCA-line downwards, i.e. when integration increases the benefits of the union increase so that we need less flexibility and/or less symmetry to make the monetary union beneficial. If there is endogeneity in integration then starting a monetary union among the EU will bring it closer to the OCA-zone .

There is interaction between integration, flexibility and symmetry that we now analyze in more detail. Let's postulate that the net benefits of monetary union (B) are a positive function of :

- the degree of flexibility (F)
- the degree of symmetry (S)
- the degree of integration (I)

We can specify the relation between net benefits (B) and the three variables, F, S, and I as follows (assuming that these relationships are linear):

$$B = \alpha F + \beta I + \gamma S$$

where α, β, γ are positive parameters. This allows us to derive the OCA-plane, i.e. the combinations of F, I and S for which the net benefits of a monetary union are zero. Set B=0, then:

$$F = -\beta' I - \gamma' S$$

where $\beta' = \beta / \alpha$ and $\gamma' = \gamma / \alpha$. A graphical representation of this relation is given in figure 3. We have normalized the variables such that

$$0 < I < 1 \text{ and } -1 < S < 1$$

Thus, S can be positive and negative depending on whether shocks are symmetric or asymmetric. Figure 3 synthesises the three trade-offs:

- the trade-off between flexibility and integration
- the trade-off between symmetry and flexibility
- the trade-off between symmetry and integration

The figure also highlights the interaction between these tradeoffs. To illustrate this, let us concentrate on the trade-off between symmetry and flexibility, which shows that when symmetry declines more flexibility is needed to make OCA beneficial. It can be seen that this trade-off depends on integration. Start with zero integration and let it gradually increase.

Then the relationship between symmetry and flexibility is shifted downwards, i.e. one needs less flexibility for any given level of symmetry.

There are more such interactions. Let us focus on the trade-off between integration and flexibility. This trade-off is influenced by the degree of symmetry. An increase in the latter leads to a downward shift of the trade-off between integration and flexibility. Finally, there is a trade-off between integration and symmetry. This trade-off is influenced by the degree of flexibility. When flexibility increases the trade-off between integration and symmetry shifts downwards so that one needs less of both integration of and symmetry to make a monetary union advantageous.

Figure 3.

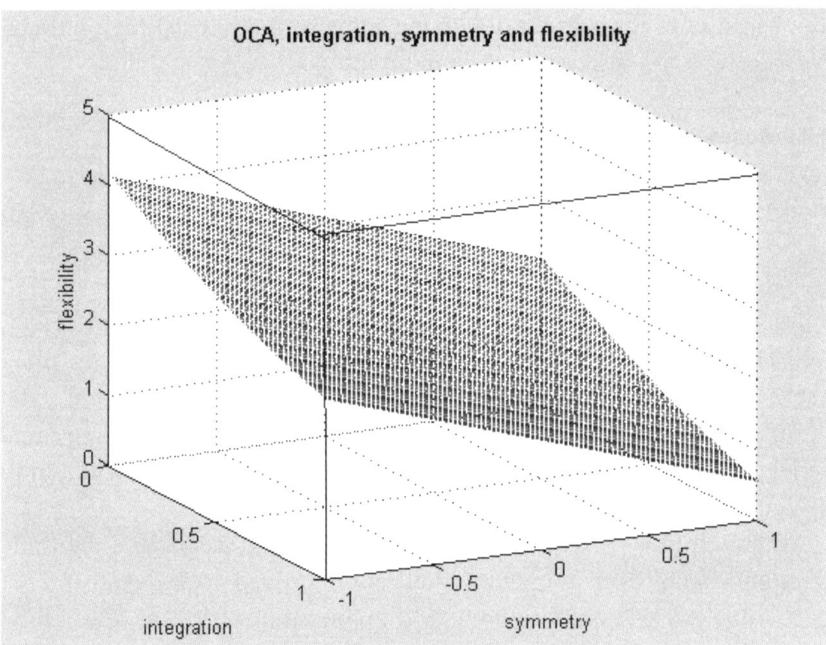

These interactions are important for understanding endogeneities and their interdependence. Let us assume that the European Union 25 as a whole is located below the OCA-plane. A decision to form a monetary union then sets in motion different endogeneities. First, integration is likely to increase. This has the effect of improving the symmetry-flexibility trade-off thereby facilitating the movement into the OCA-zone. A second endogeneity is symmetry. The decision to enter monetary union has the potential to increase symmetry. This in turn improves the trade-off between flexibility and integration, thereby facilitating the movement into the OCA-zone.

In this sense, endogeneities in integration, symmetry and flexibility reinforce each other, and speed up the process into the OCA-space. In the next section we discuss the empirical evidence on these endogeneities.

2. Endogeneity of Economic Integration

In what follows we start by discussing some research focussing on trade. We then turn to a discussion of financial integration.

2.1. Monetary Union and Trade

Several recent studies have improved our knowledge of the effects of a monetary unification (union) on trade. First, Engel and Rogers (1995) found that crossing the border between the US and Canada has an impact on relative price volatility, equivalent to an addition of, at least, 1780 miles, to the distance between cities. Second, McCallum (1995) and Helliwell (1998) conclude that Canadian provinces are 12 to 20 times more likely to trade with each other than with US states.

Third, a series of studies initiated by Andrew Rose[3] and using large panel data sets find that membership in a currency union leads to a multiplication of trade by a factor of three or more.

Although these results were received with some scepticism, the trade creation effects from monetary unification proved to be quite robust qualitatively. There are however some qualifications.[4] Recent research by

3. See amongst others Rose (2000), Rose (2001), Frankel and Rose (2000), and Rose and van Wincoop (2001).
4. For example, Quah (1999) notes that this empirical evidence pertains to a narrow set of relatively small (or even tiny) countries/territories representing about 1% of the sample used by Frankel and Rose (2002) and Rose (2000). Such entities have at times adopted the currency of a much larger partner country:

Melitz (2001) and Persson (2001) comes out with substantially lower estimates. The minimum point estimate (from Persson) still suggests a 13 per cent increase in trade from currency unification with a preferred estimate of around 40 per cent.

2.2. Some "Early"Evidence: The Effects of the Euro on Euro Area Trade

The empirical evidence discussed above relates to monetary unions in general. Does the introduction of the euro have a similar potential for trade creation? Recently this question has been analysed. Rose and Van Wincoop (2001) use an estimated version of the theoretical model of Anderson and van Wincoop (2001) to infer the impact from EMU on intra euro area trade and welfare. They conclude that intra euro area trade would expand by more than *50 percent*. Interestingly, Bun and Klaassen (2002) who use a dynamic panel model find a cumulated long-run effect of about *40 percent*. Micco, Stein and Ordoñez (2003) corroborate these findings.

The previous results relate to the likely long-term effects. As far as the short-term effects are concerned, the evidence suggests that it may take some time for these effects to be realized. Bun and Klaassen (2002) using a dynamic panel model find that the euro has increased trade by 4 percent in the first year.

Anderton and Skudelny (2001) estimate an import demand function for the euro area vis-à-vis its main extra-area trading partners which takes into account the possible impact of both intra- and extra-euro area exchange rate uncertainty. Using some panel estimates they find that extra-euro area exchange rate volatility may have reduced extra-euro area imports by around 10 per cent resulting in some substitution between extra- and intra-euro area imports. This is an important qualification of the above trade evidence.

In summary, the above trade evidence leads to some ambiguities. The theory and the empirical evidence of the trade creating effects of a monetary union is now well-established. At the same time, the evidence of such an effect in the euro area is still limited. An explanation might be that the

often the US or some other former coloniser, or a large neighbour, or an important trading or financial partner of the small country.

trade creating effects of a monetary union take a lot of time to be felt (see Mongelli, Dorrucci and Agur (2004) on this issue).

2.3. Endogeneity of Financial Integration (i.e., Insurance Schemes)

Defining financial integration is a broad and complex task as it embraces a wide array of financial intermediaries, a variety of financial market segments, and an assortment of financial instruments. Following Ferrando et alii (2004) we postulate that financial integration is achieved when all potential market participants with the same relevant characteristics: (1) face a single set of rules when they decide to deal with those financial instruments and/or services; (2) have equal access to the above-mentioned set of financial instruments and/or services; and (3) are treated equally when they are active in the market.

Financial integration generates several widely accepted benefits such as the improved allocation of capital, higher efficiency, and higher economic growth. Graphically, financial integration has the effect of endogenously shifting the OCA lines in Figures 1 and 2 downwards (i.e., raising the net benefits from EMU). Amongst others, financial markets can provide a significant source of insurance against asymmetric shocks. To the extent that monetary unification enhances financial integration, it will endogenously improve insurance against asymmetric shocks, thereby reducing the costs of a monetary union: an important endogenous component for EMU.

One interesting line of research has lead to the identification of a "border effect" also for financial market integration. Atkeson and Bayoumi (1993), Bayoumi and Klein (1997) and Crucini (1999) all find that risk sharing across the regions of a country is significantly larger than across countries. Asdrubali, Sorensen and Yosha (1996) looked at channels of interstate risk sharing in the US. They focused on shocks to gross state product and found that 39% of the shocks are smoothed through *capital markets*, 23% are smoothed through *credit markets* and 13% through the *federal government*. 25% are not smoothed. Hence, financial markets and institutions in the US contribute with 62% to the absorption of state idiosyncratic shocks. The effect is about five times more important than the federal budget.

However, the above findings do not carry over to the EU/euro area because the European Union is not currently endowed with a "Federal

Budget" i.e., a supranational shock-absorbing scheme. Also, European monetary integration is in its infancy, and financial integration is still modest overall (but rising) as we shall see. But over time financial market integration in the EU/euro area might lead to stronger international risk sharing.

2.4. Some "Early"Evidence: The Effects of the Euro on Financial Prices, Interest Rates and Equity Returns

Money markets integrated almost immediately after the introduction of the euro. The transition was smooth and swift. However, even in money markets, integration has not progressed in a uniform way in the different market segments. The unsecured deposit market may be regarded as fully integrated. The repo segment, where market participants exchange short run liquidity against collateral is less well integrated (see Berg, Grande and Mongelli (2004) and ECB, July 2001 "The Euro area Money Market Report").

Looking at bond markets it is clear that the integration of financial markets in the euro area started well before Stage 3 of Economic and Monetary Union. Yield differentials among euro area government bonds converged markedly since 1996. This convergence accelerated further after the pre-announcement of the irrevocable fixing of parities in May 1998. Since May 1998 yield differentials have only rarely exceeded 40-50 basis points while in early nineties spreads of more than 500 basis points – mostly reflecting inflation differentials – were not uncommon.[5] However, Adjaoute, Danthine and Isakov (2003) discern no obvious pattern in the dispersion of *ex-post* real yields *pre- and post*-EMU. But still there is a considerable decrease in volatility of real yields.

Adjaoute, Danthine and Isakov (2003) find some new evidence that the equity risk premium may have decreased in Europe reducing the cost of capital. There is also evidence that the structure of equity returns has changed in Europe: country factors now appear to be dominated by the factors associated with industries or sectors. Adjaoute, Danthine and Isa-

5. There are diverse explanations for this phenomenon: institutional investors have, to some extent, seized the opportunities opened by the disappearance of relevant currency matching restrictions. there was also a sharp drop in interest rate volatility for each country; and a convergence in nominal yields due to the convergence in inflation rates.

kov conclude, however, that there is little evidence in support of the hypothesis that the average European investor is now more financially diversified than in the recent past. Rather European financial markets continue to be seriously undiversified.

Angeloni and Ehrmann (2003) seek evidence of euro area-wide banking integration and the degree of interest rate pass-through using post-1999 data. They show that the pass-through of changes in money market rates is not only faster and more complete but also increasingly homogenous across the euro area. Bank retail rate spreads have also fallen steadily.

2.5. Some "Early"Evidence: The Effects of the Euro on Financial Flows, Stocks and Structures

Much attention has been attracted by the substantial increase in direct and portfolio investment flows *between the euro area and abroad* since the end of the 1990s. However, there has also been a less well documented increase in direct and portfolio investment flows *within the euro area*. Figure 6 shows both the intra and extra-euro area total foreign direct investment (FDI) and equity capital flows.

Figure 6. Foreign Direct Investment Flows Intra- and Extra-Euro Area, 1996-2001

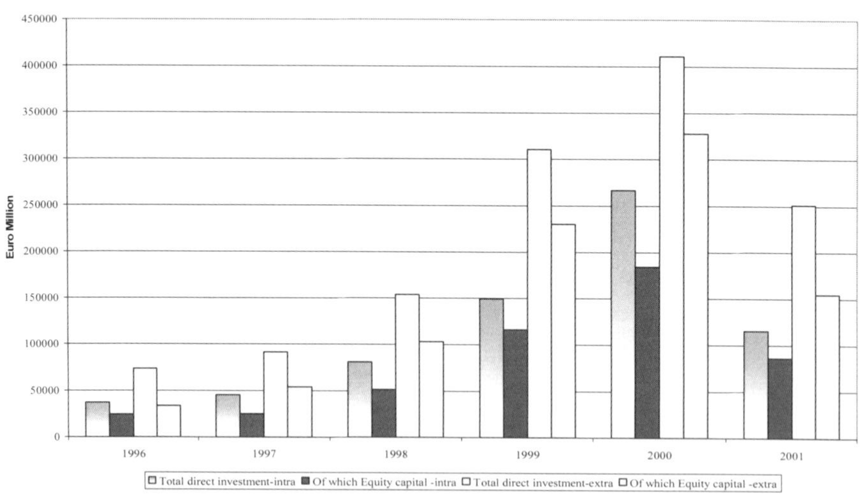

Over the sample period intra-euro area and extra-euro area FDI showed comparable patterns, posting a remarkable increase in 1999 and 2000 noteworthy that the annual percentage change of intra-euro area FDI has. There are important caveats and qualifications of these data. The most important one is that it is as yet unclear how much of this observed increase in FDI is due to the conditions of economic boom during 1999-2001.

M&A transactions show a similar development as the intra and extra-euro area FDI. M&A investments increased markedly between 1996 and 2000 posting a seven-fold increase (**Figure 7**). However, here also a qualification should be made. The large increase in M&A activity observed during 1997-2001 is probably linked to the asset bubbles and the economic boom. We observe a sharp fall since 2001. It is therefore unclear whether EMU is in any way responsible for these developments.

Figure 7. Mergers and Acquisition Activity Intra- and Extra-Euro Area, 1990-2002

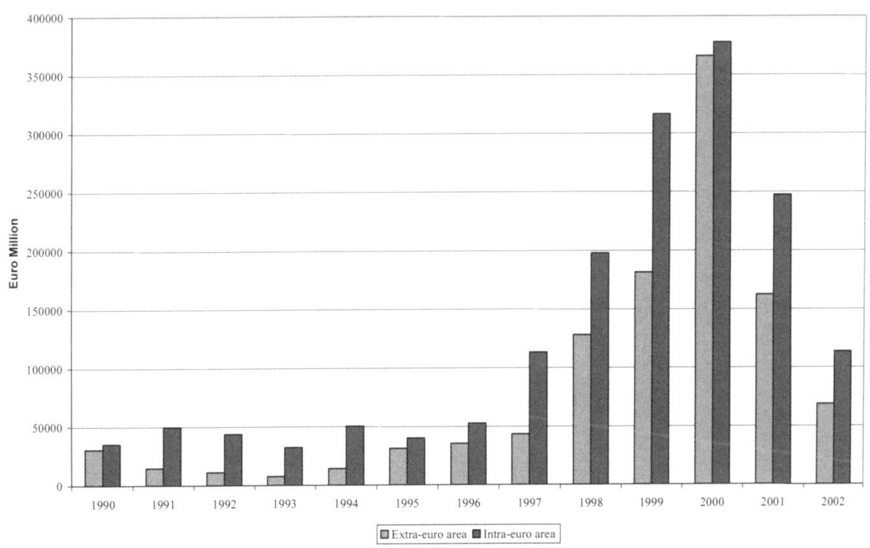

There has also been an increase in bond issuance both by non-financial corporations and by monetary and financial institutions (MFIs) – see Ferrando et alii (2004). The increased access of non-financial corporations to market finance reflects, in part, stronger competition within the European financial sector. Banks are therefore under pressure to use their balance sheet more efficiently in order to increase their return on equity. As a consequence banks are increasingly facilitating the access by corporations to capital markets. A particular significant development, in this context, is the very fast growth of issuances by smaller and less well established firms.

A look at the assets side of the balance sheet of the MFIs in the euro area – and more specifically at the loans of the MFIs – provides some indications of progress in integration in financial services. Loans represent in fact the most important asset in the balance sheet of the MFIs. Figure 9, which collects also the gross stock of the loans to euro area residents versus non-euro area residents, shows a remarkable increase of intra- euro area loans, compared to the extra-euro area loans, after 1998. However, after the year 2000 a sharp decline occurs again, leaving this ratio at a somewhat higher level than at the start of the eurozone.

Figure 9. Ratio of Loans of the MFIs to Euro Area Residents and Non-Residents.

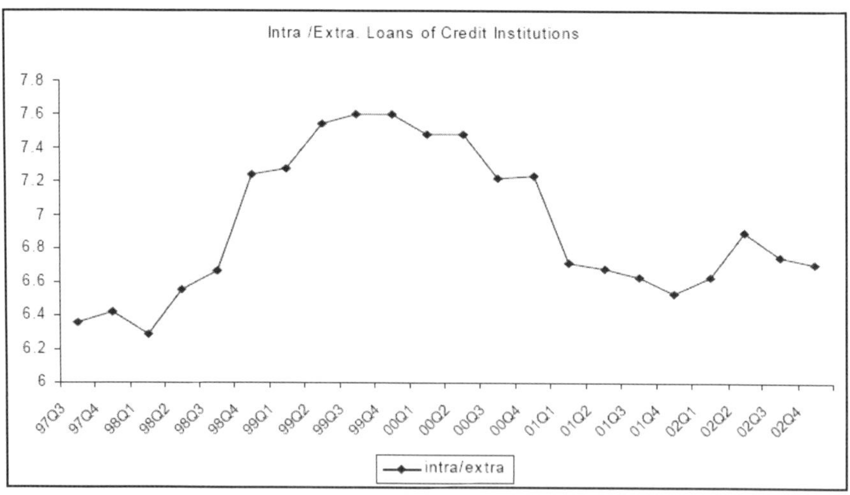

Source: ECB.MFIs database

2.6. Concluding Observations on the Endogeneity of Financial Integration (and the Insurance Schemes)

From the preceding evidence one can conclude that some progress has been made towards more financial integrations in the eurozone. There is no doubt that this progress, especially in the money and bond markets, has been due to the introduction of the euro. Yet, the eurozone is still far from a unified financial market. The view of Giovannini (2002) according to which European financial markets are still a *juxtaposition* of national markets may not be far off the mark.

3. Endogeneity of Symmetry of Shocks

3.1. Effects of Economic and Financial Integration on Income Correlation

Several authors note that the process of economic integration affects the symmetry of output fluctuations through diverse channels. According to Frankel and Rose (1998) the removal of trade barriers raises trade, allows demand shocks to more easily spread across the trading partners, and leads to more correlated business cycles. They also mention that policy shocks will become more correlated. Coe and Helpmann (1995) argue that knowledge and technology spillovers will also increase with economic integration and support symmetry of output fluctuations.

Kalemli-Ozcan, Sørensen, Yosha (2001) argue instead that higher financial integration may lead to more asymmetric macroeconomic fluctuations, possibly counterbalancing the other channels. The argument runs as follows. Economic integration leads to better risk-sharing opportunities (income insurance) through financial market integration. This in turn makes specialisation in production more attractive, rendering macroeconomic fluctuations less symmetric.

The implications for EMU of the work of all these channels could be substantial. We illustrate these with the following two distinct (illustrative) paradigms – specialisation versus endogeneity of OCA – which have different implications for the benefits and costs of a single currency.

3.2. The Specialisation Paradigm

The specialisation paradigm postulates that as countries become more integrated, they become increasingly specialized. The dynamics underlying this process is based on economies of scale and agglomeration effects. Members of a currency union would then become less diversified and more vulnerable to asymmetric shocks. Correspondingly their incomes will become less correlated. Kalemli-Ozcan, Sørensen and Yosha (2001) provide empirical evidence that financial integration enhances specialisation in production. The consequence is that an increase in integration could move a group of countries that are in the OCA-zone outside this zone, e.g., from point 1 in Figure 11 to point 2. Whether it does this depends on the relative strength of two opposing forces that result from increased integration: the increase in asymmetry which increases the costs of the union and the increase in the efficiency gains of the monetary union.

Figure 11. Specialisation Increases and Correlation of Incomes

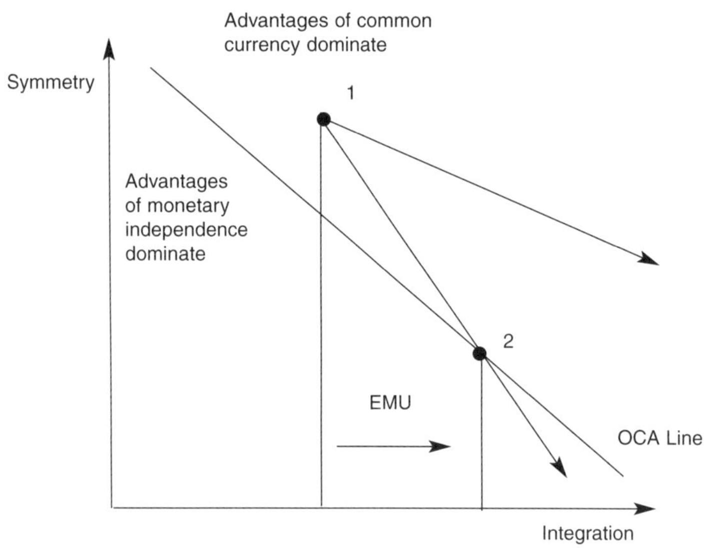

3.3. The "Endogeneity of OCA" Paradigm

The second paradigm is the *"endogeneity of OCA" hypothesis* that postulates a positive link between income correlation and trade integration. The basic intuition behind this hypothesis is that a common currency is "a serious and durable commitment" (McCallum (1995)). It precludes future competitive devaluations, facilitates foreign direct investment and the building of long-term relationships, and may over time encourage forms of political integration. This will promote reciprocal trade, economic and financial integration and it will foster business cycle synchronisation among the countries sharing a single currency. This idea is represented graphically in Figure 12.

Figure 12. A Country Joins the EU and then EMU and the "Endogeneity" of OCA Dominates

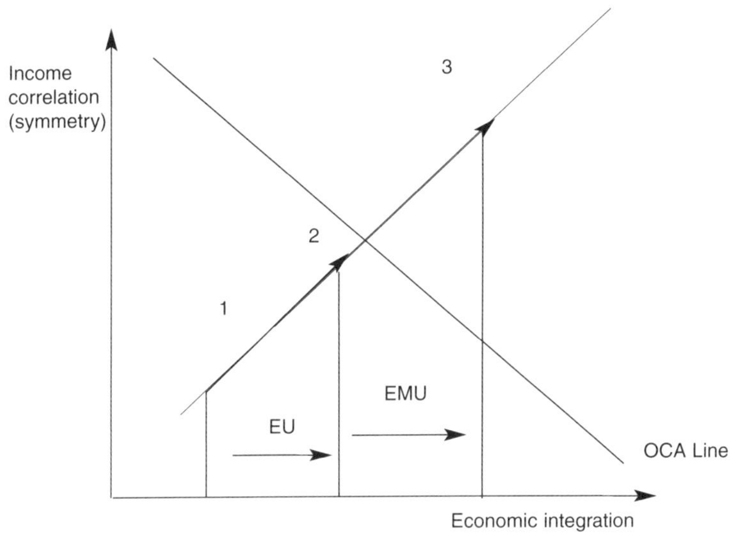

The group of countries is initially on the left of the OCA line. If these countries join together and form a union, e.g. EU, both trade integration and income correlation within the group will rise: i.e., they will gradually move to point 2. If the same countries were to start a currency area – e.g., EMU – the degree of trade integration and income correlation within this group would rise even further and the group would subsequently find itself on the right of the OCA line.

3.4. The Empirical Evidence thus far for Specialization or Endogeneity of OCA

Frankel and Rose (1996) have undertaken important empirical research relating to this issue. They analysed the degree to which economic activity between pairs of countries is correlated as a function of the intensity of their trade links. Their conclusion was that a closer trade linkage between two countries is strongly and consistently associated with more tightly correlated economic activity between the two countries. This is also confirmed in the studies of Rose and Engel (2001) and Rose(2002). Similar evidence is presented in Artis and Zhang (1995), who find that as the European countries have become more integrated during the 1980s and 1990s, the business cycles of these countries have become more correlated.

There is another piece of empirical evidence that enhances the view that economic integration may not lead to increased asymmetric shocks within a union. This has to do with the rising importance of services. Economies of scale do not seem to matter as much for services as for industrial activities. As a result, economic integration does not lead to regional concentration of services in the way it does with industries. As services become increasingly important (today they account for 70% or more of GDP in many EU-countries) the trend towards regional concentration of economic activities may stop even if economic integration moves forward. There is some evidence that this is already occurring in the USA. In a recent study, the OECD (2000) came to the conclusion that the regional concentration of economic activities in the USA started to decline after decades of increasing concentration.

3.5. Concluding Observations on the Endogeneity of Symmetry of Shocks

In summary, there seems to be some evidence indicating that in the past increased integration has led to more symmetry in economic shocks. Whether this will continue to be so in the future remains uncertain. Economies of scale and agglomeration effects may do their work in enhancing asymmetries. In addition, it is difficult at this stage to gauge the effect of financial integration on specialisation. Nevertheless we are inclined to conclude that the endogeneity of the OCA-paradigm will tend to prevail.

4. Endogeneity of Product and Labour Market Flexibility

In this section we analyse the conditions in which a monetary union will be a device to increase product and labour market flexibility. The topic of this section is probably the most difficult of all because measuring product and labour market flexibility is a delicate task. Hence, we will use also indirect measures and indicators (and some proxies of flexibility), including national income policies, labour market reforms, and so forth.

4.1. Some "Early" Evidence: The Effects of the Euro on Wages

A visible phenomenon of recent years has been an impressive progress toward nominal stabilisation in the run-up to EMU and since the start of Stage 3 of EMU. A large part of this stabilisation of nominal wages has to do with the decline in inflation observed during the same period. There may, however, be more factors involved. Calmfors (2001) and Pichelmann (2003) note that this wage moderation coincided with a reappearance of national income policies in some countries and longer contract periods in some others (the latter being the result of low inflation).

The increased use of national wage policies is probably linked to the monetary discipline imposed by a common currency. There are other areas in which the common currency affects the wage bargaining process. In particular, monetary unification may affect wage bargaining more generally by enhancing price transparency and fostering competition in product and service markets. This reduces the potential rent to be shared by workers and firms and encourages a de-centralisation of wage bargaining.

4.2. Looking at Labour Market Reforms and Policies

Is EMU encouraging or hindering labour market reforms? As so often in economics there are strikingly opposing views on this issue. One view is pessimistic and argues that a monetary union weakens the incentives to introduce structural reforms. This view is exemplified by Saint-Paul and Bentolila (2002) . These authors note that the loss of monetary policy discretion at the country level lowers the incentive to undertake large-scale reform of labour markets as it precludes a "two-handed" approach according to which macroeconomic stimulus should facilitate structural reforms. They conclude, however, that EMU increases the likelihood of having *gradual* reforms and co-ordination of reform across countries.

Other representatives of this pessimistic school of thought are Soskice and Iversen (1998) and Coricelli, Cukiermann and Lippi (2000). These authors are concerned that with EMU the "deterrence argument" might be weakened, or at least diluted, so that incentives for real wage restraints could be diminished.

A second more optimistic view is to be found in Blanchard and Giavazzi (2001). According to these authors, product market deregulation and enhanced competition decrease total rents to be shared, the incentives for workers to appropriate such rents would then decrease making labour unions weaker, reducing insider power and leading to labour market deregulation. In this connection, Jean and Nicoletti (2001) find a significant relationship between product market regulations in several sectors and wage premia.

4.3. Empirical Evidence on an EMU-effect of Labour Market Reforms

Which labour market reforms do we actually see? Bertola and Boeri (2003) conduct an insightful experiment: they take stock of reforms carried out in Europe in the field of employment protection and non-employment benefits. In a first step they look at the broad orientation of reforms: in the case of employment protection whether they are becoming more or less stringent, and in the case of non-employment benefits whether their "reward" would increase or decrease. Non-employment benefits include a variety of rewards: the most important are unemployment benefits, but various other cash transfers are also included, as well as pensions and some forms of employment protection.

The second step in Bertola and Boeri's exercise is articulated in two distinct stages. In a first stage they classify reforms as marginal or radical depending on whether the reforms are comprehensive, involve existing entitlements and reduce replacement rates of the average production worker by 10 percent or more. The second stage is a validation procedure to verify the actual behaviour of the series. This requires collecting a number of successive observations to confirm the initial qualitative assessment (and exclude that a reform has been reverted). An important working assumption by the authors is that they choose a relatively early EMU break, i.e., 1995, presuming that the convergence process led by the

Maastricht Treaty Criteria, and expectational effects of EMU even preceeding 1997 were at work.

The impact of EMU on reforms is visible since mid-1990s and particularly for reforms of non-employment benefits. The data indicate an acceleration of reforms especially in the euro area and in the field of non-employment benefits. Bertola and Boeri caution against any over-interpretation of these results as it will take more time to understand the joint effect of many reforms

A very different approach is pursued by Morgan and Mourougane (2003) who show an increasing prevalence of Active Labour Market Measures (ALMMs) across all European countries during 1985 and 2000. In percentage of GDP, ALMMs grew to about 1 % in 1999/2000 .

4.4. Some Concluding Observations on the Endogeneity of Labour Market Flexibility

In summary, there has been significant progress towards wage moderation and discipline. This progress, however, was made prior to the start of EMU, and has been maintained since. It is not inconceivable that the wage moderation occurring prior to 1999 was influenced by the expected start of EMU and the discipline imposed by the Maastricht convergence requirements.

More importantly, several empirical studies have uncovered an endogenous component in labour market flexibility. Despite the fact that the theory is unable to predict whether a monetary union gives incentives to introduce labour market reforms, the preliminary empirical evidence suggests that EMU does create incentives to introduce more labour market flexibility.

5. Conclusion

This paper brought together several strands of the literature on the endogenous effects of monetary integration. A conceptual framework within which to discuss "endogeneities of OCA" was presented. The focus was on four areas: a. the endogeneity of economic integration; b. the endogeneity of symmetry of shocks; c. the endogeneity of financial integration and the insurance provided by capital markets and d. the endogeneity of product and labour market flexibility.

We then surveyed the empirical literature to find out how strong these endogeneities are likely to be. In all the four areas our conclusion was a measured one. Since much of the empirical work is preliminary, so are these conclusions.

First, as far as the endogeneity of integration is concerned, recent theories and empirical analysis suggest that a monetary union is a strong force towards trade creation among its members. Up to now relatively little of these effects have been observed. This suggests that the trade creation effects of a monetary union take a long time to materialize. Recent empirical studies confirm this. These have found some significant euro effect on trade, but most of these effects still have to materialize.

Second, our analysis leads to the conclusion that we should expect more symmetry in shocks of the countries participating in the currency union. Although there is still a lot of uncertainty here, it is not unreasonable to conclude that there is an endogeneity effect in the degree of symmetry of shocks in EMU.

Third, the impact of the euro on financial markets is evident in some market segments such as money markets. In other segments, the introduction of the euro may be starting to contribute to greater depth and liquidity. In bond and equity markets a gradual process of structural change and increasing integration is unfolding. Evidence of significant risk-sharing is modest thus far, and there are several areas in which financial market integration has not yet had significant effects.

Fourth, although the theory is ambiguous, some empirical studies have come to the conclusion that labour market flexibility is likely to be enhanced in a monetary union. If this is confirmed by more studies, it leads to the conclusion that the start of a monetary union creates a potentially powerful endogeneity in the OCA-criteria.

On the whole our conclusion is one of moderate optimism. The different endogeneities that exist in the dynamics towards optimal currency areas are at work. How strong these endogeneities are and how quickly they do their work remains to be seen. These questions will continue to provide rich sources of future research.

References

Alesina, A. and R. Barro, 2000, "Currency Unions", NBER WP 7927, September.

Alesina, A. I. Angeloni and Federico Etro, 2001a, The Political Economy of Unions, mimeo.

Alesina, A. I. Angeloni and Federico Etro, 2001b, "Institutional Arrangements for Federations", mimeo

Alesina, A., E. Spolaore and R. Wacziarg, 2000, "Economic Integration and Political Disintegration", American Economic Review, 90 (5): 1276-97.

Anderson, J., 1979, "A Theoretical Foundation for the Gravity Equation", American Economic Review 69 (1): 106-116.

Anderson, J. and E. van Wincoop, 2001a, "Gravity with Gravitas: a Solution to the Border Puzzle", NBER WP 8079, January.

Anderson, J. and E. van Wincoop, 2001b, "Borders, Trade and Welfare", NBER WP 8515, October.

Anderton, R. and F. Skudelny, 2001, "Exchange Rate Volatility and Euro Area Imports", ECB WP 64, May.

Badi Baltagi, Frauke Skudelny, and Nuno Sousa (2001) "Intra- and Extra-Euro Area Imports Demands for Nanufactures," mimeo, ECB.

Artis, M. J., and W. Zhang (1998), "The Linkage of Interest Rates within the EMS" *Weltwirtschaftlilche Archiv*, vol. 132(1), pp. 117-132.

Asdrubali, P., B. Sorensen and O. Yosha, 1996, "Channels of Interstate Risk Sharing: United States 1963-1990", Quarterly Journal of Economics, CXI, November: 1081-1110.

Atkeson, A. and T. Bayoumi, 1993, "Do Private Capital Markets Insure Regional Risk? Evidence from the United States and Europe", Open Economies Review 4: 303-324.

Bayoumi, T. and B. Eichengreen, 1993, "Shocking Aspects of European Monetary Integration", in F. Torres and F. Giavazzi (eds.), *Adjustment and Growth in European Monetary Union*, Cambridge University Press, Cambridge.

Bayoumi, T. and B. Eichengreen, 1996, "Operationalising the Theory of Optimal Currency Areas", CEPR DP 1484.

Bayoumi, T. and M. Klein, 1997, "A Provincial View of Economic Integration", IMF Staff Papers, 44 (4), December: 534-556.

Beck, G. and A. Weber, 2001, "How Wide are European Borders? New Evidence on the Integration Effects of Monetary Unions", mimeo, work done in the context of the CEPR Research and Training Network, *The Analysis of International Capital Markets: Understanding Europe's Role in the Global Economy.*

Bertola Giuseppe (2000) "Labor Markets in the European Union," Ifo-Studien; 46(1), pp. 99-122.

Buti, M., and Suardi Massimo (March 2000), "Cyclical Convergence or Differentiation?", *Revue de la Banque/Bank- en Financiewezen.*

Calmfors, Lars (2001) "Unemployment, Labour Market Reform, and Monetary Union", *Journal of Labour Economics*, Vol 19.

Cecchetti, S., 2001, "Legal Structure, Financial Structure and Monetary Policy, in Deutsche Bundesbank" (ed.), *The Monetary Transmission Process*, Palgrave.

Christiano, L., M. Eichenbaum and C. Evans, 1999, "Monetary Policy Shocks: What Have We Learned and To What End? " In John Taylor and Michael Woodford (eds.), *Handbook of Macroeconomics*, North-Holland, Amsterdam.

Clark, T.E. and E. van Wincoop, 2001, "Borders and Business Cycles", Journal of International Economics, 55: 59-85.

Corden, W.M. (1972), "Monetary Integration, Essays in International Finance," International Finance Section No. 93, Princeton University, Department of Economics.

Coricelli, Fabrizio, Alex Cukierman and Alberto Dalmazzo (2001) "Economic Performance and Stabilization Policy in a Monetary Union with Imperfect Labour and Goods Markets," CEPR Discussion Paper no. 2745.

Crucini, M.J., 1999, "On International and National Dimensions of Risk Sharing", Review of Economics and Statistics, LXXXI, 1, February, 73-84.

De Grauwe, Paul (2000), *Economics of Monetary Union*, Oxford University Press, Fourth Edition.

ECB, 2001, *The Monetary Policy of the ECB*, European Central Bank, Frankfurt.

ECB 2003, "Measuring Financial Integration in the Euro Area", ECB Monthly Bulletin, October.

Edwards, Sebastian, 2001, "Capital Flows and Economic Performance: Are Emerging Economies Different? ", NBER Working Paper 8076 (January)

Eichengreen, B., 2001, "Capital Account Liberalisation: What Do the Cross-Country Studies Tell Us? ", mimeo, University of California, Berkeley, April.

Emerson, M., D. Gros A. Italianer, J. Pisani-Ferry, H. Reichenbach, 1992, *One Market, One Money*, Oxford University Press, Oxford.

Engel, Charles and John, Rogers, 1996, "How Wide is the Border?" American Economic Review, 86 (5): 1113-1125.

Escriva, J.L. and G. Fagan, 1996, "Empirical Assessment of Monetary Policy Instruments and Procedures in EU Countries", EMI Staff Papers, 2.

Fagan G, F.P. Mongelli and J. Morgan (2003) *Institutions and Wage Formation in the New Europe*, Edwar Elgar Publishing.

Ferrando, A., Baele, L, Hördahl, P, Krylova, E, Monnet, C, 2004 "Measuring Financial Integration in the Euro Area", ECB Occasional Paper no. 14, April.

Ferrando, A., Baele L. 2004, "Bond and Equity Market Integration", in: M. Grande, J. Berg and F. Mongelli (eds.), "Elements of the Euro Area: Integrating Financial Markets", (forthcoming).

Frankel, J. and P. Romer, 1999, "Does Trade Cause Growth? " American Economic Review, 89 (3): 379-399.

Frankel, J. and A. Rose, 1997, "Is EMU More Justifiable Ex Post than Ex Ante?" European Economic Review, 41, 753-760.

Frankel, J. and A. Rose, 1998, "The Endogeneity of the Optimum Currency Area Criteria", Economic Journal, 108, 1009-1025.

Frankel, J. and A. Rose, 2000, "Estimating the Effect of Currency Unions on Trade and Output", CEPR Discussion Paper 2631.

Frankel, J., 2001, "Globalisation, Growth and Governance", Address to a Conference held at the Gulbenkian Foundation, Lisbon, June.

Garcia-Herrero, A., V. Gaspar, L. Hoogduin, J. Morgan and B. Winkler, 2001, "Introduction, in Why Price Stability First ECB Central Banking Conference, European Central Bank.

Gaspar, V. , G. Perez-Quiros and Jorge Sicilia, 2001, "The ECB Monetary Policy Strategy and the Money Market", ECB Working Paper 69, July.

Genre Veronique and Ramon Gomez-Salvador (2002) "Labour Force Developments in the Euro Area since the 1980s," ECB Occasional Paper no. 4, July

Giavazzi, F. and M. Pagano, 1988, "The Advantage of Tying One's Hands: EMS Discipline and Central Bank Credibility", European Economic Review.

Helliwell, John, 1998, *How Much Do National Borders Matter?* Brookings, Washington D.C.

Hess, G.D. and E. van Wincoop, 2000, *Intranational Economics,* Cambridge University Press, Cambridge.

Jonung, L. 2001, "The Scandinavian Monetary Union", paper presented at the Conference *From the Athenian Tetradrachm to the Euro,* organised by the European Association for Banking History and the National Bank of Greece, Athens 8-9 October 2001.

Kenen, Peter B. (1969), "The Optimum Currency Area: An Eclectic View", In Mundell and Swoboda, (eds.), Monetary Problems of the International Economy, Chicago: *University of Chicago Press.*

Leeper, E., C. A. Sims and T. Zha, 1996, "What does Monetary Policy do? " Brookings Papers on Economic Activity, 1-63.

Lockwood, B., 2000, "Discussion of A. Rose, "One Money, One Market: The Effect of Common Currencies on Trade", Economic Policy, April.

McCallum, John, 1995, "National Borders Matter: Canada-US Regional Trade Patterns", American Economic Review 85 (3): 615-623.

McKinnon, R., 1963, "Optimum Currency Areas", American Economic Review, 52, 712-725.

Melitz, J., 2001, "Geography, Trade and Currency Union", CEPR Discussion Paper 2987.

Mongelli, F. P. (2002), ""New" Views on the Optimum Currency Area Theory: What is EMU Telling Us," ECB Working Paper no. 138, April.

Mongelli FP, E. Dorrucci and I. Agur (2004) "What does European Institutional Integration tell us about Trade Integration?", European Central Bank, mimeo.

Mundell, R., 1961, "A Theory of Optimal Currency Areas", American Economic Review, 51, 657-665.

Mundell, R., (1973) "Uncommon Arguments for Common Currencies", in H.G. Johnson and A.K. Swoboda, *The Economics of Common Currencies,* Allen and Unwin, pp.114-32.

Obstfeld, M. and K. Rogoff, 1996, *Foundations of International Macroeconomics,* MIT Press, Cambridge, Massachusetts.

Obstfeld M. and K. Rogoff, 2000, "The Six Major Puzzles in International Macroeconomics: Is There a Common Cause? " NBER Working Paper 7777.

OECD, (1999) "EMU: Facts, Challenges and Policies", Organisation for Economic Co-operation and Development, Paris, France.

OECD, (2000) "EMU One Year On,"Organisation for Economic Co-operation and Development", Paris, France.

OECD, (2000, 2001 and 2002) "Economic Outlook", Organisation for Economic Co-operation and Development", Paris, France.

Persson, T., 2001, "Currency Unions and Trade: How Large is the Treatment Effect? " Economic Policy, October.

Pichelmann Karl (2003) "Wage Developments in the Early Years of EMU" in (eds) G. Fagan, F.P. Mongelli and J. Morgan in *Institutions and Wage Formation in the New Europe*, Edwar Elgar Publishing.

Pissarides Christopher, Pietro Garibaldi, Claudia Olivetti, Barbara Petrongolo, and Etienne Wasmer (2003) "Women in the Labour Force: How Well is Europe Doing?" mimeo.

Portes, R. and H. Rey, 1999, "The Determinants of Cross Border Equity Flows: the Geography of Information, NBER Working Paper 7336.

Poyhonen, P., 1963, "A Tentative Model for the Volume of Trade between Countries", Weltwirtshaftliches Archive, 90: 93-99.

Quinn, Dennis, 1997, "The Correlates of Changes in International Financial Regulation", American Political Science Review 91, pp 531-551.

Quah, D., 2000, "Discussion of A. Rose, One Money, One Market: The Effect of Common Currencies on Trade", Economic Policy, April.

Rodrik, D., 1998, "Who Needs Capital Account Convertibility? " In Peter Kenen (ed.) *Should the IMF Pursue Capital Account Convertibility?* Essays in International Finance, 207, Princeton: Princeton University Press.

Rose, A., 2000, "One Money, One Market: The Effect of Common Currencies on Trade", Economic Policy, April.

Rose, A., 2001, "Currency Unions and Trade: The Effect is Large", Economic Policy, October.

Rose, A. and Charles Engel, 2001, "Currency Unions and International Integration", CEPR DP 2659, January.

Rose, A, (2004) "A Meta-Analysis of the Effects of Common Currencies on International Trade," NBER Working Paper no. 10373.

Rose, A. and E. van Wincoop, 2001, "National Money as a Barrier to Trade: The Real Case for Currency Union", American Economic Review (Papers and Proceedings), 91:2, May, 386-390.

Skudelny, Frauke (2003), "Exchange Rate Uncertainty and Trade: a Survey," mimeo Katholieke Universiteit Leuven.

Snower Dennis (2002) "Centralized Bargaining and the Organization of Work" in (eds) G. Fagan, F.P. Mongelli and J. Morgan in *Institutions and Wage Formation in the New Europe,* Edwar Elgar Publishing.

Soskice David, Torben Iversen, Jonas Pontusson (2000) (eds.) *Unions, Employers, and Central Banks: Macroeconomic Coordination and Institutional Change in Social Market Economies,* Cambridge University Press.

Szasz, A., 1995, "Post-Maastricht Prospects for European Integration", mimeo.

Tavlas, G.S. (1993), "The 'New' Theory of Optimum Currency Areas", *The World Economy*, pp 663-685.

Tobin, J., 1992, "Money", in Peter Newman et al (eds.), *The New Palgrave Dictionary of Money and Finance,* The Macmillan Press Limited, London.

van Wincoop, E.,2000, "Borders and Trade", Federal Reserve Bank of New York, April.

Wynne, M. and J. Koo, 2000, "Business Cycles under Monetary Union: a Comparison of the EU and the US", Economica 67: 347-374.

Wyplosz, C., 1997, EMU: "Why and How It Might Happen", Journal of Economic Perspectives, Fall.

CHAPTER 6

The ECB's Monetary Policy Strategy Revisited

Alexandre Lamfalussy

1. A Brief Reminder of Ancient History – The Role of the EMI

In conformity with its mandate, the European Monetary Institute (EMI) undertook in 1994 its preparatory work on the design of the operational framework of the single monetary policy, i.e. of the instruments and procedures to be used by the European System of Central Banks (ESCB). A year later it started discussing the definition of the monetary strategy to be pursued by the Governing Council of the European Central Bank (ECB).

Of these two undertakings, the former received priority treatment for two obvious reasons. First, the EMI was given an explicit mandate in this case by the Treaty, but only an implicit one as regards the latter. Second, it appeared right from the outset that considerable time would be needed to adjust regulations, statistics, market practices and, most important, payment and securities settlement systems to the requirements of the chosen operational instruments and procedures. All this carried heavy implications for the IT and telecommunication systems operated by the ECB, the national central banks and the banking community at large. This "lead time" issue imposed very rigid constraints: despite the notable convergence during the 1980s in the operational techniques of the national central banks, considerable differences continued to prevail in financial and banking structures, market practices and, not least, the legal environment. The time constraint (1 January 1999) did, however, work wonders, notwithstanding the unhelpful disposition of the Treaty, which imposed unanimous decisions by the EMI Council in this field. As required by the EMI statutes, the conceptual work was finished in 1996, and its conclusions published in January 1997 in a so-called "Framework Report"[1]. In September of the same year a more detailed report was published [2] which included the technical specifications for the ESCB's operational framework. After its establishment in June 1998 (and the simultaneous liquidation of the EMI) the ECB endorsed the content of this EMI report and developed it further by specifying additional provisions.

The process was far from being as smooth and conclusive when it came to defining the monetary policy strategy of the ESCB. After lengthy discussions within its key Monetary Policy Sub-Committee, the EMI published in February 1997 a (modestly titled) report on "The single monetary policy in Stage Three – Elements of the monetary policy strategy of the ESCB". The report listed a number of uncontroversial elements that should be part of any strategy. It ruled out exchange rate targeting, interest rate pegging and nominal income targeting, and retained monetary targeting and direct inflation targeting as potentially usable monetary policy strategies. It gave the pros and cons for both, but decided to leave the decision to the Governing Council of the ECB. From this it drew the logical conclusion that for the remainder of its existence the EMI should concentrate its efforts on preparing the infrastructure necessary to support the implementation of monetary policy decisions – irrespective of the strategy to be chosen. Which indeed was done.

This report makes interesting reading today when we look at the experience of the past five years. A couple of sentences are particularly striking. After having enumerated key elements that would have to be incorporated in the strategy chosen by the ECB, the report says: "The above elements can be combined in different ways. They would allow the ESCB the pursuit of both monetary and inflation targeting strategies and could also be used in frameworks which put high emphasis on monetary

1. "The single monetary policy in Stage Three – Specification of the operational framework", EMI, January 1997
2. "The single monetary policy in Stage Three – General documentation on ESCB monetary policy instruments and procedures", EMI, September 1997

targets while using supplementary elements from inflation targeting or vice-versa". This sounds quite familiar – if you make allowance for the not unimportant qualification that today's "economic analysis" is not inflation *targeting* properly defined, nor is "monetary analysis" equivalent to monetary *targeting*.

2. Recent History – The Evolving Strategy of the ECB

In October 1998 the ECB made public its monetary policy strategy. It defined price stability as a "year-on-year increase in the Harmonized Index of Consumer Prices (HICP) for the euro area of below 2%". This was meant to provide an anchor for inflation expectations and a benchmark against which the ECB can be held accountable. It was stated from the outset, and has since been repeated on innumerable occasions, that price stability thus defined should be maintained over the medium term.

To achieve this objective the ECB intended to use what has come to be known as the "two pillar" strategy. The first pillar gave a "prominent role" to money. This implied, among other things, setting a "reference value" – not a target – for the annual rate of growth of M3. The assumptions were, first, that in the medium to long run inflation is a monetary phenomenon (i.e. that money supply has no effect on output, employment or real interest rates) and, second, that in Euroland the demand for money function is stable or at least changes predictably. Under the second pillar the ECB decided to analyse a wide range of "real" or financial indicators which might affect price developments in the short to medium run. Inflation forecasts prepared by the staff were part of the tools under this pillar, as were macroeconomic projections, which however did not constrain the policy judgement of the Governing Council. Right from the beginning it was emphasised that (a) we lived in an uncertain environment, and (b) we did not have at our disposal a single, well defined, trustworthy model which would dispense policy makers from adopting a diversified approach. It is for the same reason that it was decided to cross-check the indications supplied by alternative, or complementary, analytical approaches.

In 2001 the ECB published a comprehensive and authoritative book entitled "The Monetary Policy of the ECB" (hereinafter referred to as

"Overview 2001"), which set out in great detail its monetary policy strategy as well as its operational framework. It also contained an analysis and assessment of the policy decisions taken in 1999 and 2000.

Early 2003 the ECB undertook a thorough evaluation of its monetary policy strategy supported by an impressive series of staff papers [3]. The outcome of this exercise was published in June 2003 [4], and incorporated in an updated version of Overview 2001 [5].

Two novelties strike the reader of Overview 2004. One is the reformulation of the definition of price stability as "an increase in the HICP of below, but close to, 2%", which signals the commitment of the Governing Council to provide an adequate margin for avoiding the risks of deflation. As a result, the definition of price stability became explicitly symmetrical.

The other novelty concerns the two pillars. On the one hand, the analysis of both has been amplified. Quite considerably, I am tempted to say, as regards the monetary pillar, which now includes a more general assessment of the liquidity situation based on information about the components of M3 as well as its asset counterparts, notably credit to the private sector. On the other hand, the ranking of the two pillars has been inverted: monetary analysis now follows economic analysis, whilst it preceded it in Overview 2001. The logic of this inversion is spelled out when Overview 2004 says that: "The monetary analysis mainly serves as a means of cross-checking, from a medium to long-term perspective, the short to medium-term indications for monetary policy coming from the economic analysis". [6]

Do these novelties amount to a "change", or are they just "confirmation and clarification", as argued by the ECB? [7] Well, yes and no. As regards the two pillar approach, it would seem difficult to deny that Overview 2004 does represent a change (though not a radical one) in comparison with the 1998 decision – but, on the other hand, it can be regarded as the confirmation of an evolutionary process. Indeed, anyone who cares to

3. "Background Studies for the ECB's Evaluation of its Monetary Policy Strategy", ECB, November 2003
4. Monthly Bulletin, ECB, June 2003
5. "The Monetary Policy of the ECB", ECB, 2004 ("Overview 2004")
6. Overview 2004, p. 55
7. Overview 2004, p. 7

glance through the ECB's Monthly Bulletins over the past couple of years can clearly identify an evolutionary process in the ECB's thinking. One gains the impression that the monetary analysis has become more and more a sort of controlling device which is used to render two eminently respectable services. First, it serves the purpose of ensuring that the operational conclusions drawn from a diversified economic analysis are not invalidated by potential longer-term inflation risks signalled by monetary developments. Second, when there are significant departures from the reference rate of growth of M3, it compels policy makers to explain why they did not react to such departures. Such explanations have been offered in abundance. And for good reasons, too: there was, indeed, significant overshooting of the reference rate of growth both in 2002 and in 2003. Similarly, the more general comments on the liquidity situation did not appear out of the blue in Overview 2004: they had been creeping into the Monthly Bulletins for quite some time, and had been signalled in Overview 2001.

The expression "clarification", on the other hand, applies quite well to the reformulation of the definition of price stability. Overview 2001 already stated clearly that price stability meant avoiding deflation as well as inflation. At the same time, by defining price stability as an <u>increase</u> in prices it implied that a decrease was unacceptable. But it was still a salutary decision to make more explicit the commitment to a symmetrical approach. The more so, since the current economic environment displays characteristics that are very different from those prevailing ten to fifteen years ago. I don't recall anyone mentioning in the early 1990s the possibility, let alone the probability, of deflation becoming a genuine risk.

The reader may have realised by now that I have a great deal of sympathy both for the ECB's diversified approach and for the evolutionary process which, I believe, has gone in the right direction. In what follows I spell out more explicitly the reasons for this sympathy and air at the same time some queries or concerns.

3. Monetary Policy is Operating in an Uncertain Environment

Calling the ECB's monetary policy strategy a "two pillar" approach does not do full justice to what it is in fact an eclectic, or at least highly diversified approach. The basic assumption underlying this approach is that there is considerable uncertainty regarding the working of the transmission mechanism of monetary policy.

To begin with, all ECB publications insist on the fact that we do not have at our disposal a reliable, unified model of price formation which would incorporate both shorter-term real sector price determination models (note the plural) and the longer-term monetary model. In the absence of a broadly accepted, integrated, model of price determination we are well advised to cross-check the information provided by the two pillars. In this sense the cross-checking procedure is a commendable manifestation of intellectual humility. No wonder that it triggered hostile reactions from the academic world: few economists are noted for their modesty, and even fewer would admit that their "one model" approach could lead to completely wrong policy advice.

But this is only part of the story. "Operating in an uncertain environment" does not simply mean "model" uncertainty, i.e. uncertainty about which model or models best capture the modus operandi of price determination and therefore the working of the transmission mechanism of monetary policy. It also means that policy makers are likely to be confronted with "surprises", i.e. unforeseen events which they cannot ignore in their decision making process. Terrorist attacks, geopolitical shocks, oil price hikes and natural disasters come obviously under that heading. But, more important, there are also surprises relating to key economic variables and to the behaviour of consumers, investors or indeed governments. And the problem with the emergence of new behavioural patterns is that we have no clue how fundamental they are, and how lasting they will be.

Developments in the US economy over the past ten years provide us with good examples of "surprises" of the latter kind. The first was a significant increase in the rate of growth of labour productivity from the mid-1990s onwards, followed by its atypical acceleration during the recession. At the same time, we witnessed a fairly substantial decline in the natural rate of unemployment. As a result, despite large-scale job creation and the surprising length of the cyclical upswing, inflationary risks remained subdued. There is little doubt that both the volume and the nature of IT and telecoms investment played a major (and possibly decisive) role in pushing up the rate of productivity increases. They did this after long years during which they appeared to have no impact on productivity. Equity markets took note of these developments and, with the help of the majority of portfolio advisers and quite a few economists (who announced the emergence of a "new economy" and the end of the business cycle), they typically overreacted and raised equity prices to levels that could be described as levitation.

In 2000 the boom in technological investment came to an abrupt end, and the bubble burst. Between March 2000 and March 2003 the P/E ratio of S&P 500 declined from 38 to 20, and that of US technology stocks plunged from 65 to 18 [8]. That such a meltdown did not produce a genuine financial crisis and a lasting downturn in the "real" economy owed a lot to the resilience of the banking system, but first and foremost to the fact that household consumption and investment held up remarkably well. The decisive factor in this respect was the unprecedented dose of simultaneous monetary and fiscal stimulus administered to the US economy. The result was a short and shallow recession, followed by a remarkable recovery.

It seems to me that the major question mark hanging over the sustainability of this recovery is related to the key role(and the unpredictability) of asset price levels and movements. None of the "flow" imbalances that had characterised the US economy since the mid-1990s were corrected by the recession; on the contrary, with the recovery they have deepened. In the end, however, they will have to unwind. That they have not done this so far is attributable to the sizeable wealth effects due to the level of asset prices. Among these asset prices the prospective behaviour of real estate asset prices is likely to play a major part: property wealth has as counterpart a significant debt burden in households' balance sheets, of which a non-negligible proportion is based on adjustable interest rate contracts. In short, asset-price domination has led the US econ-

8. BIS, 73rd Annual Report, June 2003, p. 105

omy into uncharted waters. This is an environment which requires cautious and flexible monetary policy, able to react (yet not overreact) to new information. Quite an assignment.

An objection could be raised against citing the uncertainties affecting the US environment to justify the ECB's diversified approach. It is of course true that, fortunately or unfortunately, Euroland has not been affected, or at least not to the same degree, by US-type uncertainties. But such uncertainties might also arise in Europe: I am not aware that in the mid-1990s they were expected to emerge in the US either. More important, Euroland has to cope with uncertainties of its own. For reasons different from those affecting the US economy, the fate of its recovery is unpredictable. The sorely needed structural reforms, without which there will be no upward shift in its potential rate of growth, may or may not succeed. Will M3 continue to grow at a rate well above the reference value? And, even if it were to slow down, will the accumulated money gap signal for the longer run a degree of liquidity which could turn out to be detrimental to price stability? Finally, there is a more fundamental uncertainty liable to affect the working of the transmission mechanism of monetary policy: how will financial integration affect our financial structures? Combined with the wider impact of financial globalisation, it may well harbour some surprises.

Now let me turn to some queries and concerns.

4. Transparency and Accountability

Operating a monetary policy strategy which is explicitly based on an eclectic approach does not make life easier for the Eurosystem's policy makers. What about the implications of such an approach for accountability and transparency – two requirements which are related to each other but are not identical? Let us look at them in turn.

Accountability is a backward-looking concept, with a strong political content. In the ECB's own words: "Accountability can be understood as the legal and political obligation of an independent central bank to properly explain and justify its decisions to the citizens and their elected representatives, thereby holding the central bank responsible for fulfilling its objectives" [9]. The Annual Reports, the Monthly Bulletins, and most important, the President's appearance four times a year before the European Parliament's Economic & Monetary Affairs Committee go a long long way towards meeting the accountability requirement. But do they go all the way? It is often argued that they should be supplemented by giving detailed (but suitably delayed) information on the internal debate within the Governing Council prior to policy decisions, on the grounds that Euro-MPs as much as the broader public are entitled to know "what is going on inside the ECB".

There are, however, powerful arguments against providing such information. There is the "infant industry" argument: the ECB is still a relatively new institution which deserves to enjoy some protection. Give the Council time to work out the rules governing their teamwork. Don't expose individual Council members to political pressure from their country of origin. While these are not negligible arguments, I would attach greater weight to the danger that revealing positions taken by individual Council members would make it more difficult for them to revise their views. Human nature being what it is, there are not many people who want to give the appearance of being volatile, and there are even fewer who would like to publicise that they have been wrong. Yet in the kind of uncertain environment in which they have to shape – as a group – the ECB's policy, it is essential that Council members stand ready to change their opinion in the light of new information or by reconsidering the validity of arguments put forward by other members.

Could these objections be met? Perhaps, by avoiding identifying the positions taken by individual members, yet summing up the course of the debate on substantive issues, and if there was voting, by signalling the kind of majority ("overwhelming", "clear", "narrow", etc.) which carried the decision. It is of course true that in a world dominated by investigative journalism there is a genuine risk that individual positions will be revealed. For the sake of enhancing accountability, this would perhaps be a risk worth taking – on condition, however, that such disclosure would

9. Overview 2004, p. 66

also be recommended under the heading of transparency, about which I have some doubts.

Transparency can be taken as a more forward-looking requirement, whose main merit is to enhance the effectiveness of a stability oriented monetary policy. It does it in two ways. In the shorter run, it gives guidance to markets about policy intentions, thereby speeding up the transmission mechanism. Second, to the extent that transparency highlights the consistent pursuit of the objective of price stability by the Council, it provides an anchor to price expectations. Such an anchor is particularly useful when there is a risk of supply shocks setting in motion a second round of inflationary or deflationary developments. An additional argument in favour of guiding the markets is to avoid major disturbances in financial markets, an argument which is not without weight in our increasingly market-centred systems.

Today the most authoritative guidance is provided by the President's introductory statement at the monthly press conference, the text of which is agreed by the Governing Council. This is complemented by the Editorial of the Monthly Bulletin, which is both backward and forward looking.

Would ex post information on the debate within the Council be a useful addition for the sake of transparency? I doubt it. Revealing a couple of weeks or months later the nature of the discussion which preceded the approval of the President's introductory statement might produce contradictory results. It might strengthen the credibility attached to the President's guidance if it turns out that there was an overwhelming majority in favour of the text – and, especially, if this is repeatedly confirmed. In the opposite case, on the contrary, the importance attached to the statement might be weakened. We just do not know which of these two outcomes, or what combination of them over time, would prevail.

To complicate the matter further one could also wonder which of these two outcomes would be better. Strengthening the guidance to the market would undoubtedly increase the effectiveness of monetary policy, and protect market participants from unpleasant surprises. But this would not be without carrying potentially high costs. Credible central banks can overdo their guidance by communicating too much. When they have acquired a high degree of credibility their utterings become the best available guide not only to what they are likely to do, but also to what the predominant view of market participants will be. This reduces the need for the latter to make up their own mind about the state of the economy. Yet, in our current environment we badly need the broadest possible participation in analysis and assessment. Moreover, the Governing Council should also feel free to adjust its view to new information. Practising unambiguous guidance may put the Council in an unwelcome straitjacket. It may not be able to get out of this without damaging its credibility *and* creating market turbulence.

5. Ensuring Price Stability: Primary or Exclusive Objective?

Article 105 of the Treaty states unambiguously that "the primary objective of the ESCB shall be to maintain price stability". But it also adds that "without prejudice to the objective of price stability, the ESCB shall support the general economic policies in the Community with a view to contributing to the achievement of the objectives of the Community as laid down in Article 2". This article lists an impressive number of tasks entrusted to the Community which include, among others, "sustainable and non-inflationary growth" and "a high level of employment". This sounds reasonably clear, but given the repeated urgings of European politicians in favour of lower ECB interest rates in a situation of economic slack, a case can be made for some clarification. Let me spell out where I can see a need for clarification.

For the sake of avoiding ambiguity I suggest agreeing on a set of initial assumptions – which, of course, reveal my own preferences. First, on the "clarified" definition of price stability which resulted from the ECB's evaluation exercise. Second, that price stability should be maintained in the medium term. Third, that it is none of the ECB's business to fine tune demand management. Fourth, that it is by ensuring price stability that monetary policy can make the most significant contribution to "sustainable growth" and to "high level of employment".

Does this mean that the ECB should consider implementing a stimulative monetary policy stance *only* if there was a genuine probability of the rate of increase of retail prices declining, in a medium-term perspective, below (and probably significantly below) 2% – on the grounds that such an outcome would represent a risk of deflation?

There is surely one case when no such justification would be needed for the ECB to resort, even on a large scale, to central bank money creation: when there is a risk of systemic financial crisis and / or of a gridlock in the payment system. Such action did actually take place after 9/11.

But what about a situation in which (a) there seems to be no danger of inflation, (b) nor a danger of deflation, (c) but in which there clearly is a shortfall of demand, that is, a negative output gap, and, moreover, (d) an output gap that appears to be sticky? The probability of encountering such a situation may not be very high, but in Euroland at least it is arguably not nil. My reading of ECB publications may have been incomplete or superficial, but I do not recollect having found a reply to this question.

6. Concluding Remarks

Looking at the evolving monetary policy strategy of the ECB I detect a sort of "changement dans la continuité" (an expression coined by Valéry Giscard d'Estaing when he became President of the French Republic) which well befits cautious and principled central bankers who at the same time respect facts and stand ready to adjust their monetary policy strategy to meeting new challenges. Am I mixing up observation with wishful thinking on my part? I hope not.

CHAPTER 7

Parallel Monies, Parallel Debt: Lessons from the EMU and Options for the New EU Members

Giorgio Basevi [1], Lorenzo Pecchi and Gustavo Piga

In 1975 Niels Thygesen, together with eight other economists – one of us among them– published in *The Economist* a "manifesto" proposing a new common currency for Europe (Basevi et al., 1975). His co-operation on this subject was pursued within a smaller group, and resulted in the publication of two reports for the EU Commission (Optica Report '75, Optica Report 1976).

The proposal in the "manifesto" was ironically re-titled, by *The Economist*, "The All Saints' day manifesto for European monetary union". In fact it had been published on 1st November, and the "Saints" should have been, according to *The Economist*, the European Governments if they had adopted and adhered to the proposal.

This amounted to launching a new currency that should have circulated in parallel to the national ones, related to them by flexible exchange rates, due to the constraint that such new currency, the "Europa", had to be kept by an automatic formula at fixed purchasing power. In fact the

1. We are grateful for suggestions and comments by Marco Pagano and Philippe Rakotovao. We also received help in collecting data from the statistical offices of the Italian Treasury, the OECD, MTS SpA, and MCC SpA. However the opinions expressed in this paper are merely those of the authors, who bear sole responsibility for its content. The research reported in this paper was partly financed with funds of the Italian Ministry for the University (Fondi ex 60%).

Europa was to be indexed to the inflation rates in the participating countries, according to the weights of their national currencies in what at that time was called the European Unit of Account.

As for the two other reports, *Optica '75* proposed again a parallel currency, but less than fully inflation-proof, since its standing in terms of purchasing power would have been the same as that of the currency of the member country with the lowest inflation rate. In the *Optica 1976* Report, while reiterating the proposal of a parallel currency along the lines of *Optica '75*, the focus was on designing a joint management of intra-European exchange rates on the basis of inflation differentials.

The proposals contained in the three documents where premature, perhaps visionary. On 7 July 1978 the European Council met in Bremen and drew the lines of the European Monetary System, which started on 13 March 1979, on the basis, among other things, of a new quasi-currency –the European Currency Unit (ECU)– composed of a basket of national currencies. Since then, it took almost twenty years before the euro was introduced, replacing the ECU on 1st January 1999.

Comparing the euro to such proposals, we note at least two differences. The euro (a) did not start as a parallel currency, but replaced with a pre-announced schedule the national currencies of the countries participating in the monetary union, and (b) it was not conceived as an automatically inflation-proof currency, but one issued by a Central Bank bound by a monetary policy aimed at price stability.

1. Parallel Currencies and Parallel Bonds

Whether the theory on which they were based was good or bad, the European authorities did not retain such proposals. Monetary union (EMU) found its way on a different track, even though some of the characteristics of those proposals can be traced in the evolution that led to EMU.

In any case, from a practical point of view, it is useless to re-open a debate that is by now obsolete. We shall rather consider some aspects that may be important in the future, more specifically for the new EU member countries, all of which are supposed to eventually adopt the euro.

From this point of view, we note that the two main elements in the original proposals – i.e. parallel circulation, and constant purchasing power– were both partly realized, albeit in a different form: the first in the EMS, the second in the EMU. In fact, they were not applied to a common currency – i.e. the ECU in the EMS and the euro in the EMU– but rather to a large part of the other type of Government debt besides currency –i.e. to Government bonds. This took place in the form of issuing (i) Government debt denominated in ECU side by side to debt denominated in domestic currency (during the EMS period), and (ii) euro-denominated and inflation indexed Government bonds (since the inception of EMU).

As for (i), while denominating a share of domestic debt in foreign currencies has been common for many countries and in various historical periods, the novelty, during the period of the EMS, was that many participating countries' Governments used to denominate part of their debt in ECU, i.e. in a prospective potential common currency. Table 1 presents data on EU countries' Government debt, where, in particular, the components of foreign currency denominated and inflation indexed bonds (IIB) are detailed. The table, albeit indirectly and approximately, also shows how the EU countries made use of foreign (among which ECU) denominated debt during the period before the EMU. In fact it can be noticed that, for the countries that became members of the euro-area, the shares of "foreign currency" generally drop in between 1998 and 1999, as debt denominated in the currencies of other member countries and in ECU was converted into euro-denominated debt (domestic currency debt) at par.

In passing, it is interesting to note that the interest rate that countries had to pay on their ECU-denominated debt was generally lower than the "synthetic" interest rate that they would have paid by issuing debt on a basket of currencies reproducing the ECU. This feature points to liquidity gains that will be relevant to our discussion of euro-denominated debt: in substance, the larger and more liquid market of ECU denominated bonds relative to at least some of its component currencies, allowed a lower ECU-interest rate.

Table 1. Composition of Central Government Debt of EU Countries and Major Foreign Countries * (percentage shares)

		1993	1994	1995	1996	1997	1998	1999	2000	2001	2002
Austria	**Total Central Government Debt**	100	100	100	100	100	100	100	100	100	100
	Non- Market. Debt	27	27	26	25	22	19	16	15	14	13
	Fixed Rate Income Instruments	62	64	66	67	70	75	79	81	85	86
	Inflation indexed	0	0	0	0	0	0	0	0	0	0
	Other	11	10	8	8	8	6	4	4	1	1
	Foreign Currency	18	19	20	19	19	24	13	12	12	11
Begium	**Total Central Government Debt**	100	100	100	100	100	100	100	100	100	100
	Non- Market. Debt	17	15	10	7	6	4	0	5	5	4
	Fixed Rate Income Instruments	64	61	71	73	73	78	81	82	82	83
	Inflation indexed	0	0	0	0	0	0	0	0	0	0
	Other	18	24	19	20	21	18	19	13	13	13
	Foreign Currency	6	6	7	5	6	6	3	2	2	1
Demark	**Total Central Government Debt**	100	100	100	100	100	100	100	100	100	100
	Non- Market. Debt	0	0	0	0	0	0	0	0	0	0
	Fixed Rate Income Instruments	100	100	100	100	100	100	100	100	100	100
	Inflation indexed	0	0	0	0	0	0	0	0	0	0
	Other	0	0	0	0	0	0	0	0	0	0
	Foreign Currency	24	19	15	14	14	12	12	12	12	12
Finland	**Total Central Government Debt**	100	100	100	100	100	100	100	100	100	100
	Non- Market. Debt	16	15	12	14	15	12	12	9	10	8
	Fixed Rate Income Instruments	72	67	71	71	73	80	80	76	67	64
	Inflation indexed	0	0	0	0	0	0	0	0	0	0
	Other	12	18	17	15	12	7	8	15	23	28
	Foreign Currency	55	52	44	40	34	32	16	15	15	13
France	**Total Central Government Debt**	100	100	100	100	100	100	100	100	100	100
	Non- Market. Debt	13	15	13	12	11	11	11	10	10	7
	Fixed Rate Income Instruments	75	74	75	75	77	76	79	79	77	78
	Inflation indexed	0	0	0	0	0	1	1	2	3	4
	Other	11	11	12	13	12	12	9	10	10	11
	Foreign Currency	4	4	4	5	6	7	0	0	0	0

Germany	**Total Central Government Debt**	100	100	100	100	100	100	100	100	100	100
	Non- Market. Debt	14	13	15	16	14	12	16	13	10	7
	Fixed Rate Income Instruments	85	85	82	80	82	84	81	85	87	89
	Inflation indexed	0	0	0	0	0	0	0	0	0	0
	Other	1	2	2	4	4	4	3	2	3	4
	Foreign Currency	0	0	0	0	0	0	0	0	0	0
Greece	**Total Central Government Debt**	100	100	100	100	100	100	100	100	100	100
	Non- Market. Debt	24	24	21	18	18	17	20	17	15	14
	Fixed Rate Income Instruments	8	7	5	1	12	22	32	43	55	67
	Inflation indexed	0	0	0	0	0	0	0	0	0	0
	Other	68	69	74	80	70	61	47	40	30	20
	Foreign Currency	n.a.	n.a.	n.a.	n.a.	n.a.	n.a.	n.a.	n.a.	n.a.	n.a.
Ireland	**Total Central Government Debt**	100	100	100	100	100	100	100	100	100	100
	Non- Market. Debt	5	9	11	13	14	16	16	16	14	15
	Fixed Rate Income Instruments	n.a.	n.a.	n.a.	n.a.	n.a.	52	61	60	58	63
	Inflation indexed	n.a.	n.a.	n.a.	n.a.	n.a.	0	0	0	0	0
	Mark.Debt/ Other**	95	91	89	87	86	32	23	24	28	22
	Foreign Currency	n.a.	n.a.	35	29	27	24	7	6	6	0
Italy	**Total Central Government Debt**	100	100	100	100	100	100	100	100	100	100
	Non- Market. Debt	13	8	8	9	9	9	9	9	9	9
	Fixed Rate Income Instruments	32	38	40	39	40	44	49	52	53	53
	Inflation indexed	0	0	0	0	0	0	0	0	0	0
	Other	55	54	52	53	51	47	42	39	37	37
	Foreign Currency	6	7	7	7	7	6	3	4	3	3
Netherland	**Total Central Government Debt**	100	100	100	100	100	100	100	100	100	100
	Non- Market. Debt	24	22	18	15	12	10	6	4	1	1
	Fixed Rate Income Instruments	75	76	79	82	85	87	91	92	93	88
	Inflation indexed	0	0	0	0	0	0	0	0	0	0
	Other	1	2	3	4	3	4	3	4	6	11
	Foreign Currency	0	0	0	0	0	0	0	0	0	0
Portugal	**Total Central Government Debt**	100	100	100	100	100	100	100	100	100	100
	Non- Market. Debt	36	32	30	28	26	25	24	25	24	24

	Fixed Rate Income Instruments	16	18	21	25	33	38	50	66	68	73
	Inflation indexed	0	0	0	0	0	0	0	0	0	0
	Other	48	50	49	47	40	36	26	10	8	3
	Foreign Currency	0	0	0	0	0	0	0	6	7	3
Spain	**Total Central Government Debt**	100	100	100	100	100	100	100	100	100	100
	Non- Market. Debt	14	14	13	12	8	7	6	6	5	4
	Fixed Rate Income Instruments	51	51	56	57	65	71	76	79	83	84
	Inflation indexed	1	1	1	1	1	1	0	0	0	0
	Other	34	34	30	31	26	21	18	14	12	11
	Foreign Currency	2	2	2	2	2	3	3	4	4	3
Sweden	**Total Central Government Debt**	100	100	100	100	100	100	100	100	100	100
	Non- Market. Debt	12	10	9	8	7	5	5	5	5	5
	Fixed Rate Income Instruments	66	64	70	67	70	69	69	64	63	62
	Inflation indexed	0	1	3	7	8	9	9	10	9	12
	Other	22	26	18	17	15	18	17	21	23	21
	Foreign Currency	32	30	28	28	26	24	21	18	19	17
UK	**Total Central Government Debt**	n.a.	n.a.	n.a.	n.a.	n.a.	100	100	100	100	100
	Non- Market. Debt	n.a.	n.a.	n.a.	n.a.	n.a.	17	18	20	22	21
	Fixed Rate Income Instruments	n.a.	n.a.	n.a.	n.a.	n.a.	63	62	58	56	55
	Inflation indexed	n.a.	n.a.	n.a.	n.a.	n.a.	15	17	18	18	19
	Other	n.a.	n.a.	n.a.	n.a.	n.a.	5	4	4	4	5
	Foreign Currency	n.a.	n.a.	n.a.	n.a.	n.a.	0	0	0	0	0
USA	**Total Central Government Debt**	100	100	100	100	100	100	100	100	100	100
	Non- Market. Debt	12	12	11	10	10	12	12	11	13	12
	Fixed Rate Income Instruments	68	68	69	70	71	70	67	67	61	59
	Inflation indexed	0	0	0	0	1	2	3	3	4	4
	Other	20	20	20	20	18	17	18	18	22	24
	Foreign Currency	0	0	0	0	0	0	0	0	0	0

Source: OECD, *Central Government Debt Statistical Yearbook*, various issues and our elaborations.

* The "Fixed Rate Income Instruments" and "Other" items include the "Foreign Currency" item. "Fixed Rate Income Instruments" include also variable-rate notes and money market instruments.

** From 1993 to 1997 "Other" for Ireland is Marketable Debt.

As for (ii), in view and after the beginning of EMU some member countries – most notably France, Greece, and Italy – started issuing part of their euro-denominated debt in the form of IIB. As indicated in Table 2, France is the only euro-zone country to issue indexed bonds also linked to the domestic inflation rate; a choice that is not neutral with respect to the risks that affect the Government budget, as we will see later on.[2]

We think it is interesting to consider the similarities and differences between these two developments on the one hand, and the inflation-proof and parallel currency approach on the other hand.

Table 2. Euro-area inflation indexed Government Bonds Outstanding

Country (date of first issuance)	**Inflation reference**	**Number of issues**	**Simple average maturity at issuance** (years)	**Simple average coupon rate at issuance** (%)	**Outstanding amount** (billion euro and share of total debt on 12/31/2003)
France (1998)	French	3	14	2.96	28.26 (3.6%)
France (2001)	Eurozone	2	19	2.8	16.14 (2%)
Italy (2003)	Eurozone	2	7.5	1.9	21.9 (1.2%)
Greece (2003)	Eurozone	1	22	2.9	1.25 (0.7%)

Source : Bloomberg

2. Why Parallel Bonds Rather than Parallel Currencies?

By issuing ECU-denominated bonds, EU Governments were applying the parallel currency approach to that part of their debt, in so far as the ECU could have become a parallel currency in EMS countries.

2. The German Finance Ministry announced, at the end of May, 2004, a plan to issue IIB on the basis of the euro-zone inflation in the harmonised index of consumer prices (HICP) for up to a maximum of 5% of the Federal Government borrowing requirement. To enact this plan, new legislation is needed, because indexation to price changes is at present forbidden in Germany.

More generally, two Government debt issues, equal in all respects except currency of denomination, could be seen as two parallel debts. In fact the market arbitrages between them, as it would do between two currencies, both circulating among a country's residents.

More specifically, when the currency of denomination was the ECU, the issuing Government was effectively choosing to denominate its debt in a currency that could have become the parallel European currency, side by side to the national currencies. Indeed, in Belgium at least, ECU-denominated bank deposits were allowed and became relatively common, even though the ECU was never issued as paper money.

Why were Governments ready to consider –and indeed to implement– the issuance of parallel bonds but not the issue of a parallel currency? The answer to this question goes some way in answering a second question, that we shall discuss later, i.e. why European Governments, after having skipped the parallel currency step and moved directly to parallel debt, took so long in taking the next step, i.e. from ECU-denominated bonds to IIB.[3]

Let us consider the first question: why parallel bonds and not a parallel currency. Governments enjoy some monopoly power in issuing domestic currency, as they can choose and enforce the currency that is legal tender. Hence they may exploit such power to extract seignorage and impose an inflation tax. By allowing a parallel currency to circulate side by side to their own national currency, Governments would lose the possibility to extract an excessive inflation tax on money denominated in their national currency: the attempt to do so would induce substitution of the parallel currency for the national currency. Indeed full substitution would take place in case the parallel currency enjoyed a constant purchasing power, as was in fact the aim of the "All Saints' day Manifesto".

The same cannot be said of Government debt, for which a status analogous to legal tender does not apply.[4] On the contrary, under free capital

3. In its critical comment attached to the "The All Saints' day manifesto for European monetary union", The Economist had already proposed, as alternative to the price-indexed parallel currency approach, one based on issuing IIB or GDP-indexed bonds ("national income equities", as they were labelled by The Economist).
4. Actually, there are cases in which Government debt has been forced into the hands of savers, in substitution of due Government payments, such as em-

capital movements, international competition for savings is very strong. Government has to pay a competitive interest rate on bonds denominated in its domestic currency: the yield must – relative to other countries' Government bonds – compensate for country risk, exchange rate risk, and liquidity risk. For Governments that are price-takers in financial markets, the premia related to all three risks must be borne by the issuer. Hence, in differentiating its issues by currencies a Government has no inflation tax to lose on its bonds.[5] On the contrary, it may reduce the overall cost of its debt by choosing the combination of exchange risk and liquidity risk that is most appropriate to international investors, without having to pay anything more or less in terms of country risk.[6]

This implies that, in the absence of other costs, issuing parallel debt is a more reasonable choice than issuing a parallel currency, at least from the Government point of view. In fact Table 1 shows that, although unevenly among EU countries, denomination of Government debt in ECU and in foreign (largely each other's) currencies had become an interesting characteristic well before EMU.[7] Other countries, however, especially "hard-currency" ones – like Germany and the Netherlands in the EMS-EMU area – never started a programme of issuing foreign or parallel currency denominated debt.[8] France launched only an ECU programme, emphasizing the symbolic political message, rather than the economic foundation of such a debt management strategy.

Therefore the puzzle remains as to why some key EU countries, especially the ones with traditionally stronger currencies, abstained from issu-

ployees salaries etc.. These, however, are exceptional cases, adopted in situation of financial crisis.

5. If investors correctly anticipate inflation.
6. However, foreign currency denomination may influence the likelihood of default in case of a currency crisis. Hence there might be positive correlation between currency risk and country risk.
7. Developing countries also have made use of foreign currency denominated debt. This occurred mainly in high inflation countries, as a substitute for inflation indexed debt. The latter, by referring to their own currencies and inflation, would not have been particularly attractive for international investors. Pecchi and Ripa di Meana (1998) show the diverse reasons of why debt denominated in foreign exchange was issued in developed countries in the 80s and 90s.
8. Outside of Europe, other hard-currency countries, like Japan and the United States, that could have issued foreign currency debt, declined to do so.

ing in foreign or parallel currencies; or did so, like France, only to foster a sense of leadership in the European monetary integration process. The answer to this is linked with a second puzzle, of why in the EU we had to wait more than twenty years to see the emergence of IIB, and this took place only after EMU was launched.

More specifically, why after a currency that is relatively inflation-proof – i.e. the euro – was adopted, only then member Governments became willing to issue IIB? This sequence may be puzzling, if we consider the attractiveness of IIB to be higher when inflation is high. Indeed, it has been argued that "delegation of monetary policy to an independent central bank is a better solution to credibility problems than increasing the costs of inflation by issuing indexed debt, foreign currency debt and short-term debt."[9] If we consider the European Central Bank independence and commitment to low inflation, such normative argument is not supported by the EMU experience so far; hence the puzzle.

3. Why Inflation Indexed Bonds after the EMU?

Although there have been different opinions on the matter, eminent economists have long advocated that Governments should issue IIB.[10] And yet, at least in the EU –and with the sporadic exceptions of Ireland, Italy, Sweden, and the more important and systematic case of the UK– the advice to issue IIB was not followed until the EMU was launched.

In fact it may be considered a paradox that IIB have not been popular in high inflation periods and inflation prone countries, such as Italy,[11] and that they were adopted in Europe only when countries had effectively

9. Falcetti and Missale (2002), p.1848.
10. See Pecchi-Piga (1997) for a survey of the literature. See also Price (1997), who provides a detailed account of sovereign indexed bonds issues.
11. Italy made only one issue, and not a very successful one. It was issued on August 1st, 1983 (a particularly badly chosen month to launch a new instrument, given the scarce activity of market makers in that period) with a 10 year maturity. Beside the fact that its technical structure was not attractive for investors (see Foresi et al, (1997)) it met the resistance of the Italian Central Bank, at the time the de facto debt manager (see for example, Banca d'Italia (1981), pp. 403-408.) that succeeded in its intention not to see the issue renewed.

reached low inflation levels. On the other hand, outside of Europe, the US case is by far the most significant. Table 3 presents data on IIB issues.

Table 3. Countries and Issues of IIB

Country	Period of issue	Average CPI inflation rate in the 3 years prior to the introduction (in %)	Indexed debt outstanding in 1999 (in % of total Government debt)
Argentina	1972-1989	18.6	0
Australia	1985-88	8.4	29.5
	1993-	3.8	
Brazil	1964-	n.a.	19.6
Canada	1991-	4.6	1.5
Chile	1956-	39.6	62
Colombia	1967-	13.7	13.2
Czech Republic	1997-	9.3	1.7
Finland	1945-	n.a.	0
France	1998-	1.7	0.6
Greece	1997-	7.6	0.2
Hungary	1995-	23.2	3
Iceland	1955-	4.3	11.5
Ireland	1983-	18.6	1.1
Israel	1955-	32.7	80.2
Italy	1983	18.5	1.2*
	2003-	2.6	
Mexico	1989-	110.7	8.4
New Zealand	1977-1984	14.2	2.3
	1994-	1.4	
Norway	1982-	9.8	0.1
Poland	1992-2000	292.2	0
Sweden	1952	8.2	12.5
	1994-	5.4	
Turkey	1994-	80.8	24.3
UK	1975	10.7	12
	1981-	13.2	
USA	1997-	2.8	0.8

Source: Borensztein and Mauro (2004), except for Italy (source Italian Ministry of the Economy and Finance)

* Indexed public debt outstanding at end 2003 as a % of total Government debt

In Europe, the UK started a major IIB program in 1981, at the peak of the inflation period. In the two years before the first issuance, UK inflation had averaged 15.5%, and in the two years after the first issuance it fell to 5%. This rapid disinflation was a concrete sign of the stabilization policies by the Thatcher Government. It amounts to one of the boldest, largest and most successful plans in the history of public debt management in terms of "beat the market" strategy. In the scenario of high inflation expectations and inadequate credibility of a successful stabilization, issuing nominal bonds would have implied much higher ex-post real returns than those that materialized with indexed bonds. However, the UK experience remains a unique experiment, and an exception to the puzzling rule, at least in developed countries, that indexed bonds are issued when inflation is relatively low and prices more stable.

The specific EMU puzzle lies in the fact that issuing IIB has become popular among EU countries –such as France and Italy, but also Greece, and possibly Germany– after they have adopted the euro, i.e. a currency institutionally meant not to be inflationary. Why did not such countries systematically issue IIB before, or at least during, the period of convergence to the Maastricht parameters, so as to make their commitment to it more credible?

A first explanation may derive from the solution to the paradox above: from a political economy point of view it is not in the interest of high inflation countries to issue IIB. On the one hand, one could argue that a Government that does not control inflation, but fears unexpected inflation surges, might consider IIB more expensive than nominal bonds. Furthermore, the Government might also fear that issuing IIB will be interpreted by the financial community as a signal of insider knowledge that inflation will increase.[12] In fact, by providing insurance against inflation, IIB create a moral hazard problem, in that individuals and/or institutions will have lower gains and less interest to fight inflation.[13] In a world where credi-

12. Actually, in the case of Mrs. Thatcher's Government, IIB were issued on the opposite basis.
13. It is interesting to note that this debate has been the focus of heated discussions even among economists that share similar philosophies. Von Hayek (1976) stated (chapter 14) that indexation would weaken the resistance against inflation, protracting it and increasing it. These measures, according to him,

tors are instead exposed to the inflation threat, as in the case when they are owners of nominal bonds, a lobby is created that can effectively support restrictive monetary policies and lack of inflationary surprises. In fact there is ample anecdotic evidence of the scepticism with which indexed bonds were considered in the financial community. In the US an IIB programme was started only when the Chairman of the Federal Reserve Board, Alan Greenspan, testified in front of the House of Representatives.[14] In Italy, IIB were resisted by the Central Bank, that substantially managed Government debt until the mid 90s, and introduced a substantial programme of (ex-post costly) liquid long term nominal bonds, even in a period of relatively high inflation.[15] If the argument above is valid, then only in times when inflation is not a threat do Governments issue

would make it easier to live with inflation and would make people less aware that their pains are to be attributed to inflation. In that same chapter Von Hayek takes side against Milton Friedman, who believed that indexation (while no substitute to a stable money) would make prices more flexible by raising the awareness of people to changes in inflation. That the issues of indexation, parallel currency, and a currency area, are strictly inter-related is confirmed by the fact that Von Hayek dedicates in the same book ample space to the issue of parallel currencies, which he views as a more practical alternative to the "utopia" of a unique European currency, and actually as a device that would make people familiar with the advantages of moving towards a unique currency in the European area.

14. "Some have voiced concern that by making it easier for investors to live with inflation rather than treating it as a fundamental problem, issuing indexed bonds, on occasion, could appear to mark official acceptance of continuing high inflation. This is not the situation today. The US economy has made considerable progress toward price stability over the past decade..." (Greenspan, as reported in Federal Reserve Bulletin (1992)). Still, Congress, in the 33rd Report of the Committee on Government Operations (1992), was adamant in requiring that the programme were to be "designed and managed in close and continuing consultation with the Fed in order to ensure its compatibility with the objective of assisting monetary management."
15. Piga and Valente (2004) show that while in the 1970-1996 period the expectation hypothesis of the term structure of interest rates held, the Italian debt manager was actively managing its debt. The puzzling finding is that it lengthened the maturity (duration) of debt when the yield curve steepened, a result that they attribute to the desire of the Italian central bank (the effective manager of the Italian debt at the times) to increase the nominal bonds constituency in the face of worsened inflation expectation.

them, to take advantage of their benefits.[16] Therefore, when the currency adopted is a less inflationary one – like the euro – it becomes more attractive for a Government to issue IIB, even though these may be relatively less interesting for national (euro-area) investors.

A second explanation points out that IIB defined with respect to national currency and national inflation rates would have been attractive to national investors, but much less so to international ones. Now that the euro exists as a wide area currency, defining IIB in terms of the inflation rate of that whole area makes them much more attractive to international investors, thereby allowing a lower liquidity premium in favour of the issuer.[17] However, EU issuers may have contrasting incentives for issuing such IIB linked to EMU inflation. If the IIB issued by different EMU countries are internationally traded, market arbitrage will align their prices. As a result those countries that have a lower (higher) than the average European inflation will experience ex-post a higher (lower) real cost of debt. Therefore, within a common currency area one might expect to see relative high inflation countries more willing to issue IIB linked to the euro-area inflation than those with lower inflation rates.[18] In fact only France, a low inflation country, issued IIB linked to national inflation, while Italy and Greece, countries with a high inflation in the euro area, did not (see Table 2).[19]

16. This argument, however, gives indications contrary to those by Falcetti and Missale (2002).
17. In fact the width of the area is the argument that best explains the diffusion of US Treasury IIB, which are, of course, anchored to US inflation.
18. It should be pointed out, however, that a euro-area country could unlikely have, over long horizons, an inflation rate consistently above average without experimenting serious competitiveness problems.
19. In a different institutional and historical context, a paradoxical situation was that of Argentina, where even some types of non-tradable services were indexed to the dollar –notwithstanding the currency board constraint—and to the US inflation rate, which was, during the currency board period, higher than the Argentine inflation rate. This indexation characterized, in particular, the tariffs of public utilities, and was done in order to entice foreign investment in their privatisation process; something not dissimilar to the need to issue bonds attractive to international investors. Similar problems may arise for the new EU members during their process of convergence to EMU, in so far as their real exchange rate may appreciate during the convergence period (see Natalucci and Ravenna (2002), and our next section).

Thirdly and more generally, IIB – whether linked to national or euro-area inflation – have stochastic properties that, compared to nominal or foreign currency bonds, make them particularly suitable in specific environments, where Governments care about budget stability. This argument has become particularly important in the light of the euro-area Stability and Stability Pact, which makes Government debt managers very careful about budget stability. Missale (2001) suggests that IIB should be issued even when they imply a high variability of interest payments (as is the case when the economy is likely to experience shocks owing to unexpected inflation). Indeed, high price variability implies not only high variability of interest payments but also a high variability of the budget primary surplus. When inflation is high, revenues increase (owing to the imperfectly indexed structure of tax brackets) more than public expenditure (owing to the imperfect indexation of outlays), and the opposite effect is true with deflation. In this case, it would be optimal to issue IIB because they stabilize the budget balance; unlike fixed-income bonds, which would have been preferred on the basis of a theory that was only concerned with interest payments volatility.[20]

A fourth possible explanation of the recent IIB emergence is related to structural changes in the traditional European public sector involvement in retirement schemes. For better risk-sharing and especially for budgetary reasons, Governments want to reduce their involvement in such schemes. These were generally based on the pay-as-you-go principle, and constructed in ways that automatically provide protection against inflation. The gradual substitution or integration of those schemes with pri-

20. Missale's paper also suggests –confirming earlier findings in Missale (1997), (2000)– that there is very little justification for the use of foreign-currency debt, either in a confidence crisis or in a stable environment. In a currency crisis, when the exchange rate is devalued and interest payments on foreign currency debt are high, output is usually low following harsh stabilization programmes. Therefore, interest payments rise in a recession when budget deficits are already high. In a stable environment, a restrictive monetary policy, coupled with an expansionary economy and an appreciating currency, would result in low interest payments owing to foreign currency debt. If the US were to issue foreign currency bonds in a recession (when interest rates are low and the exchange rate depreciates) high interest costs would add to the burden of an expanding and unstable budget deficit.

vate pension funds based on the fully-funded principle is creating a new demand for inflation protection. In fact Governments issuing default-risk-free IIB are offering to financial intermediaries and asset managers that want to create inflation-proof products, the financial instruments to hedge their positions.

A fifth explanation is that the ECB, on the one hand, and Governments in the euro-area, on the other, now have a higher need to disentangle at least three elements in the cost of issuing debt:

(a) inflationary expectations in the over-all euro area, say π_e
(b) specific country risk premium, say γ_i for country *i*
(c) specific country's debt liquidity premium, say λ_i for country *i*.

Comparing non-indexed Government bonds of two different euro-area countries, *i* and *j*, both denominated in euro and issued in the same size, should allow identification of the countries difference in (b), assuming that (c) is only a function of the amount of debt issue outstanding. Similarly, comparing a country's euro-IIB with its euro-nominal bonds would allow identification of (a), provided the size and liquidity of these two domestic markets were equivalent. If IIB had been issued before the euro with reference to national currencies, then (a) would have referred to the expected national inflation rate π_i and it would have been difficult to separate it from the country specific exchange rate risk, which is now common to all euro-area countries.

Finally, the introduction of the euro and the consequent standardization of debts instruments denominated in the new currency have increased competition among sovereign issuers, and thereby induced them to develop new financial products or try to specialize in already existing ones, such as IIB.[21]

21. Marco Pagano has stressed this point in private exchange.

4. Policy Prescriptions for the New EU Members

In the light of the preceding discussion, a number of questions arise for countries that plan to adopt the euro, particularly those whose monetary and fiscal authorities are relatively less credible, as it may be the case for the new EU member countries.

In theory, the same sequence that was discussed above could be reexamined for them: (i) would the adoption of a parallel currency of almost constant purchasing power (such as the euro) be expedient, ahead of entering the euro-area? (ii) should one accompany it, or substitute it, with the issuance of Government debt denominated in this currency, and (iii) possibly also by issuance of IIB, before entering the euro-area or only after?

Actually question (i) is practically no longer relevant, given that the EU Council and the European Central Bank have stated that the new and future EU members should not unilaterally decide for early adoption of the euro.[22] There remain the questions (ii) whether it would be useful for such countries to issue euro-denominated bonds, and (iii) more specifically to issue IIB, in advance of entering the euro-area.

If the new EU members were to follow the lead of the present members of the euro-area, the answers may be different: a qualified yes for euro-denominated bonds (in so far as some present members were issuing ECU-denominated bonds in advance of EMU[23]); a clear no, for IIB. Instead, they should mostly issue nominal bonds denominated in domestic currency, and try to develop a liquid secondary market for them. Let us consider whether indeed, in the current macroeconomic scenario, these

22. Euroisation was not seen favourably by the European Council in Nice. This stand has been reasserted by the ECB. In its policy position of December 18th, 2003 the ECB stated: "Any unilateral adoption of the single currency by means of "euroisation" outside the Treaty framework would run counter to the economic reasoning underlying Economic and Monetary Union, which foresees the eventual adoption of the euro as the end-point of a structured convergence process within a multilateral framework. Unilateral "euroisation" cannot therefore be a way of circumventing the stages foreseen by the Treaty for the adoption of the euro".
23. Even though the ECU was not really a full-fledged currency, but a parallel basket currency.

answers might constitute appropriate public debt management strategies for the new EU members.

Table 4 Economic Indicators of the New EU Members

	HICP Inflation*			Public Deficit (% of GDP)		Public Debt (% of GDP)		Debt Average Life**
	2002	2003	2004: IQ	2002	2003	2002	2003	July 2005
Cyprus	2.8	4.0	1.0	-4.6	-6.3	67.1	72.2	3.85
Czech Republic	1.4	-0.1	2.0	-6.4	-12.9	28.9	37.6	1.48
Estonia	3.6	1.4	0.6	1.8	2.6	5.7	5.8	n.a.
Hungary	5.2	4.7	6.8	-9.3	-5.9	57.1	59.0	4.29
Latria	2.0	2.9	4.3	-2.7	-1.8	15.5	15.6	5.92
Lithuania	0.4	-1.1	-1.1	-1.4	-1.7	22.8	21.9	5.41
Malta	3.1	2.6	0.9	-5.7	-9.7	61.7	72.0	n.a.
Poland	1.9	0.7	1.8	-3.6	-4.1	41.2	45.4	3.88
Slovakia	3.5	8.5	8.2	-5.7	-3.6	43.3	42.8	4.06
Slovenia	7.5	5.7	3.7	-1.9	-1.8	27.8	27.1	4.63
Reference Value*			2,9		-3,0		60,0	

– *Source:* ECB: Monthly Bulletin

* Reference value for inflation is the average of inflation in the three best performing countries of the euro zone.

** *Source:* Bloomberg.

In general, Government debt management could be used to "beat the market" when the expectations on variables that will affect interest rates differ between the issuer and the market. However, if there were wide consensus and little asymmetric information, then debt issuers would have no advantage in implementing strategies meant to prove cost effective ex-post. On the other hand, if the credibility of political commitments, like joining the EMU, were low, beat-the-market strategies should at least be considered. The matter thus depends on commitment and credibility. How credible are the new EU members' commitments in joining the euro-area soon?

The institutional set-up of convergence to the euro for the new EU members would seem more credible than the one enjoyed by some of the first entrants in the early and mid-1990s. Indeed, the new EU members do not have the choice to opt out of the euro (as the UK, Denmark and Sweden[24] did), but only to adopt it sooner or later. In fact, after accession to the EU, they are expected to join ERM II "at some point in time".[25]

How far is this point in time? While for some large new EU members proxy indicators of the probability of joining the EMU in the medium term – such as by 2008– are high, they do not yet point to a fully credible nominal convergence. Yet, markets seem to attach a high probability that they will join the EMU within a reasonable horizon. We have computed indicators of such probability with the following procedure. For those countries that have a significant and liquid domestic yield curve (the Czech Republic, Hungary, Poland, Slovakia), we have calculated the implied forward rates of the domestic curve for a period after the EMU target joining date (assumed to be in 2008). We have then related these forward rates with those implied in the Bund yield curve, adjusting for country risk premia.

More precisely, a measure of country risk (γ_i) is first computed as the difference between the country's benchmark Government euro-bond yield (r_i) and the Bund yield (r_e), assuming the same liquidity:

$$\gamma_i \equiv r_i - r_e$$

Let f_i and f_e be the forward interest rate on country i domestic denominated debt, and the benchmark euro forward interest rate, respectively. The probability of a country i joining the EMU is then related to an index of convergence c_i defined as:

$$c_i \equiv 1 - (f_i - f_e - \gamma_i)/f_i = (f_e + \gamma_i)/f_i$$

24. Actually, Sweden did not choose the opting out clause, but never entered ERM I, i.e. the mechanism that would have ensured one of the convergence criteria for being admitted to the euro-area.
25. European Central Bank (2003), p. 158.

when $f_e + \gamma_i \leq f i$, and as:

$$c_i \equiv 1$$

when $f_i + \gamma_i > f i$, i.e. when $f_i - f i > -\gamma_i$. For example, in the realistic case in which $\gamma_i > 0$, if the difference in forward rates $(f_e - f_i)$ is negative and smaller in absolute value than the country risk, it is taken as an indicator that expected inflation embedded in interest rates is lower in the new EU member country than in Germany, and therefore that the markets believe convergence will be achieved at the date to which the forward rates refer.

Figure 1. Index of Probability of Joining the EMU*

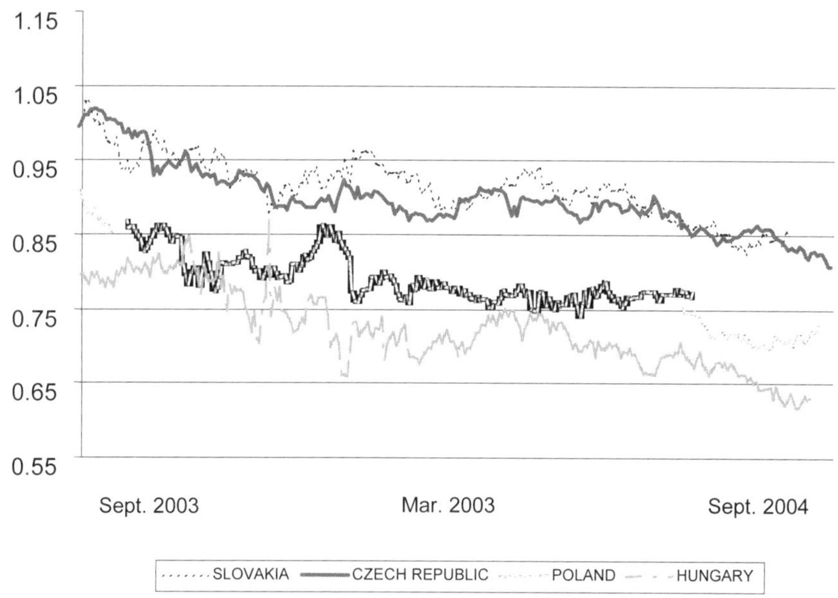

* Government Bonds used to calculate the Probability of Joining EMU: Czech Republic (17/03/2008-16/06/2013); Hungary (06/12/2008-02/12/2013); Poland (24/06/2008-24/10/2013); Slovakia (03/05/2008-22/01/2013).

Euro Denominated Government Bonds used to calculate the Country Risk: Czech Republic (23/06/2014); Hungary (06/02/2013); Poland (05/02/2013); Slovakia (14/04/2010).
Source: Bloomberg

Figure 1, which refers only to countries that present significant market data, shows that entrance in EMU, while not taken as granted for most new EU members, is substantially incorporated in current bond prices, at least on the basis of the c_i index. However, while relatively high, the computed index has had the interesting tendency to fall during the last year (2003-2004). We tentatively advance a number of explications for this.

First, recently these countries have shown a worrying relaxed fiscal stance relative to the fiscal restraint adopted some years ago. Second, while the exclusion of the opting-out clause for the new EU members has assured their entry into EMU "at some point in time",[26] the absence of a precise date has also made more uncertain their actual adoption of the euro. Third, the cooling of public opinion in some of these countries towards EU membership and EU institutions, may have been interpreted by the markets as a decrease in their willingness to accelerate entrance into EMU. Fourth, investors might fear that present EMU members are not applying enough pressure on the new EU members to adopt more restrained fiscal policies, since the EMU members themselves are currently discussing proposals for relaxing or changing some of the rules of Stability and Growth Pact, given the strains that some of its rules are imposing on their own economies. Fifth, some present EMU members may themselves be cooler now towards the new EU members' entrance into EMU. Indeed, it cannot be ruled out that the same decision-making problems that arose in the drafting of the European Constitution and the reform of the Stability and Growth Pact might disrupt the monetary policy-making process once it is opened to the new members.

What does this suggest for optimal debt management strategies? We should keep in mind, first of all, alternative financial instruments available to Government debt managers: (a) short-term and long-term nominal bonds denominated in (a1) domestic currency, or (a2) foreign (euro) currency, and (b) long-term indexed bonds linked to (b1) national inflation rate or (b2) euro-inflation rate.[27]

26. European Central Bank (2003), p. 158.
27. Inflation-indexed securities have generally long term maturities, since investors use them mainly to provide future retirement income. Professional investors, such as insurance companies, utilise IIB to hedge their financial products that provide annuities linked to the cost of living as the way to guarantee a

In this setting, a Government that were to adopt a "beat-the-market" strategy in the belief that euro adoption will occur with certainty, should choose (b1) –i.e. issue IIB linked to its national inflation rate– and (b2), to the extent that price dynamics are strongly correlated across the euro area and new EU countries; but also (a2) –i.e. euro-denominated bonds– rather than (a1) long-term nominal bonds in domestic currency.

However, beat-the-market strategies have rarely paid-off, as they are based on the somewhat unlikely assumption that markets know less than Governments about their country's economic fundamentals. In fact, Governments are getting keener to adopt debt management strategies that prevent extreme negative outcomes in terms of their objectives.

For example, the possibility of a "peso-problem" during the period of convergence before adoption of the euro might not be ruled out for some new EU members. Considering that, with their accession to the EU, these countries are expected to join the euro area at an unspecified future date, while in ERM II the standard fluctuation band around the central rate is ± 15%, markets might engage in currency attacks especially against countries with a high political willingness to join the euro-area. This would make foreign currency (especially euro-denominated) bonds and short duration domestic currency bonds (like T-Bills and floaters linked to short-term rates), rather unattractive. Both types of bonds would indeed raise the costs of a currency crisis, whether before it, to defend the stability of the exchange rate (short duration domestic bonds), or after it (foreign currency bonds), as the cost of servicing the debt would increase because of the depreciation.

Besides currency crises, another possibility is related to the so-called Balassa-Samuelson effect. These countries (more than the current members of the euro-area) may face in the near future substantial productivity shocks, positively related with permanent output, inflation, and the real exchange rate.[28] Such shocks would make nominal bonds –both foreign (euro) denominated and domestic currency denominated bonds– less

minimum standard of living in the retirement period. As already mentioned, this feature may make IIB more attractive now and for some time in the future.

28. We define the real exchange rate as the ratio between the domestic price level and the foreign price level, converted in domestic currency by the exchange rate.

attractive than IIB bonds (particularly IIB linked to national inflation), as the latter would have a more stabilizing impact on the national budget –a very desirable feature on the road to the euro.[29]

Imagine, for example, a negative productivity shock in the tradable sector that decreases real wages both in the tradable and non-tradable sector. As a result the domestic CPI declines (or, in a growth context, its inflation rate falls) and the real exchange rate depreciates. With foreign currency bonds, a real exchange depreciation increases the cost of debt when it is more painful, i. e., during a period of recession. The same would occur with long-term nominal debt, whose real return would increase. On the contrary, national currency-denominated IIB will have the attractive feature to maintain the real cost of debt constant, no matter the state of the economy; less so with IIB linked to the inflation of the currency area, which however might have the advantage of greater liquidity.

Even though Balassa-Samuelson effects may be of little relevance, IIB could still play a significant role in the new EU member countries. Indeed, if shocks in aggregate demand prevail, that simultaneously consist in unexpected increases in the price level (inflation) and output, smoothing the deficit/GDP ratio is helped by issuing IIB. As monetary management might be particularly relevant in the convergence toward EMU, aggregate demand shocks might indeed be relevant and issuing IIB (albeit

29. A similar argument is developed by Natalucci and Ravenna (2002). According to them, the new EU members will enjoy a productivity growth in their tradeable goods sector higher than the old members, in order to catch up with them. Hence their real exchange rate will have to appreciate. Imposing on them the ERMII requirement of a relatively fixed nominal exchange rate will make their adjustment more painful. In fact, according to the authors (p. 4), these countries "may face a trade-off between complying with the inflation criterion and respecting the nominal exchange rate requirement for EMU membership. [...] We then evaluate the business cycle implications of relaxing either the exchange rate requirement or the Maastricht inflation criterion. We conclude that allowing for a sustained appreciation of the nominal exchange rate would deliver a lower volatility of both the output gap and inflation". The similarity of the Natalucci and Ravenna argument with ours is that, just like abandonment of the nominal exchange rate anchor may facilitate adjustment for the new EU members, the choice of IIB rather than nominal bonds may facilitate the stability of the deficit/GDP ratio.

not exclusively) might have a significant pay-off in insuring deficit/GDP stability and therefore convergence.

Finally, one should not disregard the fact that many countries attempting to adopt the euro in the 1990s accompanied their strategy by a switch to long-duration nominal bonds denominated in their national currency, supported by a sophisticated secondary market infrastructure. Given that this strategy was highly costly in terms of ex-post real rates once disinflation successfully materialized, one might wonder why it was implemented. If, as Pecchi and Piga (1999) suggested, it was done also to reinforce the national anti-inflationary constituency, it is clear that if the new - EU member countries were to issue bonds in nominal euro or IIB linked to domestic inflation, this would have "an insurance effect" that should weaken the resolve of any such anti-inflationary constituency.

These considerations seem to suggest a number of policy prescriptions for the new EU members. First, that foreign (euro) denominated bonds – solution (a2)– just as they were of little use on the way to a common currency for first entrants into the euro zone, have few interesting properties (and actually some highly risky ones, as in a currency crisis), so that they should not be a relevant portion of the portfolio of any new EU member aspiring to enter the EMU.

Second, IIB –solution (b2)– especially if linked to national inflation (unless there is perfect correlation between domestic and euro inflation), might be of greater use, in so far as the Balassa-Samuelson effect might be of more relevance for such countries in the next few years than it was for the already rich group of EMU first comers, and as the process of convergence seems to have, for those countries, more credible institutional features, and inflation in many of them is low already.

Third, long-duration nominal bonds in national currency –solution (a1)– should sustain the development of national secondary markets that would foster liquidity and would turn into euro-denominated assets only once accession to the EMU is finally granted. Such domestic bonds would increase the sensitivity of national bondholders to the stability of nominal values and therefore the adherence of their citizens to the value of stability, which is a cornerstone of the EMU construct.

Have the new EU member countries followed these prescriptions, and how far? If not, in what sense should they move?

Table 5. Central Government Debt by Instruments*
(shares of amounts outstanding at the end of period)

		2000	2001	2002
Czech Republic	**Total Central Government Debt**	100.0	100.0	100.0
	Non-Marketable	6.8	2.6	2.3
	Fixed Rate Income Instruments	36.1	43.4	56.2
	Index Linked Bonds	0.0	0.0	0.0
	Other	57.1	54.1	41.4
	Foreign Currency	0.0	0.0	0.0
Hungary	**Total Central Government Debt**	100.0	100.0	100.0
	Non-Marketable	36.0	28.3	25.0
	Fixed Rate Income Instruments	33.7	41.0	45.3
	Index Linked Bonds	0.3	0.3	0.3
	Other	30.0	30.4	29.4
	Foreign Currency	10.2	11.8	9.5
Poland	**Total Central Government Debt**	100.0	100.0	100.0
	Non-Marketable	47.5	35.9	31.4
	Fixed Rate Income Instruments	36.7	42.6	49.7
	Index Linked Bonds	0.0	0.0	0.0
	Other	15.8	21.5	18.9
	Foreign Currency	16.7	19.1	19.8
Slovak Republic	**Total Central Government Debt**	100.0	100.0	100.0
	Non-Marketable	10.9	4.7	10.2
	Fixed Rate Income Instruments	80.9	67.3	63.2
	Index Linked Bonds	0.0	0.0	0.0
	Other	8.2	28.0	26.5
	Foreign Currency	38.8	21.5	19.3

Source: OECD, *Central Government Debt Statistical Yearbook*. various issues and our elaborations.
* The "Fixed Rate Income Instruments" and "Other" items include the "Foreign Currency" item. Fixed Rate Income Instruments include also variable-rate notes and money market instruments.

Looking at the data on the composition of debt (Table 5), it appears that the share of foreign-denominated assets of most of these countries (the Czech Republic being a relevant exception) is higher than the one of most EMU applicants in the mid 90s (with the relevant exceptions of Austria,

Finland, and Ireland, see Table 1), for which a share was denominated in each other's currencies and in ECU, as shown by their already mentioned drop at the end of 1998. A moderate shift of the new EU members debt toward a larger share of domestic denominated bonds would therefore be desirable and possible. The decision to issue IIB related to a euro index or a national index of inflation will have instead to be decided by looking at the advantages of liquidity in such a segment (higher for the euro-related index) and the advantages of national inflation protection (higher for the national index).

On the other hand, looking at the debt average life (Table 4), it is quite surprising that these countries do not present serious budget risk problems, as it was the case for countries such as Italy and Spain before joining the EMU. In fact, they present a debt average life that is more or less in line with those of the other EMU countries. On the contrary Italy and Spain had very short debt maturity even few years before joining the EMU.

In conclusion, we think that the European Commission should take a particularly close view, now and in the next few years, at the evolution of the composition of new EU members' debt. As the popular acceptance of the euro in those countries will be strictly correlated with the severity of stabilization policies, it would be a considerable political mistake to let public debt management destabilize economic policies and act as fuel on what could otherwise be a small and extinguishable fire.

References

Banca d'Italia (1981). "Considerazioni finali del Governatore della Banca d'Italia", in Relazione Annuale all'Assemblea dei partecipanti. Rome.

Basevi G., M. Fratianni, H. Giersch, P. Korteweg, D. O'Mahoney, M. Parkin, T. Peeters, P. Salin, N. Thygesen. "A Currency for Europe. The All Saints' Day Manifesto for European Monetary Union". The Economist. November 1st. 1975.

Borensztein E., P. Mauro (2004). "The Case for GDP-indexed bonds". Economic Policy. vol. 38. April. 165-206.

European Central Bank (2003). Annual Report.

Falcetti E., A. Missale (2002). "Public Debt Indexation and Denomination with an Independent Central Bank". European Economic Review. vol. 46. No. 10. December.

Foresi S., A. Penati, G. Pennacchi. "Reducing the Cost of Government Debt: the Role of Index-Linked Bonds." in De Cecco. M., L. Pecchi, G. Piga (eds.). *Managing Public Debt: Index-Linked Bonds in Theory and Practice*. Cheltenham: Edward Elgar. 93-115.

Greenspan. A. (1992). Statement before the Commerce, Consumer, and Monetary Affairs Subcommittee on Government Operations. US House of Representatives; in *Federal Reserve Bulletin*. August.

Missale, A. (1997) "Tax Smoothing with Price Indexed Bonds: A Case Study of Italy and the United Kingdom",. in De Cecco. M., L. Pecchi, G. Piga (eds.). *Managing Public Debt: Index-Linked Bonds in Theory and Practice*. Cheltenham: Edward Elgar. 50-92.

Missale, A. (2000). *Public Debt Management*. Oxford: Oxford University Press.

Missale, A. (2001). "Optimal Debt Management with a Stability and Growth Pact". Public Finance and Management. 1 (1). 58-91.

Natalucci F.M., F. Ravenna (2002). "The Road to Adopting the Euro: Monetary Policies and Exchange Rate Regimes in EU Candidate Countries". Board of Governors of the Federal Reserve System. *International Finance Discussion Papers*. n. 741. December.

Optica Report '75. "Towards Economic Equilibrium and Monetary Unification in Europe". Commission of the European Communities. 16 January 1976.

Optica Report 1976. "Inflation and Exchange Rates: Evidence and Policy Guidelines for the European Community". Commission of the European Communities. 10 February 1977.

Pecchi, L., G. Piga (1999). "The Politics of Index-Linked Bonds." Economics and Politics. 11. 2. 201-12.

Pecchi, L., A. Ripa di Meana (1998). "Public Foreign Currency Debt: A Cross-Country Evaluation of Competing Theories". Giornale degli Economisti e Annali di Economia. Vol. 57. N. 2. 251-288.

Piga G., G. Valente (2004). "The Term Structure of Interest Rates and the Public Debt Issuance Policy: A Note". Finance Letters. Volume 2. Issue 2.

Price R. (1997). "The Rationale and Design of Inflation-Indexed Bonds". *IMF Working Paper*. WP/97/12.

Von Hayek. F.A.. *The Denationalization of Money: an Analysis of the Theory and Practice of Concurrent Currencies*. Institute of Economic Affairs. London. October 1976.

Part III

The Fiscal Framework of the EMU

CHAPTER 8

What Went Wrong with the Stability and Growth Pact?

Lorenzo Bini Smaghi[1]

The July 2004 judgment of the European Court of Justice closed the *annus horribilis* of the Stability and Growth Pact (SGP). In June 2004, the Heads of State and Government, in conjunction with the Constitution for the European Union, adopted a declaration committing them to strengthening and clarifying the implementation of the SGP.

Several proposals for reforming the SGP have been put forward.[2] However, before rushing to reform the Pact, an assessment should be made of what is, or has been, wrong with it. Changes that are not justified by clear evidence of a shortcoming of the SGP should be considered with great caution.

Views differ on how the SGP has performed. One view is that the SGP has led to wrong budgetary policies in the Member States. This view is shared by those that consider that budgetary policies in Europe have been excessively tight and are largely responsible for the slow economic growth and those, at the other extreme, that believe that budgetary poli-

1. I wish to thank Marco Buti, Carlo Monticelli, Roberto Rinaldi, Gelsomina Vigliotti and Ignazio Visco for their comments and suggestions on earlier drafts of the paper, and Federico Giannusso and Manuela Nenna for their contribution to the Appendix. The views expressed in this paper are exclusively of my own responsibility.
2. See in particular the Communication by the European Commission (2004b).

cies have instead been too lax, as the larger countries in particular have failed to adjust their underlying budget position.[3] According to the former, the SGP should be relaxed and allow for more room for manoeuvre. According to the latter, the SGP should instead be tightened and made more binding.

A more balanced view, which combines parts of the previous ones, is that budgetary policies in the euro area have been somewhat pro-cyclical: too expansionary in good times and too tight in bad times. Was this the fault of the SGP? It is interesting to note that, according to the IMF:

"The SGP has been instrumental to the pursuit of sound policies. Specifically, it needs to be given credit for the shift to a largely appropriate euro-area fiscal policy stance in a challenging cyclical environment. This improvement in policy behavior is remarkable when viewed against the standards of the area's own procyclical fiscal policy history and the concurrent drastic weakening of underlying fiscal positions in other major currency areas."[4]

This IMF view is supported by recent academic research, in particular by Gali and Perotti (2003). The data confirms that the large pro-cyclicality in budgetary policy, which used to be one of the weaknesses in European policy-making, has been markedly reduced, although not fully eliminated, since the inception of the euro. Automatic stabilizers have been allowed to play and, although adjustment towards balanced positions has been insufficient, the underlying structural balance in the euro area has not deteriorated as in other major industrial countries.[5]

To sum up, the glass is half empty, but also half full. This doesn't mean that everything is fine and well with the SGP and that no improvements

3. See European Commission (2004).
4. IMF Concluding Statement of the 2003 mision. A similar judgment was expressed in the May 2004 concluding statement of the euro area article IV consultation.
5. The average euro area budget deficit has remained substantially unchanged during the past 6 years, in both nominal terms (from 2.3 per cent of GDP to 2.7 per cent) and cyclically adjusted terms (from 1.8 to 1.7 per cent). The overall debt has remained unchanged, slightly above 70 per cent of GDP.

are needed. There are two main problems that need to be addressed in a revision of the SGP.

First, the implementation of the procedures underlying the SGP has been difficult. It entailed much learning-by-doing, with unavoidable mistakes and tensions between EU institutions and with the Member States, in which undermined the credibility of the Pact. Experience has shown that some of the current provisions of the Pact have created obstacles in achieving the desired result and thus need to be changed.

The second problem is that the SGP has been more about stability than growth. This has nothing to do with budgetary policy itself but with its (lack of) interaction with other policies, in particular structural reforms. The political survival of the Pact requires that more attention be given to growth, by further reducing its pro-cyclicality and by integrating it with the Lisbon Agenda.

The next two sections examine these two issues and possible solutions. The main conclusion from this paper is that most of the initial shortcomings of the SGP have largely been addressed over time through learning-by-doing. This process has however generated conflicts and led to undermining the credibility of the Pact. Some limited changes are thus needed, but the reform process should avoid the risk of overshooting, making changes that would modify the nature of the SGP and possibly entail different type of problems for the future.

1. The Hard "Learning-By-Doing"

At the start of EMU there was little or no experience at all with fiscal policy frameworks in monetary unions that could be used as a guide for the application of the SGP. Implementation had thus to be based on learning-by-doing, which explains much of the problems and shortcomings of the Pact. Reviewing the experience in implementation is useful to understand some of the changes that the Pact might need.

1.1. From Maastricht (1991) to Amsterdam (1997): From Procedures to Rules

Some of the difficulties in implementing the SGP derive from the change in philosophy that took place in Europe between the signing of the Maastricht Treaty and the start of EMU. There are two main changes worth mentioning.

The first change is that while the Treaty aimed at achieving budgetary discipline through a procedure (the so-called Excessive Deficit Procedure), the SGP is based on a set of specific rules for national policies. According to the Treaty, the identification of an excessive deficit should be the result of a judgment, taking due account of a series of elements, including two reference values and other parameters, such as *"whether the government deficit exceeds government investment expenditure and... all other relevant factors, including the medium-term economic and budgetary position of the Member State"*.

The preparatory work of the Monetary Committee made this point very clear. For instance, the Chairman's Report on "The State of the Committee's Discussion on Excessive Deficits in EMU", dated 25 June 1991, stated in particular that:

"This procedure must address deficits representing gross errors of budgetary policy which jeopardize the stability of the Union or of a Member State. It must be designed to identify such deficits and enforce their reduction. By its nature the initiation of this special procedure should not be a frequent event in full EMU".

The Report went on to state that:

The Council's excessive deficit procedure will involve the exercise of judgment. It should on the other hand be started automatically when there is evidence that one of the agreed principles may have been broken. The principles and the reference values can be seen as together constituting 'trigger mechanisms'".

On the level of the reference values, while the 60 per cent debt: GDP ratio, which was about the EU average at that time, received a broad consensus, the reference value for the deficit was the subject of discussion until the very end:

"As a Chairman, I have the impression that the figure ultimately agreed will be in the range of 3-4%".

The SGP, agreed at the Amsterdam June 1997 European Council, marked a drastic change in philosophy. The European Council Resolution committed:

"all parties, the Member States, the Commission and the Council, to implement the Treaty and the SGP in a strict and timely manner".

If the implementation of the excessive deficit procedure had to involve the exercise of judgment, as initially thought, how could such a judgment be implemented in a "strict and timely manner"? In fact, the drafters of the SGP did not intend the Treaty's Excessive Deficit Procedure as a procedure, but as a rule. This is reflected in the text of the Regulations, starting with the first recital:

"the provisions of this Regulation constitute a new integrated set of rules for the application of article 104c". [6]

What was the reason for such a change? The main one was that not all members of the Council trusted that the procedure foreseen in the Treaty would be implemented in a rigorous way. Since membership in the Monetary Union was less restricted than initially thought, there was a risk, according to some, that countries traditionally less acquainted with budgetary discipline would create obstacles to a firm implementation of the Treaty. The lack of trust led Finance Ministers to accept tying their hands with rules that turned out to be so strict as to hamper, on some occasion, the exercise of judgment.

The second change in philosophy that took place after the signing of the Maastricht Treaty had to do with the purpose of budgetary surveillance. Whereas initially the main objective of budgetary surveillance was to avoid excesses, the SGP gave the EU a role in prescribing countries' budgetary policies, in particular the target of achieving a position close-to-balance or in surplus over the cycle. While the Treaty limited itself to defining reference values for the deficit and the debt, on the basis of which the Council would decide whether a country's budget would be

6. Regulation 1467/97 of 7 July 1997.

excessive, the SGP put at the center of budgetary policy cooperation a specific budget target, similar for all countries. In short, although this might not have been fully understood by the signatories, the SGP shifted power from the Member States to the Union.

What were the reasons for this change in philosophy? The justification was that:

"adhering to the close-to-balance objective will allow all Member States to deal with normal cyclical fluctuations while keeping the government deficit within the reference value of 3% of GDP".[7]

In sum, the SGP was supposed to create an instrument for crisis prevention, to help countries avoid reaching the reference values. This interpretation is not fully convincing. Had this been the case, the target for budgetary positions over the cycle would have been to be below the so-called "minimal benchmark", which measures the level of the cyclically-adjusted deficit consistent with allowing automatic stabilizers to play fully while respecting the 3 per cent limit even in the case of particularly unfavorable, but still possible, cyclical conditions.[8] This approach would have implied that, for most countries, a deficit around 1 per cent of GDP would be broadly appropriate. In fact, from the start of EMU countries were asked to produce budgetary plans achieving a zero-balance budgetary positions within the four years program horizon. As the Commission itself recognizes:[9]

"an additional safety margin, estimated to be in the order of 0.5% and 1% of GDP, was also deemed necessary... In aggregate, these estimates imply that broadly balanced budgets are an appropriate medium-term target for most Member States, and that a surplus would be advisable for some".

As new safety margins were added to previous margins, the SGP evolved from a preventive to a prescriptive instrument. Countries' balanced bud-

7. European Commission (2004b).
8. See European Commission (2004b) and Buti et al. (1997).
9. See European Commission (2004b), p. 65.

getary targets were systematically missed, because they were unnecessarily ambitious and did not take the underlying economic conditions into due account. As an example, until June 2002, nearly one year after September 11, countries were requested to achieve budget balance by 2003 or 2004, with an adjustment of 1 per cent of GDP or more in spite of the sharp slowdown of the economy. These targets were not only pro-cyclical; they were not credible. They were not respected, thus partly reducing the pro-cyclicality of budgetary policies, but undermined the credibility of the Pact itself.

The second reason for the change in philosophy was that the excessive deficit became a criterion for entry into the euro area. The fear that entry might be decided mainly on political, rather than economic, grounds transformed the excessive deficit procedure into a rule and the 3 per cent deficit: GDP ratio from a trigger point to a ceiling. This interpretation continued after the start of EMU, to the point that any deficit above 3 per cent would be considered as "excessive" by definition, while any notch lower would not. For example, the 3.2 deficit recorded by the Netherlands in 2003, with an economy in recession, was considered excessive, while the 2.8 per cent deficit in Portugal in 2000, with a booming economy, was not. Entry into EMU limited the Council's ability to exercise judgment. Again, the fear that Member States would help each other out, in exchange for future favors, led the Council to bind its ability to exercise judgment with rules that proved ex-post not easy to implement in a rational way.

The third reason derives from the deterioration of the economic and public finance environment in Europe during the 1990s. The growth potential initially assumed for the euro area as a basis for setting the 3 per cent reference value proved to be over-optimistic. The 3 per cent deficit was calculated as being consistent over the medium term with a 60 per cent debt: GDP ratio, on the assumption of a 3 per cent real GDP growth and 2 per cent inflation. Over the 1990s, trend growth in the euro area declined from 3 to around 2 per cent. The appropriately calculated reference value consistent with a 60 per cent debt: GDP ratio should thus be reduced accordingly, to around 2 per cent.

The problem with this reasoning is the confusion between a limit and an average. What the above debt dynamic rule suggests is that a 3 per cent average deficit entails a declining debt: GDP ratio towards a 60 per cent level. If the 3 per cent becomes a ceiling, instead of an average, the debt converges towards a lower level than 60 per cent.

Public finances deteriorated in the course of the 1990s also as a result of the ageing population, an issue which was not raised in the discussions leading to the Maastricht Treaty. Aiming at a budget close-to-balance or in surplus was advocated as a way to tackle the unresolved pension problem in many countries. This was the wrong reasoning, however. For most countries with increasing pension expenditure no reasonable surplus can be sufficient to compensate for future deficits in the Welfare system. The only reasonable solution to the ageing problem is a reform of the pension system. In fact, the SGP's major failure has been the lack of incentives for countries to adopt structural reforms aimed at improving the sustainability of their public finances, as will be examined in the next section.

A reform of the SGP should start by going back to the roots of the Maastricht Treaty, focusing more on the objective of avoiding excesses rather than on prescribing specific policies for the member states, which is a primary responsibility of national Parliaments. The 3 per cent deficit and 60 per cent debt should be considered again as reference values, that trigger an assessment of whether the deficit is excessive or not, rather than being used automatically. The assessment should take all elements into consideration, particularly debt sustainability and the cyclical position of the country. Some of the existing provisions of the SGP do not allow to take these factors into account. For instance, the provision whereby it is only the country concerned that can invoke the clause of "exceptional circumstances", to justify a deficit above 3 per cent, should be removed.[10] Had this clause not existed, the Council would have had no difficulty in considering the 3.2 per cent deficit of the Netherlands in 2003 as not excessive (contrary to what actually happened), given the recession experienced by the country.

1.2. The Difficult Fight for Automatic Stabilizers

As mentioned above, the SGP was initially based on nominal budgetary targets, to be achieved within set deadlines and without taking into account the underlying cyclical position. This gave rise to problems since

10. This restriction applies when GDP contraction is less than 2 per cent.

the very beginning. In April 1999, Italy's Minister Ciampi wrote to the Commission and the EU Council indicating that, in light of the lower than previously expected growth (1.3 per cent instead of 2.5), the Italian deficit target for that same year would have to be revised upward, from 2 per cent of GDP indicated in the Stability Programme to 2.4 per cent. Keeping budget target unchanged with a slower than expected growth would have required the immediate adoption of corrective measures that would have produced a pro-cyclical effect. At the May 1999 Ecofin Council, the incoming Italian Minister Amato had to face a line of fire against Italy's request. The main argument was that the budgetary objectives set in the Stability Programmes could not be considered as "moving targets" and could not be adjusted in light of economic developments. According to this view, the SGP was based on nominal targets, which should not be changed. The assessment of any deviation from the targets should be made only *ex-post*.

Only after an intense discussion in the Ecofin was Italy allowed some room for manoeuvre and avoid having to take corrective action. Although the Pact proved to allow for some flexibility, the media interpreted the decision as a first breach of the Pact. It took quite some time, and many difficult discussions, in the EFC and on the Council, to move away from purely nominal targets and take cyclical developments fully into consideration in the assessment of budgetary positions. The concept that automatic stabilizers should be allowed full rein, so long as the 3 per cent reference value was not breached, was not agreed until as late as June 2002, three years after the start of EMU.

One of the drawbacks of the 1999 Italian experience is that Finance Ministers became aware of the difficulties they would encounter in discussing openly potential budgetary problems as soon as they emerged. It proved easier to keep nominal targets unchanged, even if unrealistic in light of changing economic environment, and eventually wait for the final budgetary data to reveal divergences. This created the incentive to admit budgetary overruns as late as possible, most often too late to make any timely correction.

One example of the distortion created by the SGP is that the latter requests that the correction of an excessive deficit be implemented in the year following the one in which the excessive deficit is identified (not the year in which the excessive deficit occurs). Thus, the later a deficit is identified as being excessive, the longer is the time allowed to correct it. No wonder excessive deficits have only been identified in the following year.

1.3. From Judgment to "Justice"

The 1999 Italian case made it clear what a country, and particularly its Finance Minister, experiencing budgetary difficulties should expect from the implementation of the SGP: a public trial. The Pact contains no incentives, except for the threat of sanctions, to achieve cooperative solutions. Country ownership for policy recommendations is not a priority. The result is that the implementation of the SGP has often given rise to conflicts, between institutions and between Member States.

The 25 November 2003 episode is worth recalling. On that date, after long discussions with France and Germany, the two countries finally agreed to take action, broadly in line with what the Commission had requested, to correct their excessive deficits by 2005, rather than 2004 as previously requested. Both countries had agreed to the commitments and the policy recommendation. There was, however, a divergence of views regarding the article of the Treaty under which the policy recommendations should be issued. France and Germany requested article 104(7) to be applied: the Commission wanted to apply article 104(9). The lawyers were brought to the table. What mattered, at that point, was not the substance, and in particular the fact that the peer pressure had produced the desired policy result, but the procedure. What seemed to be the only matter for budgetary policy in the Union was the legal interpretation of the Regulation. The fundamental warning by Lord Keynes – "lawyers on tap, not lawyers on top" – was sadly ignored!

Eight months later, the European Court of Justice indicated that the Commission had the choice of proposing the policy recommendation according to either article 104(7) or 104(9). The decision of the Council to vote down the Commission Recommendation under article 104(9) could have led the Commission to present the same Recommendation under article 104(7). The Commission chose not to do so, thus leaving a vacuum in the procedure. This is why the Council adopted so-called "political" Conclusions, that actually proved to be unlawful in the absence of a new Commission proposal.

The 2004 experience with the Early Warning to Italy shows how peer pressure can work, even without resorting automatically to all the steps provided by the formal procedures.

The lesson to be learned is that the diversity of cases and circumstances, both political and economic, make it impossible to implement budgetary discipline only through rules and automatisms. Judgment must be exercised, as the founding fathers of the Maastricht Treaty suggested. Constraints on the exercise of judgment are bound to lead to conflicts and sub-optimal results. On the other hand, a totally unconstrained exercise of judgment may not lead to optimal results either, given the incentives that countries may have to absolve each other, in exchange for future favors. This creates the usual trade-off between rules and discretion. The SGP may have erred on the side of excessive rules. An adjustment may thus be required, aiming at ensuring greater accountability in the decision-making process.

2. Too Much Emphasis on Stability and None on Growth

This is the greatest criticism to the SGP. There can be two ways of putting greater emphasis on growth. The first is to take more account of cyclical conditions in assessing budgetary performance and in prescribing adjustment from an excessive deficit, so as to avoid short-term negative repercussions on the economy. The second is to take account of longer-term factors of growth in the implementation of the SGP so as to create incentives for reform.

2.1. More Account of Cyclical Conditions

An increasing role has been given to the use of cyclically-adjusted indicators in the implementation of the SGP, although this development has not been without its difficulties, as seen in the previous section. As mentioned earlier, there is little evidence that policies in EU Member States have been pro-cyclical over recent years. However, the implementation of the SGP has led to some pro-cyclicality, notably in the Netherlands and Portugal.[11] It is interesting to note that these were the only two countries that implemented the October 2002 Eurogroup agreement to reduce the cyclically-adjusted deficit by at least 0.5 percent of GDP, independently of the cyclical position. The two countries experienced a recession.

Pro-cyclicality has been avoided partly as a consequence of the fact that some of the policy commitments were not fully respected. This has led to a loss of credibility of the commitments, and thus of the Pact itself. The obvious example is the 2003 policy recommendations to France and Germany to reduce the deficit to below 3 per cent that were formulated on the basis of growth assumptions that did not materialize.[12] The two countries did not implement the recommendations fully and were granted one more year to make the adjustment, although this was not originally allowed for in the SGP rules. Pro-cyclicality was avoided but the credibility of the Pact suffered.

Policy objectives and recommendations, especially for countries that have excessive deficits or budgetary positions distant from balance, need to take the cyclical position into account. Indeed, it is easier to reduce the cyclically-adjusted deficit by 0.5 per cent of GDP when the economy is above potential, rather than when the output gap is negative.

When the economy is above its potential there must be incentives for stronger budgetary adjustment. The main responsibility for the budgetary problems experienced in recent years resides in the lack of adjustment in 2000, when euro area growth was strong. The euro area cyclically-adjusted deficit raised to 1.9 per cent of GDP in 2000, from 1.7 in 1999. In Germany, the increase was 0.4 percentage points, in France 0.1, in Italy 0.6. The inability to correct the deficit in good times reduced the margins of manoeuvre in the following years, when economic conditions turned out to be worse than expected.

To be fair, it is not always easy to know when the good times are there, and when they are expected to end. For instance, although the good growth performance in 2000 was largely unexpected, the sharp slowdown in the following years was also unforeseen. To be sure, the Autumn 2000 Com-

11. IMF (2004).
12. The Autumn 2002 Commission forecast on GDP growth for France and Germany in 2003 was 2.0 and 1.4 per cent, respectively. The actual results were 0.2 and –0.1.

mission forecasts projected euro area growth of 3.2 per cent in 2001 and 3 in 2002 (against an outcome of 1.6 and 0.9, respectively). Several European countries expected the good times to last longer and decided to use the extra fiscal revenues to reduce their tax burden rather than to trim their deficit. This decision, which was the subject of intense political debate ("la cagnotte" in France), was not seen at that time as being pro-cyclical.[13] The extra proceeds from the sale of the UMTS licenses also contributed to giving the illusion of better longer-lasting budgetary outcomes.

Creating incentives for greater budgetary adjustment in good times is one of the changes necessary to make the SGP more effective. This is not easy, however. The Council tried once to pressure for such a policy, but it turned out to be a mistake. This is the case of the 2001 Early Warning to Ireland. On the basis of existing projections, the Irish budget for 2001 was considered excessively expansionary and pro-cyclical. These projections were however too optimistic. Irish growth turned out to be much worse than expected, and the Irish expansionary budget policy proved ex-post to be anti-cyclical, rather than pro-cyclical.

2.2. More Incentives for Structural Reforms

One way to improve the functioning of the SGP is to create incentives, or eliminate the disincentives, for countries to undertake structural reforms in the fields of welfare and labor markets. Disincentives may exist when reforms have short term budgetary or political costs. For instance, implementing a widespread pension reform, with the creation of a second pillar, might create additional net public expenditure in the short run, subtracting room for manoeuvre for budgetary policy, especially when growth is slow. A country adopting wide-ranging welfare reforms that improves the sustainability of its budgetary position could be allowed some margin of manoeuvre in the short term, in particular to adopt fiscal reforms.

This approach has begun to be implemented pragmatically, for instance with the Council Opinion on the 2003 Austrian Stability Pro-

13. The Spring EU Commission forecasts considered that the 2000 average euro area budgetary position was actually restrictive compared to 1999 (-0.8 against -0.9 per cent of GDP). The same assessment was made by the OECD.

gramme, which looked favorably at the 2005 tax cut, by about 1 per cent of GDP, in light of the beneficial effects on debt sustainability produced by the pension reform enacted in 2003.

The framework underlying the analysis of fiscal sustainability should be strengthened and more prominence given to this indicator in the implementation of the SGP. Suggestions along these lines have already been put forward in the literature.[14] A stronger fiscal sustainability framework would create a link between the SGP and the European reform agenda, in particular in the context of the Lisbon process, by making the incentives for countries to accelerate structural reforms more explicit. If structural reforms are effective, by raising labor participation, reducing unemployment, increasing the growth potential of the economy, and reducing the cost of pensions to society, they improve the sustainability of a country's debt. A debt sustainability framework, similar to that available in the OECD, IMF and the European Commission, can calculate the impact of these reforms on the dynamics of the public debt. The Appendix gives a simple example of how structural reforms can be incorporated into the SGP through the debt sustainability analysis.

The proposal to incorporate debt sustainability analysis into the SGP differs from earlier proposals (for instance the Autumn 2002 Commission Communication) to discriminate budgetary policies according to the level of the debt.[15] The economic literature does not provide a clue about the optimal level of a country's debt, which may differ according to a series of factors, including national savings. What is essential for budget discipline is not so much the level of the debt, but that a country's debt is sustainable. This requires a forward-looking assessment of all liabilities, particularly those arising from population ageing.

3. Conclusions: Fix It, But Don't Break It

Where the SGP really needs changes is in the procedures, to create the right incentives to achieve discipline and address problems *ex-ante* rather

14. See for instance Balassone and Franco (2000), Buiter and Grafe (2003).
15. See for instance Sapir et al. (2003).

than *ex-post*. The assessment of budgetary policies should lead to peer pressure and develop country-ownership rather than providing solemn judgments on whether countries' policies are right or wrong. This requires a completely new interaction between the Member States, the Commission and the Ecofin Council.

In this section, we offer a few suggestions on areas where the SGP could be rejuvenated, with a view to fostering consistent and credible implementation.

The European Council Resolution on the SGP lists a set of separate commitments by the Member States, the European Commission and the Ecofin Council. There are no joint commitments, perhaps on the assumption that if each party did its duty the Pact would be implemented smoothly. This is not the way the world, and democracies, work, especially when judgment, most often political judgment, is at stake. It is possible, and even frequent in real life, that judgments on the appropriateness of a given policy differ. There is therefore a need for mechanisms of reconciliation, to ensure that institutions work together and cooperate to find solutions consistent with the spirit of the SGP. The lessons of the past few years suggest the following.

First, even when the parties involved (the Council and the Commission) dissent, no void should be allowed in the implementation of the SGP and the Treaty. A situation similar to what happened on 25 November 2003, whereby a negative vote by the Council implies the suspension of the Treaty provisions, should be avoided. The Council and the Commission should be induced to find a solution before coming to a showdown. This entails specific changes to the Regulations.

Second, a country which intends to adopt the necessary measures to correct an excessive deficit should be encouraged to do so by all means. Before issuing any warning or recommendation, the policy intentions of the country should be discussed and analyzed in depth, allowing for the necessary time. The policy recommendation ultimately addressed by the Commission and the Council to such a country should be "owned" by the latter and take the form of a cooperative agreement rather than an imposition by the European Union. As in the spirit of the Treaty, sanctions should be considered only as a very last resort, to be exercised against a country that is unwilling to cooperate to achieve budget discipline.

Third, the assessment of budgetary positions and policy recommendations made to a country should consider both the short and the longer-term policy measures, placing greater emphasis on the latter when countries are grappling with debt sustainability problems. The objective of close-to-balance or in surplus should not necessarily be the same across countries but consistent with the need to avoid breaching the 3 per cent reference value and take into account debt sustainability. This requires, *inter alia,* the development of analytical tools that are able to take into account the longer-term impact of structural reforms and the short-term cost of these reforms.

Incentives should be provided to highlight and address problems as soon as they emerge, rather than *ex-post*. This requires that the discussions on budgetary issues are loaded with fewer tensions. If there is one lesson to be drawn from the first years of the SGP, it is that countries do not want to address budget policy issues in the form of court judgments, but through cooperative, peer pressure mechanisms. It is the task of the Commission to help the Council to implement these mechanisms in the most efficient and useful way, for the Union and for the member countries themselves.

This approach requires each party involved to take account of the views and interests of the others in its own process and to give priority to the whole purpose of the SGP, which is to ensure budgetary discipline. In particular, the Commission cannot consider itself to be a mere technical body, since it has the right of initiative and is responsible for providing the Council with policy recommendations. The procedure for presenting such policy recommendations should take national economic and political conditions into account. The Council should implement the SGP with a view to preserving its credibility over the medium term. A credible and efficient SGP is in the interest of the Finance Ministers themselves. If there are incentives in the short term to help countries in difficulty, in exchange for similar favors in the future, a systematic bias towards leniency would in the end undermine the credibility of Finance Ministers themselves.

None of the above-proposed improvements to the Pact require new rules, but few specific changes to existing procedures aimed at creating better interactions between the Community institutions.

Appendix
Integrating Structural Reforms into the SGP

This note provides an example of how Debt Sustainability Analysis can be used in the context of the SGP to create the appropriate incentives for countries to adopt structural reforms in line with the Lisbon Agenda.

A country's budget constraint can be described according to a standard equation (where all variables are GDP ratios):

$$b_t = g_t^A + g_t^{NA} - t_t + ib_{t-1} \quad with \quad t = 1, \; 2,...50$$

where, b_t is the public debt, g_t^A are the age-related expenditures, g_t^{NA} are the non-age-related expenditures and t are the tax receipts. This is the framework which is also used by the EPC for assessing debt sustainability.

We consider a very simple case of a stylized country whose GDP grows at a steady state rate of 3 per cent, with a real interest rate of 3.1 per cent. Tax receipts and non-age-related expenditures grow at the same rate as GDP. Age-related expenditures grow instead at a rate faster than GDP (3.5 per cent from t+2 onwards). The initial debt: GDP ratio is 60 per cent. The basic assumptions can be easily changed.

Starting with an initial deficit of 1 per cent of GDP and unchanged policies, the debt: GDP ratio decreases in the first 6 years but starts increasing thereafter, as age-related expenditure rises. As shown in the figure, in the baseline scenario the debt gets on an unstable path, approaching 160 per cent of GDP in t+50.

Under these conditions, a policy aimed at reducing the tax burden would add to the instability, even if in the initial years the deficit would remain below the 3 per cent range. A 1 per cent tax cut would increase the debt: GDP ratio from the first few years of the simulation, and accelerate the increase thereafter. The deterioration of the debt path is overestimated, given that for the sake of simplicity it is assumed that the tax cut has no effect on GDP growth. However, the pre-existing non-sustainability of the debt is likely to hamper any stimulative effect of a tax cut.

Let us now assume a new scenario, where the country implements a pension reform that aligns the growth of age-related expenditure to GDP growth. In this scenario, the debt: GDP ratio falls throughout the simulation period to below 40 per cent after 20 years, and 20 per cent in t+50. The pension reform makes the debt profile sustainable.

If such a reform is politically costly, and the country has difficulties in getting it approved, what kind of incentive can be used to encourage the country to embark on it? Merging the previous two exercises shows that if the country simultaneously adopts the pension reform and the tax cut, the debt remains sustainable even with a deficit close to 2 per cent for several years. The debt and the deficit are overestimated, also in this scenario, given the assumption of the neutrality of tax cuts with respect to GDP. Any positive effect would contribute to reducing the deficit over time.

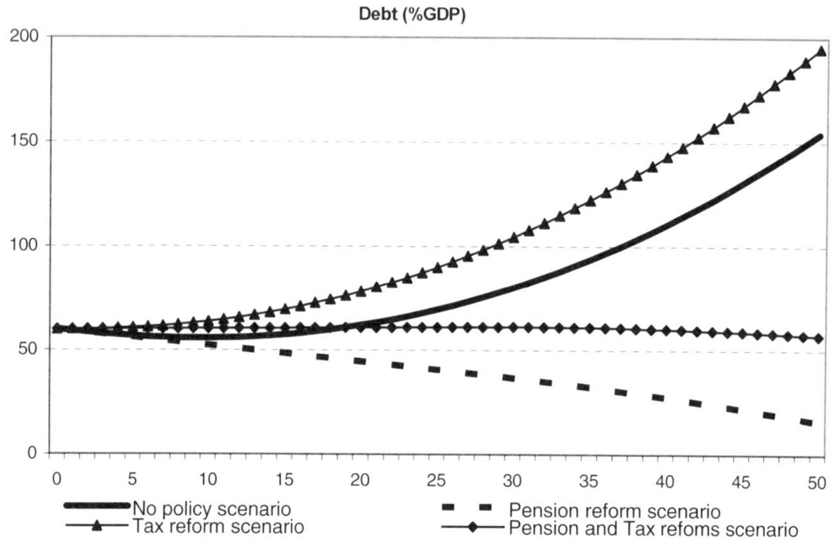

The "combined policies" scenario shows that the longer-terms benefits of a pension reform can be brought forward to benefit the present generation, and thereby be made politically more "palatable", through a tax cut that raises the budget deficit above the baseline, for several years. Such a deficit is nevertheless sustainable and could therefore be tolerated in the context of the SGP.

This framework can be used to assess other types and combinations of reforms, and link them to short term budgetary policy.

References

Balassone, F. and D. Franco (2000), "Assessing Fiscal Sustainability: a Review of Methods with a View to EMU", in Fiscal Sustainability, Banca d'Italia.

Bini Smaghi, L. (2004) "Reflections on Economic Governance", Aspen European Dialogue, Venice, February.

Buiter, W. and C. Grafe (2003), "Reforming EMU's Fiscal Policy Rule: Some Suggestions for Enhancing Fiscal Sustainability and Macroeconomic Stability in an Enlarged European Union, in *Monetary and Fiscal Policy Policies in EMU,* ed. by M. Buti, Cambridge University.

Buti, M., D. Franco and E. Ougene (1997), "Budgetary Policies During Recessions. Retrospective Appreciation of the Stability and Growth Pact", Recherches Economiques de Louvain, 63, pp. 3221-66.

European Commission (2004), "Public Finances in EMU", European Economy, n.3.

European Commission (2004b), Five Years of EMU.

Gali. J and R. Perotti (2003), "Fiscal Policy and Monetary Integration in Europe", Economic Policy, n. 37, pp 533-572.

International Monetary Fund (2004), World Economic Outlook, August.

CHAPTER 9

The Fiscal Framework Under Stress

Daniel Gros

The rules for fiscal policy have remained the most contentious issue of the entire EMU framework ever since the Maastricht Treaty enshrined a clear ceiling for deficits and a procedure to enforce them. Since the agreement on the Stability and Growth Pact (SGP) – which filled in some of the details of the 'Excessive Deficit Procedure' of Article 104 of the Treaty and which contains the (non-binding) exhortation for member countries to aim at a balanced budget or a small surplus over the cycle – the controversy has even increased.

Gros and Thygesen (1990), (1992), (1996) and (1998) were one of the first among the few academic defenders of the fiscal rules contained in the Maastricht Treaty. The argument was, and remains quite simple: financial markets do not apply a graduated pressure on governments to reign in deficits. Yields on government bonds do not really increase with higher deficits until a breaking point is reached and the capital market totally rations credit to government in question, basically because the promise to pay ever higher interest rates ceases to be credible above a certain threshold.

The first part of this chain of arguments has been vindicated since the establishment of the euro. The very small remaining differences in the yields on government debt seem to be driven more by liquidity effects (determined essentially by the size of issues) than differences in creditworthiness. (Bernoth et al. (2004)). The second part of this argument, namely that in a crisis situation governments could find themselves cut of from financial markets, has unfortunately not been observed yet.

This contribution essentially shows that two developments, demographic decline and a fall in productivity, reinforce the position originally taken by Gros and Thygesen in the early 1990s that the 3 % limit on government deficits should not be regarded as a straightjacket. Section 1 lays the groundwork by describing the demographic decline that Europe is facing over the next decades. Section 2 then illustrates the impact of this demographic decline on public finances in a long-run perspective. Section 3 discusses the implications of lower potential growth for the operation of the SGP in the short run. Section 4 concludes.

1. Ageing: The Main Challenge for Fiscal Policy

It is evident that no fiscal framework is forever. One has to judge the fiscal rules for EMU in light of the problems that are most likely to appear in the foreseeable future. If one does this for the euro area (or the expanding EU in general) there can be no doubt that the major challenge for fiscal policy over the next decade will be the accelerating ageing of the population. That ageing constitutes a fiscal policy problem of the first order of magnitude has now been established by scores of studies. And it is pretty obvious. One does not need complicated models to understand that there will be problems when the number of pensioners increases, but the number of tax payers is falling.

A first important point is that the word "ageing" does not describe adequately the problem Europe is facing. It is true that average life expectancy is increasing continuously in all developing countries. But the main reason why the proportion of the elderly is now expected to almost double over the next 50 years in Europe is that on average fertility has fallen so much below replacement levels so that natural population growth has now turned negative, and will stay negative for the foreseeable future. Lower birth rates imply of course that the average age of the population increases. It is important to realise that low birth rates are a phenomenon that is specific to Europe (and Japan), but not the US as can be seen from the demographic projections for the EU and the US presented below.[1]

This table concentrates on old age dependency ratios, which constitute a measure of the consequences of ageing for public finances since an increasing proportion of elderly implies higher pension and health expenditures. Table 1 shows that for the EU-15 the old age dependency will, on average, double by the year 2050 to reach over 50%. The prospect for the new member states is actually even worse in the sense that their fertility rates have fallen to even lower levels. By contrast, the dependency ratio of the US will increase much less and will remain about a third lower than that of Europe. Among the major member countries Germany stands out as having to face a considerably faster ageing process than France, for example.

Table 1. Old Age Dependency Projections

	2000	2025	2050
Japan	25.1%	47.0%	64.6%
USA	18.8%	29.3%	34.6%
France	24.5%	36.0%	45.9%
Germany	24.2%	39.4%	52.9%
EU-15	24.4%	36.1%	51.0%
EU-28	21.5%	31.9%	48.5%

Sources: US Census, http://www.census.gov/ipc/www/idbnew.html, own calculations.

Besides higher spending on pensions and health care, the fall in fertility in Europe has one further implication: at given productivity growth rates the overall growth rates diminish due to shrinking populations. Moreover, for Europe the ageing comes together, at least in the medium run, with a fall in productivity growth (Thygesen (2001) and (2003). This phenomenon has been documented by many observers and even official institutions have taken it into account by lowering their estimate of

1. These projections are already based on the assumption that fertility in Europe will somewhat recover than that the increase in life expectancy will slow down.

Europe's potential growth rate over the next years. Section 3 shows why this is relevant for fiscal policy.

2. Implications of Ageing for Fiscal Policy

Standard theorems about optimal fiscal policy imply that a country confronted with a predictable increase in expenditure should react already today by running lower deficits or a higher surplus. This can be easily shown in a bare bones tax smoothing model.

The key assumption in such a model is that due to ageing of the population desired public spending will increase in a generation, i.e. in about 20 years. A supplementary assumption would be that the new steady state starts then.

The model itself is completely standard, including the following element:

The starting point is a social loss function. The social loss is increasing in the tax rate (= tax take as % of GDP), denoted by t, and is increasing in the deviation of public expenditure, g (again as % of GDP) from a target, denoted by G. Time is divided in two periods:

Period 1 (runs from present to 2020)
Period 2 (runs from 2020 to infinity, new steady state)

The core is thus the usual quadratic social welfare loss function:

(1) $\text{Social loss} = [\alpha t_1^2 + (g_1 - G_1)^2] + (1+\delta)^{-1}[\alpha t_2^2 + (g_2 - G_2)^2]$

where the parameter α denotes the weight of taxes in social loss and δ is the inter-temporal discount factor.

The objective for policy makers is to minimize this social loss subject to the inter-temporal budget constraint:

(2) $t_2 = g_2 + (1+\rho)(g_1 - t_1)$

where ρ denotes the (real) interest rate on public debt. Minimization with respect to taxation over time implies:

(3) $2\alpha t_1 = (1+\rho)^{-1}[2\alpha(1+\delta)t_2]$,

or

(3)′ $t_1 = [(1+\delta)/(1+\rho)]\ t_2$

This yields the well known result that if the interest rate equals the discount rate (i.e. if $\delta=\rho$):

(4) $t_1 = t_2 = t$

Minimization with respect to government spending (g_1) implies:

$$(g_1 - G_1) = [(1+\rho)/(1+\delta)]\ (g_2 - G_2)$$

with the same assumption as above this obviously also implies that $(g_1 - G_1) = (g_2 - G_2)$, i.e. the difference between actual and desired spending should be the same during both periods. As tax rates are also constant at the optimum this implies that the same should be true to the deficits:

(5) $(g_1 - t) - (g_2 - t) = G_1 - G_2$

In other words: as it is optimal to keep tax rates constant it is also optimal to have in the first period a stronger fiscal policy if target expenditure is higher during the second period. Another way to see the same result would be to focus only on the first period deficit (or rather surplus):

(6) $(t - g_1) = (G_2 - G_1) / (2+\rho)$

An implication of the latter equation is that the first period should have a surplus, if future desired expenditure is higher than the present one. What are the magnitudes? Table 1 above showed that the old age dependency ratio will double for the EU-15 over the next two generations. If the income of the elderly is to be maintained constant in relation to the average income of the entire population this requires, ceteris paribus, a doubling of the expenditure on pensions. Since the expenditure on pensions is already above 10 % of GDP in most member states this would translate into an increase in expenditure of over 10 % of GDP (even without taking into account the higher health care costs).

Recent official estimates come to much lower number because they discount a large drop in replacement ratios and an increase in the effective retirement ages. But even under these optimistic assumptions a study of the EPC suggests that ageing will lead (ceteris paribus) to additional expenditure of 3-5 % of GDP, on average for eurozone member countries. As shown in the table below, according to EPC estimates the average for the largest euro area member countries is 3.7 % if one compares 2000 to 2050.

Table 2. Government Spending on Pensions

	2000	2030	2050
Public Pension expenditure as % of GDP	12.1	15.3	15.8

Source: EPC 2001.

But even if one accepts the much more optimistic official estimates of the fiscal burden from ageing the tax smoothing approach still implies that it would be optimal to run budget surpluses today. Based on equation (6) the required surplus today would be between 1.2 and 2 % of GDP if one uses an inter-general discount rate of, say 50 %, and an increase in age related fiscal pressure of 3-5 % of GDP,[2]

3. Implications of Low Growth

What is the link between fiscal policy and potential growth? Many academic observers (especially those from the US) have dismissed the 3% deficit of the Maastricht Treaty as arbitrary and useless. Gros and Thygesen (1992) already showed that the 3 % deficit limit fitted into an environment in which one wanted to keep the debt/GDP ratio at 60 % and

2. See Bini Smaghi (2004) for another approach to this issue.

nominal GDP growth could be expected to be around 5 % (2.5 % real growth plus 2.5 % inflation).

But this assumption concerning growth is longer justified. As shown above, growth of most member countries is declining under the combined impact of lower productivity growth and a shrinking working age population This has huge implications for the sustainability of fiscal policy. Table 3 below shows what combinations of growth and trend deficits would lead to what steady state debt level.

For a slow growth economy like Germany even a deficit of only 2% of GDP that persisted over the cycle would barely keep the debt to GDP ratio close to the 60% limit (see Table 3). Continuing deficits of 4% of GDP by all member countries would bring the EU debt ratio to 100% per cent of GDP. The contrast between Germany and the US is particularly striking. The latter could run indefinitely deficits about twice as high (4% of GDP) and still end up with a similar debt ratio (67% of GDP).

Table 3. Steady State Debt Levels (as % of GDP)

		Cyclically adjusted deficit in % of GDP			
		2%	3%	4%	5%
Trend growth of real GDP in % p.a.	Germany: 1.5%	57	86	114	143
	EU today (?): 2%	50	75	100	125
	Maastricht: 3%	40	**60**	80	100
	New members (?): 4%	33	50	67	83
	New members with B.S. effect	29	43	57	71

Source: Own calculations. The calculations assume an inflation rate of 2% so that nominal GDP growth is 2 percentage points higher than the real rates indicated in the first column, the only exception is the last row where it is assumed that the new members have a trend inflation rate that is one percent higher than that of the rest of the eurozone.

Another implication of lower potential growth is also straightforward: The observed standard deviation of growth rates in most euro area countries has been around 1 to 1.5%. If potential growth is really 1% and we assume, to make a concrete example, that the standard deviation remains also at 1%, one must expect that actual growth will be negative every 5 or six years.

More in general the slow down in potential growth requires a re-assessment of what is considered 'sluggish' growth. For example, a growth rate of 1.5% could certainly be considered 'sluggish' by politicians if they compare this figure to their own goal of 3% as agreed in Lisbon. However, in reality 1.5% might already be very close to (and for some countries above) potential growth, and would thus not qualify as 'sluggish'.

The justification for looking not only at one annual growth rate when determining whether there are 'exceptional circumstances' that justify an exemption from the 3 % deficit limit is that what matters is the accumulated output gap, which could be larger after a long period of positive growth which is below potential than after a short recession. The practical problem with this idea is that a reduction in potential growth is usually recognised only after growth has been low for some time. However, at the beginning of a period of low growth it is difficult to decide whether this is temporary or permanent. The temptation to regard it as temporary will be impossible to resist when this has the implication that higher deficits are allowed. Moreover, even on a purely technical basis, the experience of 2003 shows that output gap estimates are subject to large revisions as new data comes in. For example, when the very low growth rate for 2003 was put in the model that determines the German potential growth rate the estimate of the output gap had to be revised downwards substantially, with the consequence that the estimate of the cyclically adjusted deficit increased by almost 0.5 % of GDP.

Quantifying potential growth is an extremely difficult technical judgment which leaves much room for disagreement even among experts as one can see by looking at the differences in estimates of potential growth coming from such respected institutions as the OECD, the IMF and ECB. If estimates of potential growth rates acquire immediate political importance it will be extremely difficult to shield the staff of the Commission from political pressure or to impede the Council to just come up with higher estimates.

4. Concluding Remarks

The fiscal framework for EMU established by the Maastricht Treaty and later specified in more detail by the Stability and Growth Pact is routinely criticized as too tight. This contribution argues that tight limits on fiscal policy are today needed even more than when the Maastricht Treaty was signed. The basic reason for this result is that the ageing of Europe's population will put fiscal policy under enormous strain. Standard tax smoothing arguments imply that fiscal policy should react to a future anticipated increase in expenditure by running surpluses today. Hence the real issue for the EU (and in particular for the euro area) should not be whether or not the 3 % limit can be observed, but how member countries can be brought to achieve the fiscal surpluses that are needed in the face of ageing.

Unfortunately it seems that fiscal policy seems far from taking the ageing challenge into account. The larger euro area countries (France, Italy and Germany) have now been running deficits at close to, or above 3 % of GDP for several years. Moreover, after the difficulties to enforce the Excessive Deficit Procedure against France and Germany of November 2003, even the Commission, which should be the guardian of the Treaty seems to have lost sight of the purpose of the Maastricht Treaty.

Looking at the Communication of the Commission on the Stability Pact of September 3rd, 2004 the most important content seems to be one that is missing. The crucial argument that is not made by the Commission is that the deficit that still keeps debt/GDP ratio constant goes down with lower growth. Another 'dog that did not bark' is that, as argued here, lower potential growth makes it difficult to maintain that negative growth rates should qualify as an exemption.

The fiscal framework established for the euro is under stress, it is being ignored by politicians at the very time its economic rationale has actually become even stronger.

References

Bernoth, Kerstin, Jürgen von Hagen, Ludger Schuknecht (2004) "Sovereign Risk Premia in the European Government Bond Market",Discussion Paper, revised version of No. B26, 2003, ZEI, Bonn.

Bini Smaghi, Lorenzo (2004) "What Went Wrong with the Stability and Growth Pact?" in this volume.

Thygesen, Niels and Gros, Daniel, (1990) "Concrete Steps toward Monetary Union", in CEPS Papers No. 44, Centre for European Policy Studies, 1990, Brussels.

Thygesen, Niels and Gros, Daniel, (1992) *European Monetary Integration: From the European Monetary System to European Monetary Union,* Harlow: Longman, 1992.

Thygesen, Niels and Gros, Daniel, (1998) *European Monetary Integration: From EMS to EMU,* Addison Wesley Longman, London and New York, 2nd edition 1998.

Thygesen, Niels (with Daniel Gros, Juan Jimeno, Carlo Monticelli, Guido Tabellini) (2001) "Testing the Speed Limit for Europe", *Third Report of the CEPS Macroeconomic Policy Group,* Centre for European Policy Studies, Brussels 2001.

Thygesen, Niels (with Daniel Gros, Juan Jimeno, Thomas Mayer and Angel Ubide) (2003) "Adjusting to Leaner Times", *Fifth Annual Report of the CEPS Macroeconomic Policy Group,* Centre for European Policy Studies, Brussels, 2003.

Thygesen, Niels (1996) "Should Budgetary Policies Be Coordinated further in Economic and Monetary Union – and is that Feasible?", in Banca Nazionale del Lavoro Quarterly Review, Special Issue, 1996, pp. 5-31.

Thygesen, Niels (1999) "Fiscal Policies, the Stability Pact and the Policy Mix in EMU", in Hallett, Andrew Hughes, Michael M. Hutchison and Svend E. Hougaard Jensen (eds.), *Fiscal Aspects of Monetary Integration,* Cambridge University Press. 1999, pp. 15-37.

CHAPTER 10

How Should We Cope With the Crisis of the EMU Fiscal Framework?

*Edmond Alphandéry**

This paper does not lengthen the impressive string of proposals for reforming the Stability and Growth Pact. Building on the reasons for its failure, it concludes that when we focus blame on the architecture of the excessive deficit procedure, we overlook the primary cause of the current crisis. Fiscal profligacy is the result of failure on the part of Member States to take full ownership of rules for fiscal discipline. Statistics show that Member States that have adopted rigourous, expenditure-driven consolidations have obtained better results in terms of economic growth. Using a composite index representative of the fiscal stance of each EU Member, this paper shows a correlation between efforts made to improve fiscal position and rates of growth. The majority of EU Member States need to reduce the relative weight of their public expenditures for their own sake. Therefore, fiscal discipline in the European Union should be driven first and foremost by domestic considerations. Accordingly, European institutions should focus instead on creating a legal environment that will encourage Member States to adopt stringent, rules-based domestic fiscal

* My thanks to Olivier Garnier, Philippe Trainar, Henri Lepage and Pierre Grand-Dewyse for their suggestions. The usual disclaimer applies.

frameworks, and on promoting incentives that will induce them to stick to their own fiscal objectives.

1. The Early Failure of the Excessive Deficit Procedure

During Stage Two of EMU and the very first years of the euro, the prevailing expectation was that Member States would find it easy in the future to comply with SGP rules. A striking illustration of this optimism appears in a book published in 2002 (Barrel and Dury, 2002). Investigating on the ability of Member States to live up to SGP criteria through an evaluation of *"monetary and fiscal policy by deterministic simulations"*, the two authors concluded that (providing countries stayed within the budgetary targets laid down in their stability programmes) *"there is little evidence that the SGP will be breached under any policy rule"* (sic) ! Indeed, during the first years following the Amsterdam Treaty, fiscal deficit figures suggested that the Pact's principles were by and large being respected.

The scenery has changed dramatically in the last two years, however. Soon after the Euro Group decided to hold the excessive deficit procedure for Germany and France *"in abeyance for the time being,"* Portugal, the Netherlands, Greece and Italy joined *"the violators from November 2003,"* (as Niels Thygesen calls them, see Thygesen (2004a)). *"Half or close thereto of the participants in the Euro area, including the three largest economies, will be found to have transgressed the fiscal rule to which they have commited themselves."*(Thygesen, op. cit.).

At first glance, this apparent about-face is due to the economic downturn that hit Europe in early 2001. But a careful analysis of fiscal policies since the adoption of the SGP in 1997 tells a different story. During the period 1998-2002, the marked decline (of some 1.5% of GDP) in interest rate expenditures *"more than compensated for a clear deterioration in the primary budget surplus by around 1% of GDP."* (Briotti, 2004). The *"cyclically adjusted primary balance,"* which is a much better indicator of fiscal stance, yields a different picture of the consolidation efforts undertaken before and after adoption of the SGP.[1]

Table 1. Cyclically Adjusted Budget Balances in the EU

	Cyclically adjusted primary balance (Annual average change in GDP ratio)	
	1996-1997	1998-2002
Belgium	0.4	0.0
Denmark	0.8	0.0
Germany	0.7	– 0.3
Greece	1.4	– 0.3
Spain	1.3	0.1
France	1.3	– 0.3
Ireland	0.4	– 0.9
Italy	1.3	– 0.6
Luxembourg	–	–
Netherlands	0.8	– 0.3
Austria	1.6	0.1
Portugal	– 0.4	0.0
Finland	0.0	1.0
Sweden	2.9	– 0.3
United Kingdom	1.6	0.0
Euro 12	1.0	– 0.3
Euro 15	1.1	– 0.2

Source: Maria Gabriella Briotti (2004); a plus sign means fiscal stance has improved, a minus sign signals deterioration. The sign (-) indicates that data are not available.

During Stage Two of EMU, the fear of not being admitted to the Euro area acted as a "Maastricht effect" in favor of fiscal consolidation. But during

1. This paper sheds light on another interesting aspect of fiscal policies : tax increases played a major role in many « pre-euro » budget adjustments ; but expenditures-based adjustments performed much better than revenue-based adjustments : they proved to be less procyclical and more resilient to « consolidation fatigue » and to business downturns. The study shows that over the period 1992-2002, countries that favoured expenditures cuts for their budget consolidation (Spain, Ireland, the Netherlands, Finland and outside the Euro zone, Sweden and the United Kingdom) « *implemented a larger budget adjustment than countries which adopted a tax-based strategy (tax increases)* » (i.e. Belgium, Germany, Greece, France, Italy, Austria, Portugal and outside the Euro zone, Denmark).

the 1998-2002 period, fiscal stance in EU countries as shown in Table 1 was broadly neutral or expansionary. Therefore, we can conclude that procedures put forward by the SGP to *"maintain sustained and lasting budget discipline"*[2] have proven ineffective since their inception.

2. Why did the Excessive Deficit Procedure Fail?

Faulty implementation of the stability programmes has been largely overlooked as an explanation for this counter-performance. Olivier Garnier, a French economist who surveyed the 1998 French stability programme for the period 1999-2002 (later extended to 2003), recalls that France's public deficit commitment for year 2003 was in the GDP range of (0.3%, 0.5%), a forecast that was in compliance with the *"close to balance or surplus"* SGP requirement at the time (Garnier, 2004). The actual deficit reached 4.1% in 2003. According to Garnier's calculations, no less than 55 billion euros are missing! The main reason for this huge shortfall is not the slowdown in economic activity, however. Initial government projections over the period were based on two scenarii, with expected annual growth of either 2.5% or 3.0%. In fact, the GDP gap accounts for only 1 percentage point of the (3.6%, 3.8%) budget overruns with respect to the French commitment for 2003. Looking at national account data, Garnier notes that nearly three-fourths of the discrepancy is due to a public expenditure spree. In the initial stability programme, annual growth in public expenditure was estimated at 1% in real terms, versus an actual increase of 2.4%. Had France complied with its 1% objective, the 2003 public deficit would have been in the range of (1.5%, 2%) of GDP, well under the threshold triggering the excessive deficit procedure.

The first French stability programme of December 1998[3] contained several basic flaws which shed light on the reasons for its failure : the programme was not considered to be a binding obligation by French authori-

2. Juergen Stark,(2002, p. 83): « *It is not clear that this stability framework [the Maastricht Treaty] could withstand external pressures and that the participants in monetary union would be capable of fulfilling their Treaty obligations at all times* », Genesis of a Pact, in Brunila, Buti and Franco.
3. Une stratégie pour la croissance et pour l'emploi, décembre 1998.

ties[4]; the fiscal stance remained an intermediary objective, the ultimate goal of economic policy being *"high growth and lower unemployment"*[5]; changes in public revenue or expenditure were thought to be no obstacle to economic growth.[6] Moreover, many of its technical aspects were far from satisfactory. Growth rate assumptions were exaggerated from the outset, and were not subject to realistic revision after the economic downturn. Furthermore, the programmes contained very few (if any) indications of the reforms that were in fact indispensable for meeting the announced medium-term targets (the health sector reform is a striking example).

Unfortunately, the European Commission did not highlight any of these dangers,which have existed for as long as the Pact itself. On the contrary, the record shows that, during its first four years of surveillance (1999-2002), the Commission gave full approval of all of France's successive programmes to the European Council, even though it was increasingly uneasy with them.[7] In January 2003, the Commission's stance shifted abruptly, and an *"early warning"* was addressed to France. Since these programmes seem to have been intended to appease domestic public opinion, they were not easily suited to serious scrutiny by professional economists.[8] It is clear that the European Commission has never been ready to undertake a thorough and fair examination.

France does not seem to be an exception. In a recent study, Fàtas et al. (2004) noted that *"the SPG has achieved little, if any, strengthening of fiscal discipline in EMU ..Most Governments chose to let spending grow with revenues or trend output over the period [1999-2002]."*

4. *«Il n'implique pas le choix d'un pilotage automatique indépendant de la force des vents ou de l'apparition de récifs inconnus »*, op. cit.
5. *«L'objectif doit être d'atteindre une croissance forte entre 2000 et 2002, si possible 3% par an »*, op.cit.
6. *«Poursuivre la réduction des prélèvements obligatoires pour favoriser l'emploi » ; see also « le rythme de réduction du besoin de financement des administrations dépendra du dynamisme de l'activité afin de ne pas peser sur la croissance de l'économie »*, op. cit.
7. Recommendations of the European Commission, March 2000, January 2001, 2002, 2003 and 2004.
8. *«Cette amélioration du solde structurel traduit la grande maîtrise des dépenses sur l'ensemble de la période de programmation »*, annexe du programme pluriannuel des finances publiques, 2003-2004, ler semestre 2000, p. 14, op.cit.

Had the doctrinal principles underlying the Pact been less controversial, none of these infringements would have been possible. The fiscal discipline imposed by the Maastricht Treaty was generally welcome, and raised no serious criticism at the outset, because *"the likelihood of incurring unfavourable market reactions to expanding the public deficit, pushing up interest rates through perceptions of higher currency and/or credit risk and, maybe, facing an attack on currency which was a feature of the European Monetary System (EMS), had earlier been a deterrent to individually fiscal behaviour and now needed some form of replacement by peer pressure based on a rule" (quoted from Thygesen (2004b)).* In their eagerness to specify the treaty rules with the aim of permanently enhancing fiscal discipline in Stage Three of EMU, the authors of the SGP reopened the Pandora's box of the theoretical debate about the impact of fiscal profligacy on the functioning of a monetary union. And as the arguments of fiscal discipline advocates were not beyond dispute, it is likely that this battle worked in favour of those who were reluctant to abide by the rules of the Pact.

Today, experts remain divided. Economists on one side emphasize that the Pact restricts fiscal policy flexibility, a factor that carries some weight in a monetary union whose Member States can no longer make use of the monetary instrument. On the other side , proponents of strict common rules claim that the brunt of a lax budgetary stance on the part of one Member State may have to be borne by the other Members. (De Grauwe, 2003, Ch. 9, and Beetsma, 2002)

Nonetheless, most experts (including opponents to the Pact) acknowledge that *"budget deficits and debt levels should be reduced in many [Member] countries,"* and that *"fiscal orthodoxy is badly needed to increase the flexibility of a monetary union." (de Grauwe, op.cit.)* These common sense arguments can hardly compete with the simple *"Keynesian approach,"* whose plea for public expenditure and deficit spending during economic downturns effortlessly reconciles economics with short-term political interests.

The drawbacks of the Pact, which have been largely described in the literature, seem to argue in favour of revision (Alphandéry, 2002). However, in line with the stance that Niels Thygesen (2004b) recently adopted before the European Parliament, and also with the position of the ECB and the Euro system, I too believe that the existing general framework should remain untouched. In my opinion, any overhaul would lead to a deadlock:

- Sweetening its provisions is tantamount to admitting that principles underlying criticisms of the Pact were well not founded. In this case, the thin layer of credibility that the common fiscal discipline framework still retains – thanks to the decision of the European Court of Justice – would probably dissolve. Furthermore, since the *"penalty procedure"* has already proven to be totally ineffective, one may question the use of improving rules that are not unforceable.
- On the contrary, beefing up the current procedure would be fruitless as well, since there is no political majority at the European Council to support this proposition.

In its current proposal for reforms, the European Commission looks rather embarrassed. If improvements which it plans to introduce in the implementation procedure (with more emphasis laid on the 60% public deficit criterion or on the preventing arm of SGP during good times ..) do not raise serious contest, its position becomes less comfortable when it comes to the reform of the Pact itself. The Commission feels compelled to stress that it does not intend to modify the Treaties. But some of the suggested changes (about the notion of *"exceptional circumstances"* or the deadline granted to countries for correction when necessary may have, if adopted, a far reaching impact on the appreciation in the future of the binding dimension of the rules by Member States.

In order to clarify where efforts should presently be concentrated, we propose in Table 2 a simple grid for evaluating the various dimensions of the excessive deficit procedure (weak, medium, strong). Criteria currently used for multilateral surveillance are the simplest one can find. As such, they are more transparent than many substitutes. And with sufficient political will, they are relatively easy to monitor by Member States (Buti et al.). These major advantages outweigh the numerous drawbacks reported in the literature.[9] Furthermore, being committed to these rules will undoubtedly help Governments to avoid entering *"unsustainable territo-*

9. For instance the « *cyclically adjusted budget deficit* » raises serious difficulties which appeared in 2003 in the surveillance procedure of German fiscal orientations by the European Commission ; See : *The Six Lives of the Stability Pact* CEPS, Daniel Gros et alii (2003) ; also Thygesen (2004a).

ries" through the accumulation of public debt.[10] Whether they leave enough room for stabilization purposes remains an open question, however, even though recent experience shows that Member States were in a position to let fiscal automatic stabilizers work without restraint.

Admittedly, problems do arise during the implementation process. The quality standards required, not only for the stability programmes presented to the Commission but also for multilateral surveillance, clearly need to be enhanced. Furthermore, introducing targets in terms of a *"yearly cyclically adjusted budget surplus"* in order to prevent successive lax bias in upturns and restritive bias during downturns, complemented with public expenditures ceilings, would undoubtedly help cure the main drawbacks of the current procedure. But doing so does not require any overhauling of the rules enshrined in the Maastricht and Amsterdam Treaties.

Table 2. Dimensions of the Excessive Deficit Procedure

		Strong	Medium	Weak
Criteria	– Simple	x		
	– Transparent	x		
	– Easy to monitor	x		
Rules	– Help government to avoid entering unsustainable territories	x		
	– Leave room for stabilization		x	
Implementation	– Examination by the Commission			x
	– Enforcement			x
	– Ownership of fiscal discipline by each and every Member State			x

The most serious question remains unanswered: that of ownership by each and every Member State of rules of fiscal discipline. This is the most crucial prerequisite to the success of any common fiscal rule.

10. When the rate of growth of public debt due to budget deficit is higher than the rate of growth of the economy. According to Niels Thygesen (2004a), « *long term projections of public finances over the next 3-4 decades suggest a clear absence of sustainability in several countries, barring revisions of policy* ».

3. Promoting Domestic Fiscal Discipline

Experts readily agree on the various explanations for the current fiscal profligacy of many Member States (consolidation *"fatigue"* after entry into Stage Three of EMU; implementation of so-called *"countercyclical"* fiscal policies ; the *"pro-deficit bias"* of the Eurozone, etc.). Similarly, few would deny that these countries are, in the longer run, acting counter to their own interests. The list of serious motives for adopting strong and lasting measures for reforming their public sectors is long: the inevitable rise of interest rates in the future which will increase their debt service (with countries running up excessive debt levels being threatened with entry into *"unsustainable territories"*); ever-growing public expenditures related to demographic trends in all the Member States in the years ahead ; and, for many of them, global levels of public spending and therefore taxes that hinder economic growth.

The last argument, which remains a matter of lively debate, deserves closer scrutiny. In a recent study published by the CEPR, Fatàs et Al (2004) analyze the impact of the *"quality"* of public finances on growth, considered along two dimensions: the overall tax burden and the structure of public spending. According to growth theory, authors write, countries with a lower share of taxation on income should incur lower distortionary effects on overall wage costs and on desincentives to work. Concerning the structure of spending, lower current public expenditures (such as social transfers) relative to public investment (RandD, infrastructure, etc.), by enhancing productivity, should have a beneficial impact on the growth trend.

Plotting the average rate growth of each EU country (1992-2002) against their average tax burden, Fatàs et al. (2004) show a *"clear negative association between the tax burden and the trend growth rate."* More recently, the European Commission confirmed the correlation found in Fatàs : *"countries with small public sectors have recovered high growth rates in recent years."*[11]

Also in both papers: *"during expenditure-driven consolidations, GDP growth increased by 0.6% relative to the E.U. average ..The growth rate remains persistently higher than the EU average after expenditure-driven consolidation."*

11. Public finances in EMU, European Commission, 2004, p. 181.

(Fatas et al., op.cit.) This positive effect is not visible in tax-driven consolidations.

In the interest of delving further into this relationship, we build in Table 3 a composite index of the fiscal policy of each EU Member State and observe how it relates to its rate of growth. The index is made up of two components : the relative level of public expenditures (measured for each country as the difference with respect to the average level for the 15 EU Members in 2002, column 1), and a composite index of past fiscal adjustments, comprised of the changes over the period 1995-2002 in cyclically adjusted primary balance representative of their fiscal stance on the one hand (column 2), and in *"cyclically adjusted public expenditures,"* representative of the "the quality" of this fiscal adjustment on the other hand (column 3). Adding the three figures (in column 4) yields an index of the global fiscal stance of each Member State, in which the current public expenditure level weighs one-third and efforts (size and "quality") they have undertaken to improve their overall fiscal position accounts for the remaining two-thirds.

If we plot this index (column 4) against each country's average growth rate over the last three years (column 5), graph 1 shows a correlation between the "quality" of fiscal policies and the outcome in terms of growth. It appears that countries with insufficient fiscal policies (Belgium, France, Germany, Italy or Portugal) have managed low average growth rates. On the contrary, Member States that have followed more stringent policies (Finland, Ireland, Spain or the United Kingdom,) have benefited from higher growth (Greece being an exception).

Table 3. Fiscal Policy and Growth in the EU

	1	2	3	4	5
Country	Government expenditures/GDP in 2002 : average E15-Member	Change in cyclically adjusted primary balance related to GDP (1995-2002)	Change in cyclically adjusted primary expenditure ratio to GDP (1995-2002)	**Global fiscal stance**	**Annual average growth rate (2001, 2002, 2003)**
Belgium	– 2,6	+ 0,8	– 0,5	– 2,3	+ 0,8
Denmark	– 7,8	+ 1,6	+ 3,3	– 2,9	+ 1,0
Germany	– 1,2	– 0,1	+ 0,5	– 0,8	+ 0,3
Greece	+ 1,1	+ 1,5	– 2,5	+ 0,1	+ 4,2
Spain	+ 7,8	+ 3,1	+ 2,9	+ 13,8	+ 2,4
France	– 6,5	+ 1,1	+ 0,5	– 4,9	+ 1,2
Ireland	+ 13,5	+ 3,4	+ 3,2	+ 20,1	+ 4,8
Italy	– 0,1	– 0,2	+ 0,1	– 0,2	+ 0,8
Luxembourg	+ 1,9	–	–	–	+ 1,7
Netherlands	+ 0,2	+ 0,1	+ 4,4	+ 4,7	+ 0,2
Austria	– 4,6	+ 3,6	+ 4,5	+ 3,5	+ 1,0
Portugal	+ 1,2	– 1,0	– 4,4	– 4,2	+ 0,3
Finland	– 1,8	+ 5,1	+ 7,9	+ 11,2	+ 1,8
Sweden	– 10,8	+ 4,3	+ 5,6	– 0,9	+ 1,6
UK	+ 6,7	+ 3,2	+ 2,4	+ 12,3	+ 2,0
Euro 15	0,0	+ 1,2	+ 1,9	+ 3,1	–

Note: (+) signals a positive fiscal effect; (–) a negative effect.

Sources: Briotti (2004) and European Central Bank.

Graph 1. Global Fiscal Stance and Growth Performance

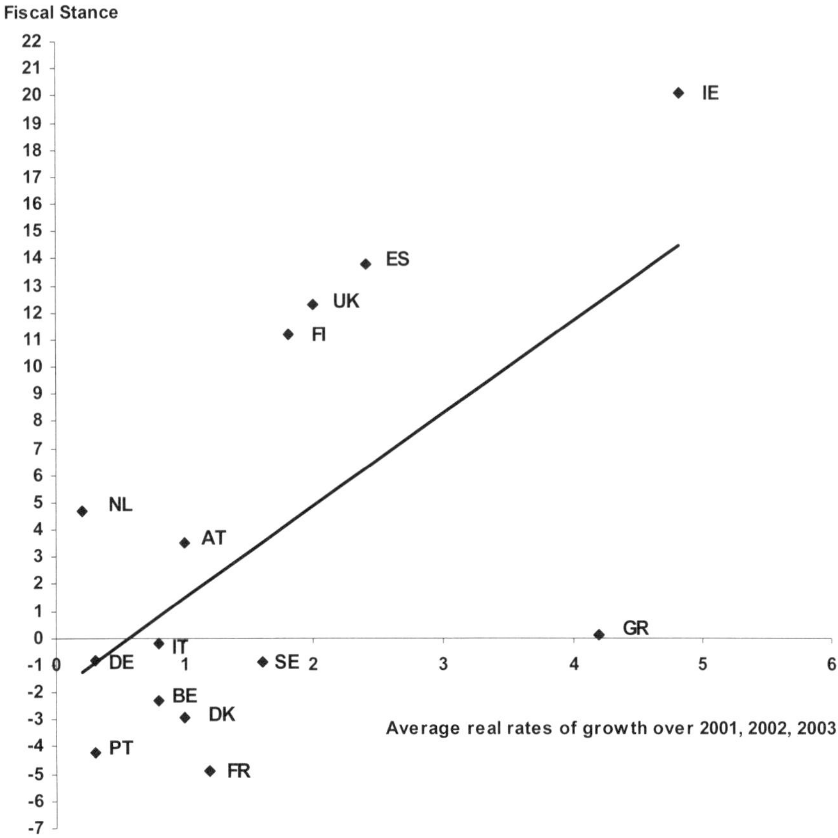

This is not surprising if we accept the following line of reasoning : a country like France, which has a relatively high level of public expenditure and has made little progress in its fiscal policy, had over the last years to bear these two combined impediments to growth. A country with higher public spending than average, that has nevertheless embarked on a rigorous fiscal policy, such as Finland, has been posting higher growth. And the correlation holds true in the opposite sense as well: a Member State like Ireland, whose efforts in terms of fiscal restraint have been modest, nevertheless has a good economic record due in part to its relatively low ratio of public spending. And a country like Austria, which has significantly improved its fiscal position, has been prevented from reaping all benefit from it because of the relatively heavy weight of its public sector.

Although many other variables obviously have an impact on comparative growth rates (the size and openess of each country, the relative impact of interest rates on the economy ...), that a majority of Member States must make clear and long-lasting improvements in their public finances hardly needs to be argued, not only for the smooth working and sustainability of the Eurozone, but first and foremost for their own sake. And as many studies have shown, many of them must get a better grip on their public expenditures if they wish to reach this aim.

The focus of reform should therefore shift from SGP rules to greater involvement on the part of each and every Member State in its own fiscal standing. The European Commission rightly emphasized the decline of ownership on the part of Member States of the common constraints of fiscal discipline.[12] The question we need to address in this regard is two-fold: under what conditions would political ownership by Member States facilitate improvements in their fiscal stance ? And, at the European level, what kind of incentives might induce Member States to pursue this objective with diligence ?

In its last report on public finances in the EMU, the European Commission sheds some light on the first point.[13] Surveying the performance budgeting of Member States, it observes that practices are *"widely diverging,"* domestic sanctions generally absent and that there is *"scope for learning from international experience."*

As the Commission rightly points out, one of the major preconditions for "quality of public finances", resides in the efficiency of national budgetary institutions. As expenditure-based adjustments have a more lasting and effective impact on fiscal consolidation than tax increases, any efficient reform of budgetary institutions should be centered on improving control over public expenditure.

During the last decade, various countries around the world have successfully experienced self-imposed fiscal rules (Australia, Canada, Fin-

12. Strengthening the coordination of budgetary policies, European Commission, 11 November, 2002.
13. Public Finances in EMU, 2004.

land, New Zealand, Sweden, and the United Kingdom, among others, see Dabán et al., 2003). Most of them focused their fiscal consolidation around expenditure restraint, and reaped positive results, notably in terms of their growth rate. It is worth noting the basic common improvements these legal budgetary rules and procedures have promoted:[14]

- **Greater transparency:** In Australia, for instance, thanks to the *Charter for Budget Honesty Act* adopted in 1996, many publications facilitate public scrutiny : *budget and economic fiscal outlook, mid-year economic and fiscal outlook, final budget outcome, pre-election economic and fiscal report, etc.*
- **Increased accountability:** In New Zealand, the *Fiscal Responsibility Act* seeks to strengthen reporting requirements.
- **Better control over public expenditures:** For example, the Canadian *Fiscal Spending Control Act* sets nominal spending ceilings that are legally binding.
- **Improved budgeting within a multi-year program framework:** In Finland, ceilings are imposed on total government spending within a four-year time horizon.
- **More cautious forecasting:** In the Netherlands, since 1994 the four-year ceilings on public expenditures are based on lower than expected GDP growth assumptions.
- **More flexibility:** In Sweden, the *fiscal rules* introduced in 1996 provide sufficient margins to finance discretionary expenditure increases.
- **More secure fiscal discipline:** The *Code for Fiscal Stability* adopted in 1997 in the UK is intended to prevent any relaxation that may occur with change of a political majority. France in this respect is a textbook case since over the last twenty five years it experienced a reversing of its ruling majority after each legislative election. It has to be protected against misleading political interpretation that may be drawn from abiding by the current SGP rules (in good times as recently happened, a Government can follow a lax fiscal stance while still remaining under the 3% threshold and get the political benefit of it, whereas its successor should pay a high price for the necessary consolidation).

14. This description draws heavily on the International Monetary Fund: "Euro Area Policies: Selected Issues", August 2004.

The main features of fiscal governance that each and every Member State should adopt are therefore straightforward. The self-imposed rules implemented by all of the countries surveyed have proven to lead in the common direction that Europe needs.

The IMF (2004) timely recalls that *"institutional* reform was a theme of the Maastricht Treaty which – in its excessive deficit procedure protocol – calls for Member States to *"ensure that national procedures in the budgetary area enable them to meet their obligations in this area deriving from the Treaty"*, and it suggests that *"there could be a section in stability programmes on ongoing institutional reforms"*.

As for the second part of the interrogation, the answer is much less obvious. In fact, fiscal stance (as measured by the cyclically adjusted primary expenditures) clearly deteriorated from 2000 to 2003 in nearly all the EU Member States, including those that adopted internal rules-based control of their public expenditures (Finland, Sweden, the UK, the Netherlands).[15]

Adoption of such rules is therefore a necessary but not sufficient precondition. It needs to be backed by strong political will and a culture of fiscal discipline. At the European level, we not only must find the road towards widespread adoption of domestic rules-based expenditure control and internal enhancement of budgetary institutions through the passage of laws or constitutional amendments ; we must also find the incentives that will foster long-lasting good domestic fiscal governance.

Instead of trying to enhance the credibility of SGP (an attempt which will probably fail because of the inoperability of the penalty procedure), the European Commission would be better off concentrating on the ways and means for European institutions to provide a general European framework that would help each and every Member State adopt domestic rules of fiscal discipline and, within the current multilateral surveillance apparatus, to promote the procedures required to verify that each respects the budgetary rules it has imposed on itself, as well as the objectives it has freely chosen to attain in conformity with its Treaty commitments.

15. With the exception of Austria and Luxembourg ; see European Commission, Public Finances in EMU, 2004, p 193.

References

Alphandéry, Edmond: *Need We amend the Stability and Growth Pact ?* paper presented at the « Euro 50 Group » conference, Paris, November 26-27, 2002, unpublished. This text is available on « Euro 50 Group » internet site: http://www.Euro50.org (go to « past roundtables »).

Barrel, Ray and Karen Dury (2002), *Will the SPG Ever Be Breached?* in Anna Brunila, Marco Buti, Daniele Franco eds, The Stability and Growth Pact, Palgrave, 2002, Chapter 10, pp 235-255.

Beetsma, Roel (2002), *Does EMU Need a Stability Pact ?* in A. Brunila, M. Buti and D. Franco, (2002), pp 23-52.

Briotti, Maria Gabriella, Fiscal Adjustment Between 1991 and 2002 : Stylised Facts and Policy Implications, ECB Occasional Paper Series, N° 9, February 2004.

Brunila, Anna, Marco Buti and Daniele Franco, eds. (2002), *The Stability and Growth Pact,* Palgrave, 2002.

Buti, Marco, Sylvester Eijffinger and Daniele Franco (2002) *«Revisiting the Stability and Growth Pact : Grand Design or Internal Adjustment?»,* CEPR Discussion Paper.

Dabàn, Teresa, Enrica Detragiache, Gabriel di Bella, Gian Maria Milesi-Ferretti, and Steven Symansky : "Rules-Based Fiscal Policy in France", Germany, Italy and Spain, IMF, 2003.

De Grauwe, Paul (2003), *Economics of Monetary Union,* Oxford University Press.

De Larosiére, Jacques (2004), "Reflexions à propos du Pacte de Stabilité et de Croissance, mimeo, January 2004.

Fatàs, Antonio, Jürgen von Hagen, Andrew Hughes Hallett, Rolf R. Strauch and Anne Sibert, Stability and Growth in Europe: "Towards a Better Pact", CEPR, MEI 13.

Garnier, Olivier *Le Pacte de Stabilité : un bouc émissaire bien commode,* Les Echos, 7 mai 2004.

Gros, Daniel et alii (2003), *The Six Lives of the Stability,* Pact Centre for European Policy Studies, December 2003.

Stark, Juergen (2002), "Genesis of A Pact", in Brunila, Buti and Franco (2002).

Thygesen, Niels (2004a), *Reform of the Stability and Growth Pact, A Note for the Economic and Monetary Affairs Committee of the European Parliament,* 2nd quarter 2004.

Thygesen, Niels (2004b), "The Stability and Growth Pact : Any Need For Revision?", A Note for the Economic and Monetary Affairs Committee of the European Parliament, 4th quarter 2002.

CHAPTER 11

EMU and Tax Policy

Mario Monti

1. The Internal Market and Taxation

The internal market is the cornerstone of the European Union: the main objective of the Treaty of Rome is to provide for the creation of a "common market" based on the free movement of goods, people, services and capital. The Single European Act of 1986, following the 1985 White Paper on the completion of the internal market, enshrined formally the date of 31 December 1992 to be the date of completion of the internal market project. Since that date, the Union is characterised by one market, where all internal borders, including all tax frontiers between Member States, are abolished.

In the area of taxation, several arrangements were introduced to preserve Member States' tax sovereignty, while eliminating specific cross border taxation. These include a transitional methods for intra-Community VAT sales of goods[1], the directive on direct taxation of cross border dividend distributions between subsidiaries and parents of different Member States[2], the directive on direct taxation of certain cross-border mergers, divisions and exchange of shares between companies of differ-

1. 91/680/EEC: Council Directive of 16 December 1991 supplementing the common system of value added tax and amending Directive 77/388/EEC with a view to the abolition of fiscal frontiers, OJ L 272of 17/09/1992.
2. Council Directive 90/435/EEC of 23 July 1990 on the common system of taxation applicable to parent companies and their subsidiaries in different Member States, OJ L 225 of 20.08.1990.

ent Member States[3], the directive on direct taxation of cross border royalties and interest payments between related companies[4], and the directive on direct taxation of cross border savings[5], only to mention some.
The Single Act defines the internal market as "an area without internal frontiers in which the free movement of goods, persons, services and capital is ensured in accordance with the provisions of this Treaty".

In 2002, the introduction of the euro further completed the economic and legal framework needed to affirm and strengthen the principles of free movement and undistorted competition in the common market, with a view to establishing a true single domestic European market. It created the necessary economic convergence to foster closer ties between Member States, in particular between the Member States acceding to the Euro zone, but also those not yet taking part in the third phase of the economic and monetary union, including the countries participating to the European Economic Agreement, the acceding countries to the European Union and the candidate countries.

The completion of the single market and the liberalisation of capital movements preceding the introduction of the common currency made clear the need to examine the particular effects of tax competition between Member States and the compatibility of certain national tax measures with the common market. In fact, the establishment of an economic and monetary union and the entering of several Member States into its third phase of development proved that it was more essential than ever to have some form of control of tax competition.

At the same time, the issue of the effects of unbridled tax competition on the process of consolidation of national budgets was being considered with some preoccupation. It was felt that the revenue losses deriving to the Member States because of international tax competition, and the fear

3. Council Directive 90/434/EEC of 23 July 1990 on the common system of taxation applicable to mergers, divisions, transfers of assets and exchanges of shares concerning companies of different Member States, OJ L 225 of 20.8.1990.
4. Council Directive 2003/49/EC of 3 June 2003 on a common system of taxation applicable to interest and royalty payments made between associated companies of different Member States, OJ.
5. Council Directive 2003/48/EC of 3 June 2003 on taxation of savings income in the form of interest payments, OJ L 157, 26.6.2003.

of distortions to competition between undertakings due to the use of certain tax arrangements in a sense contrary to the common interest, would create the need to develop a comprehensive policy to tackle harmful tax competition with every possible means, including the strict application of state aid rules to direct business taxation measures.

More recently, the European Council of Lisbon of March 2000, by setting the objective for the Union to become *"the most competitive and dynamic knowledge-based economy in the world by 2010"*, stressed the importance of an internal market without any obstacles to competition, including those deriving from tax impediments and distortions to the free flow of investments across the Member States' jurisdictions. Against this background, it appeared evident that while tax obstacles were responsible for additional complexities in intra-Community business transactions, including multiple effective taxation of cross border business activities, tax competition was responsible of inappropriate relocations of business activities across the EU and could artificially affect the competitive standing of European businesses in a way which was contrary to the common interest.

The rationale for countering international or cross-border harmful tax competition has been explored both by practitioners and academics (see Ceriani and Giannini, 2003). Against the opinion of those invoking harmonization of tax rules across the EU as the only solution to eliminate fiscal distortions, it was eventually recognized that each Member State should preserve full sovereignty in determining the appropriate size and composition of its budget (on both the expenditure and revenue sides), with the sole limitation of the EU Treaty provisions, and that taxes constitute a key element in determining the attractiveness of a jurisdiction *vis-à-vis* investment decisions. It is interesting in this regard to compare the differences in corporate tax rates in the EU, Japan and the USA.

Table 1. Levels of Corporate Tax Rate in the European Union, Japan and the United States, 2004

Country	Corporate Tax Rate
Austria	34%
Belgium	33%
Cyprus	10%
Czech Republic	28%
Denmark	30%
Estonia	0%
Finland	29%
France	33,33%
Germany	25%
Greece	35%
Hungary	16%
Ireland	12,50%
Italy	33%
Latvia	15%
Lithuania	15%
Luxembourg	22%
Malta	35%
Netherlands	34,50%
Poland	19%
Portugal	25%
Slovakia	19%
Slovenia	25%
Spain	35%
Sweden	28%
United Kingdom	30%
United States	35%
Japan	30%

"Fair" competition among jurisdictions based on budget and other public policies is not only legitimate, but also desirable. Low taxation, per se, may prove to enhance economic growth and, needless to say, is a perfectly legitimate choice of Governments. Tax competition becomes "unfair" when special preferential regimes are introduced, with the main objective of attracting mobile activities from abroad. In other words, it is unfair when tax policies deliberately attempt to "poach" the tax base of other jurisdictions. The use of those special regimes may permit some taxpayers to act as free riders, who benefit from public spending in their home country and avoid contributing to its financing.

Thus, a coordinated approach to limit or eliminate the negative effects of harmful tax competition is critical to preserve tax sovereignty, and limitations of Member States' discretion in shaping their tax systems to attract the location of foreign investments are also necessary to prevent European undertakings from taking too much advantage of national treasuries' expenditures programs.

It should be stressed that the recently adopted Constitution for Europe does not provide for any new tools to tackle this issue. Article 94 EC remained unchanged in substance (new Article III-65 bis). Nevertheless, there exists a possibility of enhanced cooperation also in the field of direct taxation. New Article III-328 allows the Member States participating in such cooperation to adopt decisions by qualified majority in fields where normally unanimity is required. Moreover, the Constitution may be amended, inter alia in the taxation field, by a simplified procedure. The Council has also at its disposal the possibility of adopting a unanimous decision which would allow taking further actionsby qualified majority in certain areas such as taxation where unanimity in the Council is required. With respect to Treaty rules preventing Member States interventions in the economy affecting or risking to affect intra-Community competition and trade, the Spaak preparatory Report to the Treaty of Rome[6] indicated that State aid control was justified to prevent Member States from providing derogatory or special treatments to certain undertakings by derogation from the general law of a Member State, thus reducing the production costs of such undertakings with respect to the production costs normally borne by other companies of the same Member State. These costs reductions constituted a distortion because they are not balanced internally within the system, as they constitute an artificial derogation from the normal costs borne in the Member State system;nor they are balanced

6. Cf. *Rapport des chefs de délégation aux ministres des affaires étrangères / Comité intergouvernemental créé par la Conférence de Messine* (Commonly referred to as the Spaak Report), prepared by the Intergovernmental Committee on European Integration, 1956, p. 57-63.

externally, due to international trade adjustments rules, the latter ones applying to the existing equilibrium between Member States systems, taken as a whole, but not to the differences generated by inconsistent internal rules of a Member State.

Notwithstanding this clear rationale, distinguishing between tax provisions that are hidden forms of State aid and those that are just the expression of acceptable differentiations in national tax laws has proven very difficult, while being of paramount importance in situations where Member States compete with their tax systems to attract investments, through specific tax measures.

2. Tax Competition

Tax competition is an inter-jurisdictional phenomenon. Itmay be defined as the attempt by sovereign tax jurisdictions to attract investments or to prevent them from expatriating from such jurisdictions by offering an attractive tax environment to investors. The geographic scope of fiscal attraction may operate either internationally between different national territories, or between sub-national jurisdictions of the same national territory, or a combination of the two.

Although by no means a new phenomenon, tax competition attracted relatively little attention until the mid-1990s. Then, in May 1996, the Member Countries entrusted OECD to study the problem and to define how to avoid harmful tax competition on investment and financing decisions and its consequences for national tax bases.[7] The OECD's Committee on Fiscal Affairs launched a review on the harmful nature of certain tax havens or preferential tax regimes aimed at attracting mobile activi-

7. That request was endorsed by the G-7 countries at the Lyon Summit in June 1996, where the heads of government affirmed that tax schemes aimed at attracting financial and other geographically mobile activities can create harmful tax competition between states, carrying risks of distorting trade and investment, and could lead to the erosion of national tax bases. They urged the OECD to vigorously pursue its work in this field, with a view to establishing a multilateral approach under which countries could operate individually and collectively to limit the extent of these practices.

ties. The results of this review have been published in a report issued in 1998.

These results showthatthere are at least threetypes of tax competition, which could influence the location of investment,(a) competition to attract substantial foreign direct investment, such as manufacturing, (b) competition to attract the more mobile types of direct investment, such as financial services and centres for multinational enterprises, and (c) competition to attract passive, or portfolio, investment.

The OECD reportfocused only on the second type of tax competition, such as financial and other service activities, including the provision of intangibles. The first type of competition, tax incentives designed to attract investment in plant, building and equipment, were provisionally excluded, although it was recognised that it is not always easy to distinguish between regimes directed at financial and other services on the one hand, and at manufacturing and similar activities on the other. The third type of competition, passive portfolio investment, namely the tax treatment of interest on cross-border saving instruments, and in particular bank deposits, was not to be considered in the report. The OECD Committee was examining instead the feasibility of separate proposals to deal with cross-border interest flows, including the use of withholding taxes and exchange of information to ensure that cross-border interest flows do not escape taxation.

The OECD Member Countries who had introduced their own preferential tax regimes would have had little incentive to eliminate them and risk their favoured activities being relocated to another country offering similar tax privileges.The 1998 report made specific recommendations for a concerted action to gradually eliminate the harmful measures and to intensify international cooperation to combat harmful tax competition, including a Forum on Harmful Tax Practices with the aim of promoting the recommendations and guidelines.

However, the impact of the 1998 report was substantially lessened by the fact that two of its member countries, Luxembourg and Switzerland, dissociated themselves from its recommendations and declared that they would not be bound by it. While both countries accepted that tax competition can be harmful, and that concerted action against it is justified, they complained that the report took a "partial and unbalanced approach," and disagreed with several features of the report, in particular that the report was limited to financial activities and excluded industrial and commercial activities, and that it gave the impression that its purpose was not so much to counter harmful tax competition, as to abolish bank secrecy.

3. The EU Action Against Harmful Tax Competition

The topic of tax competition was first presented in a discussion paper of April 1996 prepared for the informal meeting of Economic and Finance ministers at Verona. The meeting largely agreed with the analysis put forward by the Commission. This showed a decreasing revenue trend of direct taxation on investment and portfolio capital, as opposed to the discouragingly increasing trend of taxation on dependent workers, as well as the difficulties those trends created for the proper functioning of the internal market and for employment.

The following chart wasannexed to a paper presented to a later meeting of the Finance ministers. It summed up the situation,but it also constituted a very powerful visual representation of the potentially negative effects of taxation on employment. This issue was important not only per se, but also to underline that taxation problems should not be considered in isolation: part of the Commission strategy leading to the adoption of the so called "tax package" was focussed precisely on that.

Figure 1. Implicit Tax Rates in the EU 1981-1995

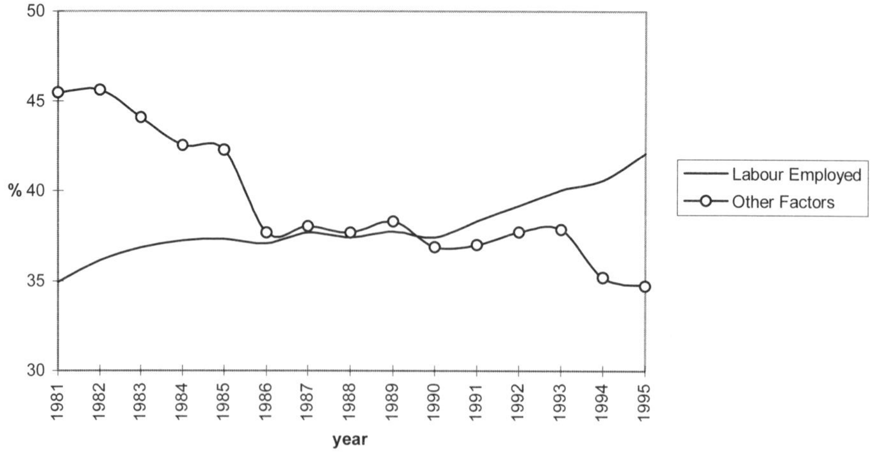

The ECOFIN subsequently instructed the Commission to develop proposals to deal with those problems by establishing a high-level group of personal representatives of the ministers. The success of the proposals to be presented by the high-level group depended on an objective and reasonable approach balancing the interest of the large manufacturing countries with that of the small financial havens of the EU. Therefore, the Code included among the potential harmful measures the tax incentives for manufacturing activities, regional schemes and headquarters schemes whose profits are determined in manners which substantively depart from the international accepted principles.

In December 1997[8], the ECOFIN Council approved a package of proposals on direct taxation, which included the adoption of a Code of Conduct to counter harmful tax competition and eliminate cross border taxation of royalties and interest payments between related parties in the field of business taxation, and the guidelines for a directive on the taxation of income from savings. The Code of Conduct was not conceived as a legally binding and enforceable agreement but, rather, as a set of principles agreed on by the Member States. The Code applies only to business taxation and concerns those measures that affect, or may affect, in a significant way the location of business activity within the European Union.

The Code was based on criteria similar to the OECD's to identify the preferential tax regimes of the Member States. However, unlike the OECD's initiative, the Code was not solely concerned with tax competition attracting more mobile and immaterial types of investment such as the financial or coordination activities, but also with tax competition to attract substantial foreign investments, such as manufacturing. The Code did not itself determine which particular tax regimes were to be considered harmful, but established criteria for determining whether a particular tax regime falls within its scope.

The task of applying the criteria to existing national tax measures was left to a group of experts constituted in June 1998 and chaired by Ms Dawn Primarolo, UK Paymaster General. The subsequent report of the group listed 40 special tax regimes within the Member States and a further 26 in the associated and dependent territories of the Member States,

8. OJ C 2 of 6/1/1998, p. 1.

which were considered harmful within the meaning of the Code and were required to be eliminated. Almost all of the identified regimes had been eliminated by the end of 2003, although some measures benefit from a grandfathering clause allowing tax concessions to continue until the end of 2010.

As it might be expected, there is a substantial degree of overlap between the Primarolo list and the list of preferential tax regimes identified by the OECD[9]. However, unlike the OECD report, the Code included certain holding company regimes, and also several tax incentives for substantial activities aimed at developing regional territories or specific industries and activities, such as the special Irish manufacturing rate, or the regimes in favour of the shipping activities.

Above all it is worth noticing that recently the idea was voiced to link the benefit of European Structural Funds to the respect of certain fiscal criteria. Member States whose corporate tax rate is below the Union's average would be, according to these proposals, denied the benefit of structural funds. In the context of an enlarged Europe, the relocation of certain undertakings to the new Member States which enjoy lower tax rates and cheaper workforce is certainly an issue. Its importance should, however, not be overestimated. Attractive tax rates or low workforce costs are certainly not the only factors that are to be taken into account by an undertaking when deciding about it relocation. Other factors such as: the quality of the infrastructure (including roads, railways and waterways), the cost of energy, the educational level of the workforce or the administrative environment also play an important role, because they have a direct impact on production costs. Moreover, the imposition of such a clause could be seen as an attempt to impose a certain degree of harmonization (towards a minimum rate) and unjustified in light of subsidiarity principle.

9. Cf. the OECD 2000 Progress Report on Harmful Tax Competition.

4. The Application of State Aid Rules to Measures Relating to Direct Business Taxation

Most of the practices potentially harmful according to the criteria adopted by the ECOFIN in December 1997 were also possibly in contrast with the norms on State aid contained in articles 87 to 89 of the Treaty. The Code therefore invited the Commission to clarify the scope of application of State aid rules to measures relating to direct business taxation, and to pursue under Section J of the Code [10]a strict application of these rules against the various regimes listed by the Code.

A Commission Notice issued in November 1998[11] confirmed that virtually any tax measure providing an advantage to particular economic activities, or investments, or regions, may fall within the scope of the existing state aid provisions and be prohibited by the Commission, unless deemed compatible with the common market under one of the exemptions provided for in article 87(3) of the Treaty. However the Notice provided no clarifications on the specific problems deriving from a State aid review of direct business tax measures and on the interplay between competition and taxation.

The State aid rules had been in existence for more than 40 years, but had only rarely been invoked against tax measures. It was only following a new, and more vigorous, approach to State aids in the field of direct business taxation taken by the Commissioner for Competition that the Commission initiated to focus on this form of competition distortion.

10. Section J of the Code of conduct: "*The Council notes that some of the tax measures covered by this code may fall within the scope of the provisions on State aid in Articles 92 to 94 of the Treaty. Without prejudice to Community law and the objectives of the Treaty, the Council notes that the Commission undertakes to publish guidelines on the application of State aid rules to measures relating to direct business taxation by mid 1998, after submitting the draft guidelines to experts from the Member States at a multilateral meeting, and commits itself to the strict application of the aid rules concerned, taking into account, inter alia, the negative effects of aid that are brought to light in the application of this code. The Council also notes that the Commission intends to examine or re-examine existing tax arrangements and proposed new legislation by Member States Case by Case, thus ensuring that the rules and objectives of the Treaty are applied consistently and equally to all*".
11. OJ C 384 of 10.12.1998, p. 3.

In July 2001, the Commission started the investigations of 11 allegedly harmful company tax regimes in eight Member States, and pleaded for existing tax regimes in four other Member States to be discontinued[12]. By June 2003[13], the Commission announced that the Member States had reached an agreement on the measures to be considered harmful within the meaning of the Code, and their elimination. The fiscal aid initiative was considered having played a critical role in pushing Member States to commit themselves to such a reduction of tax distortions.

By October 2003 the Commission was able to report that 15 investigations had been completed[14], and that, in each case, the Member State con-

12. Cf. Commission press release of 11 July 2001 IP/01/982. The procedures concerned the following harmful schemes:, 1) the German Coordination Centres scheme, 2) the Spanish Biscaye Province Co-ordination Centres, 3) the French Headquarters and Logistics Centres scheme, 4) the Irish Foreign Income scheme, the schemes for 5) Luxembourg's Centres de Coordination and 6) Luxembourg's Finance Companies, 7) the Netherlands' International Financial Activities scheme, 8) the Finnish Aland Islands' Captive Insurance scheme, 9) the UK's Gibraltar Qualifying Offshore Companies, and 10) Gibraltar Exempt Offshore Companies, 11) the Belgium's Centres de Coordination scheme, 12) the Greek Foreign Companies Offices scheme, and 13) Italy's Trieste's Financial and Insurance Services scheme. The fiscal aid package also included two non-harmful measures: 14) the French Central Corporate Treasuries scheme, and 15) the Swedish Foreign Insurance Companies scheme.
13. Cf. Conclusions of the Ecofin Council of 13 June 2003 with respect to the fact that *"at the final adoption of the tax package and in the context of agreement on the assessment of the results reached on the rollback of the harmful measures, extensions beyond the end of 2005 of the benefits of the following measures are granted"*. The measures whose duration has been extended to 31 December 2010 include: 1) Belgium's Coordination Centres Regime, 2) Ireland's Foreign Income Regime, 3) Luxembourg's 1929 Holding Companies Regime, 4) the Netherlands International Financing Regime and 5) Portugal's Madeira Free Zones Regime (the phase out period of the latter ends in 2011).
14. The Commission's investigations were all closed with an assessment by the Commission confirming that these measures constituted State aid, respectively for: 1) the scheme for Control and Coordination Centres in Germany, Cf. Commission Decision of 5 September 2002 (OJ L 177 of 16.7.2003), 2) the scheme for Coordination Centres in Biscaye, Spain, Cf. Commission Decisionof 22 August 2002 (OJ L 31,6.2.2003,p. 26), 3) the scheme for Headquarters and Logistics Centres in France, Cf. Commission Decision of 13 of May (OJ L 23 of 28.1.2004, p. 1), 4) the scheme implemented by Ireland for Foreign Income, Cf. Commission Decision of 17 February 2003 (OJ L 204, 13.8.2003, p. 51), 5) the scheme for Luxembourg's Finance Companies, Cf. Commission De-

cerned was now in compliance with EU rules. Among the regimes ruled invalid were those for Belgian coordination centres and US foreign sales corporations' arrangements, the French headquarters and logistic centres, the Irish foreign income tax scheme, the Netherlands international financing activities scheme, Luxembourg's coordination centres, and Sweden's Åland Islands insurance company tax scheme.

Also in its 2003 report[15] on the application of the Notice, the Commission did not clarify the interplay between its action in the field of direct

cision of 16 October 2002 (OJ L 153, 20.6.2003, p. 40), 6) the scheme for Coordination Centres in Luxembourg, Cf. Commission Decision of 16 October 2002 (OJ L 170,9.7.2003,p. 20), 7) the scheme implemented by the Netherlands for International Financing Activities, Decision of 17 February 2003 (OJ L 180, 18.7.2003, p. 52), 8) the Finnish scheme for the Åland Islands' Captive Insurance Companies, Cf. Commission Decision of 10 July 2002 (OJ L 329, 5.12.2002, p. 22) 9) the scheme for Belgian Coordination Centres, Cf. Commission Decision of 17 February 2003 (OJ L 282,30.10.2003), 10) the scheme for Central Corporate Treasuries in France, Cf. Commission Decision of 11 December 2002 (OJ L 330 of 18.12.2003, p. 23), 11) the scheme for Foreign Company Office in Greece, Cf. Commission Decision of 11.7.2001, on the acceptance by Greece of the appropriate measures proposed by the Commission (OJ C 108 of 4.5.2002), 12) the scheme for Italy's Financial and Insurance Centres of Trieste, Cf. Commission Decision of 11 December 2002 (OJ L 91 of 8.4.2003, p. 47), 13) the scheme on Foreign Insurance Companies of Sweden, Cf. Commission Decision of 30 January 2002 (not yet published).

The review of two measures of the original package – notably 14) the qualifying companies in Gibraltar (United Kingdom), and 15) the exempt companies schemes in Gibraltar (United Kingdom) – has been recently finalised with final negative decisions without recovery taken in the context of the review of Gibraltar corporate tax reform. The proposed corporate tax system of Gibraltar has been considered to provide for incompatible aid measures to undertakings established or operating in Gibraltar (cf. the Commission press release IP 04/404 of 30 March 2004, decisions not yet published).

The fiscal aid package has been further completed by other final decisions taken by the Commission on other harmful measures, most notably with respect to 16) the scheme for US Foreign Sales Corporations in Belgium, Cf. Commission Decision of 25 June 2003 (OJ L 23 of 28.1.2004, p. 14), and 17) the scheme on reduction of corporate income tax of the Azores (Portugal), Cf. Commission Decision of 11 December 2002 (OJ L 150 of 18.6.2003, p. 52).

15. Cf. the 2003 Draft Report on the implementation of the Commission Notice on the application of the state aid rules to measures relating to direct business taxation, not yet finalised, but available on the website:http://www.europa.eu.int/comm/competition/state_aid/legislation/business/rapportaidesfiscales_en.pdf.

business taxation and competition distortions influencing the location of business activities across the common market, nor it indicated its strategy on the future monitoring of harmful tax competition.

These clarifications are indeed needed considering that State aid rules are much broader in scope than the Code of conduct: they apply to any tax measures providing for a special advantage to a particular economic activity, or to investments in a particular location in the Member State, while not being limited – as the Code is – to tax benefits granted exclusively to non-residents, or benefits that are ring-fenced or granted in situations in which no real economic activity or substantial economic presence exists.

In fact, the Commission practice in addressing business tax aids has evolved over the last few years in parallel with the surge in interest in the issues, whose most evident representation is the political agreement reached by the Member States in signing up the Code of conduct. It would therefore be the appropriate time to ask ourselves whether the Commission practice of a strict application of State aid rules to measures relating to direct business taxation should be continued in the future.

The currently perceived trend towards accrued tax competition deriving from the accession of new Member States and the confirmation of unanimity vote in tax matters in the recently approved European Constitution Treaty is definitively against the hypothesis of an extraordinary exercise bound to be discontinued in conjunction with the end of the Code of conduct.

The future European policy should provide answers to the question of the relationship between state aid and autonomous fiscal policy, bearing in mind the final completion of the internal market and the elimination of all national distortions to competition. Against this background, a substantive reflection on the practice of the Commission in reviewing direct tax schemes and on the rationale of application of State aid rules to international tax distortionsisappropriate. In fact, to be successful any actions to tackle harmful competition must be multilateral in scope. Thus, enhanced cooperation or other restricted initiatives to fight against tax distortions will always find a limit in the pursue of individual interests of Member States. In that respect, the application of State aid rules thus confirms its critical role in addressing distortions of competition deriving from direct taxation regimes affecting the location of business activities across the common market, even and most importantly in an enlarged European Union of 25 and more Member States.

With a view to pursuing the objective of fighting against harmful competition, the Commission has evolved in its traditional approach with respect to the notion of selective tax measures, and their effects on competition between undertakings. The evolution of the Commission approach over time can be best illustrated by the example concerned with the Commission appraisal of tax measures introduced by Ireland to attract the location of business activities.

In 1980, the Commission had raised no objection to Ireland's reduced 10 percent corporate tax rate for the manufacturing sector, instead of the ordinary 45 percent corporate tax rate applicable to other sectors of the economy. This regime replaced as of January 1981 Ireland's export sales relief scheme under which manufacturing companies were given relief from corporation tax on profits deriving from export activities[16]. In examining again the scheme following the December 1997 ECOFIN resolution on the Code of conduct, the Commission found that the reduced rate for manufacturing activities constituted a selective aid distorting trade between Member States, although not directly aimed at export activities[17].

It is interesting to examine the arguments set forth by the Commission in its proposal for appropriate measures addressed to Ireland with a view to terminating this existing aid scheme, pursuant to Article 88, paragraph 1 of the Treaty. In particular, in its letter to Ireland, the Commission considered that the selective character of the tax incentive was not regarded as met in 1980, while it appeared clearly fulfilled in 1998. In 1980, Ireland had replaced an export incentive directly affecting trade with a new tax measure having the purpose of stimulating direct investments in a specific business sector, independently from its effects on trade. However, in 1998 the Commission held the view that the aid was selective because, and according to the case law[18], whether or not a measure constitutes State aid does not depend on the purposes for which the aid is granted, but on its effects.

16. Letter SG(80) D/8756 of 17 July 1980 on «Export sales relief».
17. OJ C 395 of 18.12.1998, p. 19.
18. Case 173/73 Italy v. Commission [1976] ECR, p. 709, paragraph 13.

The Commission observed that in the Irish case, "a lower rate of corporation tax has the effect that investors in the sector concerned (in this case manufacturing) are more likely to invest in the territory where the rate applies. The measure therefore distorts competition for mobile investment between Member States". The measure was deemed to impose a lower rate of tax on manufacturing companies without any justification based on the nature of the Irish tax system. The reason of the lower rate was in fact to attract mobile investment in the manufacturing sector to Ireland, through the reduction of the sector's costs of production, which was considered to be non structural relative to the tax system. The Commission also found that the measure was distorting competition and trade between Member States because "undertakings benefiting from a lower rate of tax need to generate lower gross profits for a given return on their investment. This enables them to charge lower prices which will therefore improve their competitive position in trade between Member States".

The Commission's shift to a tighter approach in reviewing the State aid aspect of tax measures applies also to the nature of the activities concerned, which can also be financial or immaterial, unlike the manufacturing activities considered in the Irish scheme. In reviewing the aid scheme in favour of the coordination centres established in Belgium, the Commission viewedthat the specific tax advantages in favour of financial or immaterial business activities could lead to competition being distorted and trade between Member States being adversely affected[19]. Referring to certain case law, according to which *"the mere fact that the aid strengthens the firm's position compared with that of other firms which are competitors in intra-Community trade is enough to allow the conclusion to be drawn that intra-Community trade is affected"*[20], the Commission considered that *"the centres, thanks to the advantages they enjoy, are strengthening their competitive position in the sector of services provided to members of the group – in which sector they compete directly with organisations including financial institutions, trusts and consultancies specialising in tax, recruitment, IT, and so on – in addition to strengthening the competitive position of firms belonging to the group which are active in numerous economic*

19. Commission Decision of 17 February 2003 on the aid scheme implemented by Belgium for Coordination centres, OJ L 282 of 30.10.2003, p. 25.
20. Case 730/79 Philip Morris v. Commission [1980] ECR I-2671.

sectors. These are all sectors characterised by intensive international and intra-Community trade, where large multinational corporations compete directly with other multinational or local firms of different sizes"[21].

Following this interpretation, all direct tax advantages relating to all business activities, no matter how immaterial, can affect competition and distort trade between Member States, provided that a direct or indirect connection can be established between such advantages and the undertakings competing in the common market. It must still be tested whether the Commission considers that certain pure tax structures such as the holding regimes, including those listed by the Code, are susceptible to constitute aid. However, even if immaterial, these forms of arrangement could produce direct distortions in the provision of certain managing services (favouring intra-group providers, instead of external suppliers), and could have sufficient spill-over effects on other trade activities to alter the natural development of the common market and influence the businesses' location.

Following this increase in the scope of State aid review with respect to certain measures relating to attracting the location of business activities, it would be appropriate considering what objectives the State aid policy would pursue in this field.

Rationale of the application of State aid rules on measures relating to direct taxation.

The rationale of State aid control in the specific area of direct business taxation has hardly been investigated. Taken from a single market perspective, Member States' corporate tax systems show several inherently territorial characters, as they are aimed at favouring "national" companies (taxpayers) against "foreign" competitors (non-taxpayers).

Firstly, the vast majority of Member States' tax systems follow a territorial approach. Under this approach, the jurisdiction of establishment of an enterprise reduces its tax claim on income deriving from business activities exercised in another jurisdiction, in recognition of the fact they are normally taxed in the other jurisdiction. Thus, by simply manipulating the amount of business income to attribute to business functions abroad, a

21. Commission Decision of 17 February 2003 on the aid scheme implemented by Belgium for Coordination centres, supra, point (100).

tax planning exercise commonly known as transfer pricing, a multinational enterprise is able to substantially modify its global tax burden.

Secondly, the benefit deriving from the allocation of business income to a foreign jurisdiction may never be recaptured in the home country because of the methods to relieve multinational undertakings from double taxation available in their home country. Member States' tax reliefs with respect to business income earned abroad mostly take the form of exemptions, as the income produced abroad is not taxed by the Member State where the company is established. Although some States may provide for a limited credit with respect to the amount of taxes paid by the company in other States where the company conducted its business, the exemption method is more generally applied when the foreign business activities of a multinational enterprise controls a separate foreign entity in another Member State, and this represents the standard in the European Union.

For example, following the transposition of the Parent-Subsidiary Directive on the tax reliefs for direct investments of multinational holdings, the vast majority of Member States fully exclude from tax the profits earned by a subsidiary and further distributed to a holding company.

The benefits of conducting one's business activities abroad through a controlled company are most evident because of yet another reason. Unlike the corporate tax system of other countries applying the worldwide taxation principle, the European corporate tax systems are not neutral towards outward foreign direct investments made by a multinational. By taxing the profits of a foreign controlled entity upon their distribution (repatriation), a Member State tax system effectively defers taxation of those profits. This tax deferral has the effect of reducing the effective tax burden of multinationals, because of the time-value of deferred tax payments. The conclusion in economic terms is that the European tax systems do not ensure capital export neutrality, in that national undertakings are better off investing abroad rather than doing business home, whenever they find favourable tax regimes overseas.

The above observations lead to the conclusion that Member States' tax incentives having the effect of stimulating the localisation of economic activities across Member States' jurisdictions are likely to produce spillover effects well beyond the boundaries of the single Member States putting them into place. They are also likely to alter the natural development of the common market in a sense contrary to the common interest because based on the territorial nature of taxation. Further, they can determine a long term reduction in general welfare due to inefficient allocation of investments across the Union. It ultimately seems that direct tax incentives are effectively susceptible to produce noticeable changes in the price and availability in the common market for factors of production across the Union.

The distortions of competition deriving from these tax rebates are even more evident when other elements are considered. The tax savings deriving from deferred tax liabilities suggest to multinational enterprises to implement tax relocation strategies to report artificial (tax driven) returns and thus distort the investors and the markets evaluation of the companies' performances.

In order to sustain their growth rate over the long term, multinational enterprises have to continuously look for new tax minimisation strategies. To limit market distortions deriving from the tax incentives consolidating their effect over time, it not only seems appropriate to pursue State aid control on cross border tax measures, but also to investigate them sooner rather than later, as the effects of these tax measure are more dramatic when first introduced. In a tax environment where enterprises continuously compete for the most optimal tax deal, we can expect that a derogation in the tax break would be quickly absorbed and replaced by new incentives. It this framework, small and medium enterprises are more likely to engage in harmful tax competition, based upon the relocation of their financial and immaterial functions, considering the reduced costs involved in such relocations.

5. The Specific Scope of the Notion of Fiscal Aid

The notion of fiscal aid is an objective one, and it embraces all forms of interventions imputable to States, whatever their form, having the effect of influencing the location of business activities across the Community. Nevertheless, we should bear in mind that only those tax measures substantively derogating from the normative benchmark set forth by a national tax system are susceptible to constitute aid.

This limitation serves the purpose of distinguishing between ordinary exclusions from taxation and extraordinary exemptions from taxation. National tax systems are normative constructs translating the power of legislators to spread the tax burden when dealing with different business situations, while pursuing substantive equal treatment among taxpayers. Against this background, a tax advantage would fall under the scope of State aid analysis only if it appears to derogate from the normative benchmark or the general scheme of a tax system.

Under the tax expenditure theory developed by Surrey and McDaniel (1985), the way to identify the benchmark or normative structure of a tax system is to define the fundamental issues that characterise corporate taxation of a country, including the definition of what is included in the tax base, what are the tax rates, whether company's profits are taxed twice or there is an integration of these profits when received by the shareholder, how taxes are administered, and most significantly how cross border transactions are taxed. Under this analysis, it is recognised, for example, that certain exclusions from taxation do not derogate from the general tax system and cannot be subject to State aid analysis, if it is part of the normative benchmark of a Member State provided by the legislation.

On the other hand, often legislations and tax treaties contain provisions that derogate from the benchmark or normative response to the fundamental tax issues mentioned above. These provisions essentially fulfil further objectives *vis-à-vis* the mere adaptation of the tax burden to specific business situations or forms; they are intended to address specific economic policy objectives, which are outside taxation, and should be analysed from a State aid viewpoint. Under State aid rules, certain derogations from the standard set forth by the tax system at hand can still be justified by the nature or general scheme of the tax system, in that they pursue general economic policy objectives that, although outside the tax system, are pursued through the tax system, provided that such measures apply without substantive distinctions to all firms and to the production of all goods, and although some firms or some sectors may benefit more than others from them.

We thus come to the conclusion that the notion of State aid is an objective one: Member States enjoy limited discretion in shaping their tax systems to favour the location of business activities in their particular regions or dependent territories at the expense of other Member States. The reasons supporting a strict application of State aid rules on fiscal aid schemes aimed at influencing the location of business activities across the EU are therefore strong.

However, there are two issues of a political nature to be considered.

First, it is argued that the extreme rigidity of State aid rules would prohibit economically independent regions to introduce differentiated taxation rules, while such rules would allow small Member States, sometimes much smaller than some regions, to fully enjoy the benefits of tax competition.It must be remembered, though, that the EC State aid rules are clear in this respect; when the distortions of competition result from the divergence between general measures applicable in different Member States, such distortions must be legally assessed differently than a differential tax treatment *within* a Member State.Only the latter can be considered as selective and therefore amounting to state aid.

The open question remains to what extent the application of principle of regional selectivity is desired in fiscal cases. In other words, to what extent the measures adopted by regions with fully autonomous tax competence, and especially with little intra-state budgetary transfers, can be caught by State aid rules. From the political and economical point of view such regions or dependent territories have very often only limited links with Member State concerned. Moreover, it may seem to be economically problematic, though legally justified, to apply in such a case as a system of reference for the region or dependent territory the "central" tax system of the State.

The second relevant political issue is how to make sure that State aid control in the field of direct business taxation does not end up creating a less favourable tax environment for EU undertakings as opposed to third country competitors, resulting in an incentive for European multinationals to relocate outside the EU. Against this background and with an eye to the development objectives set in place by the Lisbon agenda, the Commission pursues a policy of market liberalisation and of abolition of the remaining tax obstacles to market integration (quite relevant in the area of direct business taxation): in fact the fight against unbridled tax competition and State aid rules aim just at that.

Some examples may help. The Commission strategy on abolition of company tax obstacles[22] in the internal market includes a series of recommendations to Member States to amend their respective tax systems, ranging from Home State Taxation rules in favour of newly created small and medium enterprises[23], to a common Tax Base for EU multinationals on the basis of the International Accounting Standards principles[24], to a common tax regime for the Societas Europae[25]. Some Member States recommend the adoption of a common tax base for all companies across the EU, while other propose a common reduced tax rate for foreign direct investment into the European Union.

It should be emphasised that future competition policy could also provide for some developments in the view oflimiting intra-Community tax competition while allowing the elimination of tax obstacles to cross border activities in a sense which is consistent with the common interest and provided that the advantages concerned are sufficiently open to all types of undertakings so not to negatively affectcompetition and trade within the internal market. In particular, we expect that several areas of State aid review of measures relating to direct business taxation to be potentially concerned with important policy changes.

In fact, under existing State aid rules, tax breaks that are not applicable across the board, or are reserved to cross border transactions or otherwise specific situations would be considered aid. Furthermore, when not aimed at investments eligible to receive aid under the existing frameworks and guidelines within the frame of Article 87(3) of the Treaty, such aid would normally be considered not-compatible with the single market and would normally constitute operating aid.

The Commission should soon clarify its policy on the notion of general tax policy measures which rests outside the scope of application of State

22. Commission Communication of 21.11.2003, supra.
23. Cf. Commission Recommendation 2003/361/EC of 6 May 2003 concerning the definition of micro, small and medium-sized enterprises.
24. The compulsory use of International Financial Reporting Standards (IFRS), formerly known as International Accounting Standards (IAS) as of 2005 has been introduced by EC Regulation N. 1606/2002 (OJ L 243 of 11.9.2002).
25. Cf. Council Regulation N. 2157/2001 on the statute for a European company and the Commission fiscal project cited in footnote above.

aid rules. The Commission has in several occasions recognised that State aid rules do not affect the discretion Member States enjoy in spreading the tax burden across different factors of production, due to their tax policy preferences, nor do they affect the way tax rules are technically shaped to pursue the internal objectives of the tax system.

More particularly, the evolution witnessed in the recent application of State aid rules in the area of direct business taxation would require some clarifications by the Commission on how it intends to exclude Member States' basic tax rules from the enforcement of the principles of non-discrimination and non-restriction underlying the notion of selective advantage under Article 87. From what is indicated above it would seem necessary to consider to what extent Article 87 prohibitions could be seen as instrumental in eliminating all sorts of discriminations and restrictions-found in Member States' tax systems. Furthermore, it should be asked whether the coherence of the tax system is to be accepted as a valid justification put forth by national tax authorities against the challenges by single undertakings excluded from certain benefits provided by the tax system.

The Commission will also clarify its policy with respect to the notion of justification of a derogation by the nature and general scheme of a tax system. Pursuant to certain case law, it would seem that the Commission has the power to exclude certain normative derogations from the notion of selective aid, because these are justified by the external economic objectives that the tax system is charged to pursue, provided such derogations are proportionate and appropriate to pursue these general economic policy preferences.

The Commission will eventually clarify its view on devolution of fiscal powers by a central federal State to its local constituencies. The Commission could possibly take the view that regional tax systems may not distort intra-Community competition and trade when the local tax measures are internally and externally consistent with themselves. More notably, it may be inferred from the legal systems of some federal structures where distortions of inter-state commerce within the federation are constitutionally prohibited, that tax disparities are "unfairly restricting trade" only if specific conditions are fulfilled.

As an example from the US experience, in a 1977 ruling on the corporate tax system of the State of California[26], the US Supreme Court ruled that in appraising the *"fairness"* of a State corporate tax system, consideration had to be given to the system's *consistency*. According to the Court, while it is impossible to impose a standard tax system as model for the States of the Union to follow, the Federal Constitution gives right to assess its inherent consistency.

The Court further developed this idea by distinguishing two elements of consistency. Under the "internal consistency" standard "the tax regime must be such that if applied by every other tax jurisdiction, it would result in no more than the income produced being taxed once". In other words, a tax system is internally consistent and not discriminatory against interstate commerce if, where adopted as the sole tax system across the States, it would ensure taxation of all income, while avoiding double taxation.

Under the "external consistency" test, the operation of a tax scheme "must actually reflect a reasonable sense of how income is generated". Thus, taxation not only has to have a sufficient and coherent relationship with the income that is subject to tax[27], but it also has to respect neutrality with respect to both inward and outward foreign direct investments. Taking this case law as a base, we consider possible to find a standard upon which considering that fiscal devolution is in principle admissible under State aid rules, while preserving the coherence of the power to introduce local tax rules with State aid rules in favour of regional development.

Another area where clarifications may be needed includes the interplay between tax treaties and other international tax preferences awarded to certain cross border transactions on the one side, and State aid rules on the other. Reciprocity in international agreements is a factor to consider and may lead to exclude the presence of aid. The reciprocal advantages

26. *Container Corporation of America v. Franchise Tax Board,* 463 U.S. 159, 103 S.Ct.2933, 77 L. ED 2d 545.
27. Although jurisdictions can abstractly tax income on the basis of whatever nexus they deem appropriate, a universal consensus exists to justify taxation only based upon residence (place of incorporation or effective management) and source (territory).

awarded to companies of the contracting states under tax treaties, could in fact justify under the apparent derogatory treatment in favour of certain undertakings deriving by Treaty rules, because of the general policy objectives pursued with such international legal instruments.

With respect to other areas where Member States take steps forward in coordinating their tax policies in the sense promoted by certain EU policy objectives to favour economic integration between undertakings of different Member States and internationalisation of EU undertakings, the Commission could consider the opportunity of issuing specific notices examining individual projects of common European interest to be considered compatible with the common market, provided they are sufficiently open and non-discriminatory towards undertakings of different sizes and sectors.

References

Vieri Ceriani and Silvia Giannini "Trends in EU Proposals on Taxation of Transational Business Profits and Tax Coordination", paper presented at the Conference on "Multinational Enterprise Taxation in The EU" – University of Siena, 24-25 January 2003.

Paul R. McDaniel and Stanley S. Surrey, Tax Expenditures in the International Context: A Comparative Study (Kluwer, Devanter, 1985).

Part IV

The Framework for Financial Stability

CHAPTER 12

European Financial Integration: Nuts and Bolts

Luigi Spaventa

Financial integration in the EU at large and in the euro-area in particular has become an important topic in the European debate, and rightly so. The most comprehensive definition of financial integration has as its benchmark a situation in which all agents in an area have the same opportunities to raise or invest funds with no discrimination in the access to markets and financial instruments based on location[1]. Standard economic arguments are sufficient to conclude that any progress in this direction yields unambiguous benefits: being associated with efficiency gains and economies of scale and scope, deeper and more liquid financial markets, wider opportunities for risk diversification and improved capital allocation, financial integration would in the end contribute to higher growth and deliver welfare gains [2].

Whereas a single European market for goods is to a large extent a reality, however, this is not the case for financial markets. This is not surprising, as the single market provisions failed to recognize the specificities of financial markets, residing in their highly regulated nature and in the complexity and peculiarities of practices and conventions. The single

1. See Hartmann *et al.* (2003), Baele et al, (2004).
2. Though not necessarily for all the agents, as, at least in the short term, there may be losers as well as winners. The political economy problem is discussed in Giannetti et al. (2002); see also Baele *et al.* (2004).

currency has provided a powerful incentive to the integration process in the euro area, but while one market for goods could develop even in a multi-currency environment, one currency was not sufficient to deliver one market in the financial sector.

Though the broad definition of, and the general arguments for, European financial integration are clear and widely accepted, a more focused analysis of the process meets with difficulties. A few broad-brush contributions consider financial integration in the most general terms and attempt to quantify, or at least to identify, its ultimate benefits. A more precise literature measures the degree of integration achieved in different markets and for different products allowing for the multi-dimensional nature of the financial sector and of the causes of segmentation. Economic analysis is however ill at ease in dealing with precise policy prescriptions, because of the intricate variety of the obstacles to integration: more often than not the implementation of strategic designs becomes a matter of changing or adjusting some institutional, legal or technical nuts and bolts.

The broad-brush renditions of the integration process entirely miss these complications, as I shall argue in section 1: whatever their analytical merits, they are therefore of little use, or may even be misleading, for policy purposes. This is made clear by a simple taxonomy of the barriers to convergence, based on the work on the degree of integration in different markets (section 2). The Commission's Financial Services Action Plan (1999) has sought to address some of these problems by means of an extended production of European legislation. The relevance of this effort will be assessed in section 3. In section 4 I shall ask what more is to be done and shall argue that, with some exceptions, more than further legislation a patient work on the nuts and bolts is now required.

1. Broad-Brush Views of Financial Integration

Though everybody broadly agrees that greater financial integration is a good thing[3], the Commission, anxious to strengthen the political case for its Action Plan, sought to obtain more precise quantitative evidence of its benefits[4]. Whereas the description of the end result is no doubt important, what matters for policy purposes is to know how fast and by which means it can be approached. I shall consider in this light two studies prepared on the Commission's request (Giannetti *et al.*, (2002)[5] and London Economics, (2002)). Alongside, I shall also consider an independent contribution by Rajan and Zingales (2003).

The bulk of the research by Giannetti *et al.* is a relevant addition to the finance and growth literature: they use an extended sample of industry level international data to establish a causal link between financial development (private credit and stock market capitalization) and manufacturing growth[6]. When dealing with financial integration in the EU, however, they confine themselves to two simulations based on the coefficients obtained from their wider sample. As the Union's less financially developed members would gain greater access to external finance in a single financial market, in a first scenario it is assumed that this would somehow allow the EU reach the same level of financial development as the US: applying the previously estimated coefficients to Europe's industrial

3. This has in fact become a mantra to be recited at the beginning of each and every official or private report regarding integration, no matter how technical its specific object.
4. A less ambitious precedent is the Cecchini Report, in European Commission (1998). A more recent attempt is the Gylgenhammer report to the European Financial Services Round Table (a private organization), according to which a single retail market for financial services would increase GDP growth rates by 0,5-0,7 percentage points.
5. This study was conducted under the auspices of the Centre for Economic and Policy Research (CEPR): the reference in some Commission documents is to CEPR.
6. Their research strategy follows Rajan and Zingales (1998), in stressing the importance of financial development for the growth of industries more heavily dependent on external funds: their sample of industry level international data is wider and their findings are confirmed when using firm level data for EU and accession countries.

structure, the result is an increase of little short of one point to the growth rate of manufacturing output. The second, slightly more realistic, scenario follows a vast literature on the importance of institutional conditions for a country's financial development. They find that the quality of accounting standards and, to a far lesser extent, the rule of law and the quality of creditors' protection[7] are the most effective predictors and in the simulation they set these three determinants at the highest EU standard in all Member States[8]: the result is an increase in manufacturing output growth by some 0.75 points, with the greatest contribution coming from improved accounting standards. In both cases the benefits are unevenly distributed, being greater, the lower the initial level of financial development or the quality index for the institutional variables: not surprisingly, Southern or Central European countries are the gainers.

The study by London Economics abstracts from the finance and growth literature and interprets integration as the merging together of the regionally fragmented European securities markets. Trading costs, measured by bid-ask spreads, would fall sharply, and this, according to an estimated relationship, would lower the cost of equity capital by some 37 basis points. It is then *assumed* that a reduction in clearance and settlement costs would (uniformly) deliver a further cut of 10 more points and that the cost of debt finance and of bank finance would decrease respectively by 40 basis points and by 20 points across the board. Feeding all these effects into a multi-country model, yields an increase of the *levels* of GDP by 1.1 percentage points and of business investment by 6 points in the long run. The country dispersion of these gains mostly depends on the initial levels of the spreads (with some Southern countries, oddly, at the lower end and some Northern countries at the higher). Little is said on the prerequisites of a single securities market: a single Europe-wide trading platform, or at least a set of inter-

7. The data for all the three variables are computed (in the case of creditors' rights) or used by La Porta *et al.* (1998), whose papers initiated the research on legal and institutional determinants of financial development. The rule of law is measured by an assessment of the law and order tradition in each country provided by the International Country Risk Report. The quality of accounting standards is measured by an indicator rating companies on the basis of how may of ninety items are included in balance sheets and income statements.
8. Sweden for accounting standards, the UK for creditors' rights, Austria, Belgium Denmark, Finland, the Netherlands and Sweden for the rule of law.

linked platforms, and "a seamless web of market supervision", with "effective enforcement of commonly agreed provisions".

Even apart from the remarkable differences in their approach and results, a general observation applies to both studies. While financial integration is certainly desirable and is likely to have positive effects on growth, it is difficult in principle to establish how much of a good thing it is by means of simulations based either on a cross-country relationship between finance and growth or on the reduced form of a more complex model. As the former is in a way a snapshot of the outcome of long-run trends, the comparative statics exercise of assigning arbitrary values to the explanatory variable has little informative value. In the second case we are presented with partial derivatives, on the assumption that all other parameters and explanatory variables remain unchanged and are unaffected by the experiment. It is in any case sobering to remember that until the 1980's a much lower level of integration and of financial development relative to the Anglo-Saxon economies did not prevent Continental European countries to outperform the United States and the United Kingdom. In the second half of the 1990's, on the other hand, an absolute and relative increase of financial development in continental Europe[9] has coincided with a structural slow-down of growth. While this is certainly not an argument against the accuracy of model-specific estimates, it sounds a cautionary note on their relevance.

Aside from this misgivings, the (widely different) notions of integration used in the two studies are both unsatisfactory. In Giannetti *et al.*, where integration is instrumental to financial development, the first simulation is void of policy relevance and the only *operational* suggestion is to raise the quality of each country's accounting standards to the best European practice. The predicted extra growth (approximately half a point), however, is not the result of markets' integration. If each country in isolation improved its own accounting standards, it would obtain the same reward, in terms of financial development and hence of growth, irrespective of what the others do: the aggregate effect for the area is just the weighted sum of each member's rewards. Suppose however that there are frictions constraining cross-border equity investment: would the indi-

9. As documented by Rajan and Zingales (2003).

vidual effects remain the same, or, conversely, would they be increased if those frictions were removed? We shall never know, first because any obstacle affecting cross-border investment decisions is implicitly assumed away, second because the coefficients of interest are estimated with reference to a panel of countries each of which is by definition a financially integrated entity. Note finally that, if we were to rely on this study's predictions, we could relax somewhat and spend less time on complex legislation: as Regulation (EC)1606 of 2002 imposes the application of best practice accounting standards (IAS, now IFRS, international financial reporting standards) to the consolidated accounts of all EU listed companies as from 2005, the predicted increase in financial development and growth is around the corner. I think that few would agree.

In the London Economics study the identification of integration with the creation of a single securities market and of its benefits with the resulting decline in trading costs is puzzling, and not only because it concentrates only on equity markets. First, it is widely accepted that, while trading costs in major European exchanges are far from high and in line with those in US markets, the true European anomaly is represented by the very high post-trading costs of cross-border transactions within the area: according to LE, however, four-fifths of expected benefits arise from lower trading costs and only one fifth from reduced clearance and settlement charges. Second, there is no evidence that the large number of stock exchanges in Europe has harmed liquidity [10]. Third, the recent trend has been towards an increasing number of competing trading venues: the new investment services directive, "recognizing the emergence of a new generation of organised trading systems alongside regulated markets"[11], has suppressed the requirement that trades be concentrated on *the* (regulated) stock exchange. Fourth, as exchanges are private entities, their

10. See Baele *et al.* (2004), who reach that conclusion on the grounds that the ratio of turnover to market capitalisation is higher in Frankfurt, Milan and Helsinki than on the NYSE if only transactions passing through the exchange trading system are considered and higher in Milan and on the LSE if also off-market transactions are considered.
11. Directive 2004/39/EC on markets in financial instruments, adding that "definitions of regulated markets and MTF [multilateral trade facilities] should be introduced and closely aligned with each other to reflect the fact that they represent the same organised trading functionality" (5th and 6th recitals).

mergers or the setting up of common platforms have no doubt important regulatory implications, but are in the end private decisions, as shown both by the experience of Euronext and by the rise and collapse of the London-Frankfurt merger initiative[12]. In sum, the creation of a single pan-European equity market may be one desirable end result of the process of integration, but can hardly be imposed by policy or even be considered a major policy objective.

Rajan and Zingales (2003) take a different and broader perspective. In their view, what matters more for the growth of developed economies is the prevalence of arm's length market finance over relationship-based bank dominated finance. Though bank loans still remain the principal means of business financing, a shift towards markets appears to have occurred in continental Europe in the past two decades, as a result of the single market and the single currency. This process will not continue, however, and integration will not yield a financial structure more conducive to growth, unless Europe strengthens its legal and regulatory infrastructure, which still trails behind that of the US[13] and is particularly weak in some (mostly Southern European) countries.

Strengthening the institutions on which markets rest should be accepted as an end in itself more than as a way to attain a specific market structure (that of the US) as the ultimate target. No jury has yet delivered a final analytically or historically convincing verdict in what Hellwig (1999) calls the "repertory play" of 'banks vs. markets' [14]. To put it bluntly, "there is no theory that explains how different financial structures of the

12. The first commandment of the City of London (2002), according to which "markets are created and developed by market participants not by rules and regulations" applies in this case: regulators were quite ready to pave the way for iX, as they did in the case of Euronext.
13. The authors' assessment is based on the following indices: shareholders' and creditors' rights (from La Porta *et al.* (1998)), days to collect a check and to evict a tenant, judicial efficiency and rule of law (both produced by country risk rating agencies), corruption, tax compliance, quality of accounting standards, the block premium paid to acquire a controlling block as a proxy of private control benefits (from Dyck and Zingales (2003)). The indices for creditor protection, quality of accounting standards and the rule of law are the same as those used by Giannetti et al.: see above.
14. See Allen and Gale (2000) and the comments by Allen (2003) and Hellwig (2003) to Rajan and Zingales.

euro area should evolve over time" (Hartmann *et al.* (2003)), nor any reason to expect that financial integration will lead to a convergence of financial structures [15]: if anything, there is evidence that in some respects financial structure in the euro-area have become more, and not less heterogeneous[16]. More importantly the role of the characters in the "repertory play" has become blurred, due to the changing role of banks, which tend to transfer their credit risks while drawing an increasing share of their revenue from commissions on the provision of financial services (especially the management of collective investment schemes) rather than from interest margins[17].

The upshot of this discussion is that European financial integration is likely to be an unrewarding task for the economists' broad brush. First, while we can take for granted that it is beneficial in the long run, a precise measure of its benefits is, as we have seen, neither reliable nor particularly interesting. Second, financial integration, especially in an area comprising so many countries with independent jurisdictions, is a complex multi-dimensional issue: as shown by the record of the progress made so far, the variety of markets and of the barriers operating therein requires detailed analysis and specific policy prescriptions.

2. The Uneven Process of Financial Integration in the Euro-Area

A number of recent studies and reports have assessed the degree of integration in different markets on the basis of price, quantity and structural indicators (Adam *et al.* (2002), Adjaouté and Danthine (2003), European Central Bank (2003), Hartmann *et al.* (2003), Baele *et al.* (2004), European Commission (2004), Financial Services Committee (2004)). Though there may be differences in the analytical details, they provide a broadly similar picture.

15. Baele et al. (2004) and European Commission (2004).
16. Hartmann *et al.* (2003) show that the importance of currency deposits and loans has become more heterogeneous in the euro area.
17. See Spaventa (2004).

The introduction of the single currency gave a boost to the process of integration, which had started in the second half of the 'nineties, though it is difficult to detect much progress since then. Progress has been uneven. Not surprisingly, in all markets fragmentation remains substantial at the retail end. The measures used, however, do not tell us the whole story. Whatever convergence has occurred in yields and in asset allocation, such convergence has not extended to the bundle of securities sold to investors in collective investment schemes: fees and commissions show a considerable regional dispersions[18] and moreover have on the whole increased. Integration has been uneven across markets. It has been fully achieved in the unsecured money market and in some derivative markets, but not in the repo market. As from 1998, almost full convergence has occurred in the government bonds market: unexplained spreads persist however between comparable bonds[19] and a unified European yield curve has not yet emerged. The steep increase in high grade euro bond corporate issuance prompted by the introduction of the euro as well as by a surge of m&a activity at the turn of the century seems to have come to a halt, while the markets for high-yield bonds and for asset backed securities remain fragmented. The evidence on equity markets is mixed. Both the importance of sector over country diversification and the percentage of stock price variations explained by pure euro-area shocks are growing and there has been a sharp decrease in the home bias, especially in the allocation policy of asset managers. On the other hand, country specific shocks are still more relevant than in a fully integrated area, the cost of cross-country relative to domestic transactions remains high, the home bias probably persists in the case of individual investors and issuers still concentrate their IPO listings in domestic markets [20]. The retail credit market is the least integrated, especially for short-term and consumer credit, with little or no effect of the euro.

18. The incidence of commissions for equity funds is far higher in Europe than in the US; within Europe it is almost four times higher in Italy than in the Netherlands, with France in the middle: see Mediobanca (2004).
19. According to Adjaouté and Danthine (2003) full yield convergence would allow savings of the order of £ 5 billion.
20. See the evidence in Lazzari and Geranio (2003).

National players still prevail in each continental European country: not only in banking, where cross-border mergers have been rare and the second banking directive has had little effect on the establishment of foreign branches, but, perhaps more importantly, in collective investment schemes[21], which, especially in some countries, are largely controlled by domestic banks.

As this patchy picture shows, there are barriers to integration operating with different intensity and in a different fashion across markets and products[22]. In very broad terms, segmentation may be the result of regional heterogeneity of otherwise similar financial products, due to reasons other than their intrinsic economic characteristics, of obstacles to cross-border trades and of obstacles to cross-border access in the supply of financial products and financial services. The extent to which these broad causes are present depends in turn on the relevance, in each market and for each product, on a variety of factors:

- cultural differences;
- differences in legal systems and in the legal infrastructure;
- differences in taxation regimes;
- differences in securities laws and regulation and in regulatory requirements and practices;
- market factors, ranging from differences in market practices and conventions, to structural obstacles to entry, to entrenched rent positions of the incumbents.

A few examples may give some flesh to this (incomplete) taxonomy. Differences in taxation, in legal regimes and in market practices and conventions increase the post-trade cost of cross-border transactions relative to domestic transactions and are thus responsible for lack of convergence in

21. See Pioneer Global Asset Management Research Unit (2002).
22. With reference to equity and bond markets, Adjaouté and Danthine (2003) note that "the remaining measures of financial integration have to be assessed at the light of our understanding of the microstructure of markets". See also Economic and Financial Committee (2002).

several markets[23], including the repo and probably the government bond markets. The prevailing domestic structure of the banking system and of the mutual fund industry at the distribution stage, which accounts for the price dispersion in retail credit markets and in commission fees, depends not only on regulatory obstacles, but also on the level of entry costs for prospective foreign competitors[24]. Differences in bankruptcy laws segment the markets for high-yield bonds and asset-backed securities. Regulatory differences make it difficult to structure financial products common to all countries in the area[25]. Differences in accounting and auditing standards, in periodic and continuous disclosure requirements, in corporate governance and investor protection differentiate two otherwise identical securities[26]. Full and successful integration of the unsecured money market, on the other hand, is explained by the absence of product differentiation and by the agreement on uniform rules and practices[27].

Three conclusions emerge from this sketch of the available evidence. First, there is no magic wand – no single recipe – that can quickly insure full integration of European financial markets. Second, spontaneous market forces are not sufficient to deliver that result. Third, the incumbents' resistances play a role, but they are not localized in the less financially developed countries: as shown by the record of the debates on a number

23. See the two reports by the Giovannini Group (2001) and (2003). The reports list fifteen barriers to convergence, of which ten are due to market practices and conventions.
24. Regulatory obstacles, including the attitude of national governments and supervisors, play a role in preventing a cross-border presence of banks. Entry costs are important in the case of mutual funds due to the difficulty of establishing a new sales network from scratch.
25 .t has been written that designing common financial products is so difficult in the present European environment that "they would probably emerge like the proverbial horse designed by a committee – a camel" (Kevin Brown, "Call the Quadruped Committee", *Financial Times,* August 4, 2004).
26. "The bundle of rights to which investors are entitled are determined by laws and are not inherent in the securities themselves" (La Porta *et al.*, 2000)
27. The euro and the presence of a European Central Bank were a major stimulus to the harmonisation of market practices, with the establishment of basic interest reference rates for interbank term deposits (Euribor) and for overnight unsecured bank deposits (Eonia). The ECB provided a substantial contribution to convergence with the development of TARGET, a large value payments system. See European Central Bank, 2003.

of European directives, financially developed systems, where self-regulation is more effective and market practices more efficient, are often reluctant to accept harmonization through mandatory rules. It is more like a jig-saw puzzle with several players: some parts will be completed if some strategic pieces are put in their proper places, while others will be hard to fill, either because the pieces are missing (culture, language, legal systems) or because some players do not cooperate.

I now turn to the active role played by European legislation in the past four years in seeking to fill some gaps of this puzzle.

3. Filling the Gaps: The Financial Services Action Plan

Removing the obstacles to integration due to national differences in market and securities laws and regulations and establishing the conditions for mutual recognition were the purpose of the Financial Services Action Plan, launched by the Commission in 1999 and finally articulated in 42 measures, of which more than half of legislative nature. After five years the Commission's pride is justified: the plan "has been delivered in full and on time – a major success for an EU programme of this scale and complexity" (2004b)[28]. Beside legislation, there have been no less important institutional innovations, first in the securities field and more recently in banking and insurance, regarding the legislative process and the role of regulators at the Community level[29].

This ambitious legislative program has met with two kinds of criticisms. One has its roots in the dispute regarding the required level of minimum harmonization, where an extreme view is that mutual recogni-

28. Not quite in full, as two proposals are still to be made and one is under negotiation.
29. Worried by the initial slow progress, in November 2000 the ECOFIN requested a Committee of Wise Men (Lamfalussy Committee) to propose operational recommendations to speed up the legislative procedure and improve the European regulatory system: the Committee's proposals, regarding a four-level approach to legislation and regulation (European Commission, 2001), were quickly approved and no less quickly implemented – another unprecedented event. The "Lamfalussy method" has been extended to banking and to insurance in 2004.

tion, full acceptance of the home country principle and regulatory competition would make harmonization almost unnecessary[30]. Leaving aside some almost theological arguments, which often conceal more mundane vested interests, it is in practice a question of measure. While attempts to establish uniformity with a one-size-fits-all approach may prove incompatible with the variety of country specific legal and market institutions, it must on the other hand be recognized that insufficient harmonisation has allowed Member States to erect regulatory barriers to mutual recognition and hence to competition. A more pragmatic and more justified criticism concerns the legislative technique. A major item of the Lamfalussy proposals was that primary legislation (subject to a lengthy co-decision procedure) should be confined to framework principles, with technical implementing measures delegated to the more flexible remit of a Securities Committee. Though approved by Council and Parliament, this procedure has received only limited application: the new directives are still replete with minute technical details which will be difficult to change[31]. Neglecting these issues, we must ask how far the results of this recent period of legislative activism may help to further European financial integration.

As particularly relevant in the present context, I shall briefly consider the directives on market abuse (2003/6), on prospectuses (2003/71), on take-over bids (2004/25), on markets in financial instruments (2004/39), the regulation on the application of international accounting standards (1606/2002), and the directive on transparency (soon to be approved following an agreement between Parliament and Council)[32].

This legislation seeks to remove the barriers to integration due to differences in securities laws and regulations regarding the provision of

30. The issue is also debated in the United States. See Romano (1998), (2001).
31. See European Central Bank (2003). The Lamfalussy proposal was also dictated by the need to update technical measures according to the experience and market developments without having to change a directive: this can only be done for the implementing measures delegated to the Securities Committee. The European Parliament has always resisted this innovation: its (predictable) reaction has been to narrow the limits of delegation.
32. I shall refer to the directive on financial collateral in the next section. There are several other important pieces of legislation (on collective investment schemes, for instance, and on distant marketing of financial services) which I shall neglect here.

financial services and the access to capital in non-domestic markets and those arising from differences in the "bundle of rights"[33] to which investors are entitled in each jurisdiction. The alleged purpose of the directive on take-overs was to level the playing field in the market for corporate control.

The directive on financial services and markets (replacing the obsolete investment services directive of 1992) is of particular importance. By providing a common legal framework for the authorisation of investment firms and for their operating conditions (conduct of business, market transparency and integrity), it removes some national regulatory barriers and puts mutual recognition on a more solid ground. The elimination of concentration requirements and a new discipline of the obligations of multilateral trade facilities and of investment firms operating on own account[34] will encourage competition between different trading venues. The prospectus directive allows issuers of a wide array of financial instruments to use the same prospectus, filed with and approved by the home competent authority[35], when raising capital or seeking admission to trading in all EU regulated markets. A European passport for prospectuses is expected to encourage cross-border access to capital especially for smaller companies: it is doubtful however that this by itself will be a sufficient incentive and offset all the other costs connected with foreign or cross listing.

33. See footnote 7.
34. The discipline of pre-trade transparency for the investment firms operating systematically on own account (the so-called "systematic internalisers") has been the most contentious issue due to the opposition of the British *(rectius* American) financial industry to the pre-trade transparency requirements (exceptionally, the Council eventually approved the directive by qualified majority). Supportive literature was provided on both sides (Lee (2002), Biais and Davydoff (2002)). It is still doubtful whether the provisions on best execution (article 21) and on pre-trade transparency (article 27, on the application of which the Commission shall have to report) will work. Precisely because of the difficulties of ensuring best execution when trades are no lomger concentrated on one regulated market, a generalized requirement of pre-trade transparency in the case of smaller size trades has a cogent validity.
35. This has been another cause of fierce debate. According to the International Primary Market Association (2002), the requirement to file in the home State even if the offer is made or admission to trading is sought in a foreign market will discourage, and increase the costs of, foreign listings.

Some relevant country differences in the quality and extent of information provided to investors should disappear with the new legislation. All listed companies in the Union will have to comply with common (high level) financial reporting standards and all will have to observe some minimal but quite stringent periodic and continuous disclosure requirements. The transparency directive provides a framework for the yearly and half-yearly financial reports, requires immediate information regarding changes in the holding of equity capital or voting rights and introduces provisions encouraging shareholders' participation at the general meetings. The market abuse directive requests the issuer to immediately disclose any inside information to the public. Following this legislation, some egregious corporate scandals prompted the Commission to propose a new directive (Com(2004)177) envisaging a more stringent harmonised approach to statutory audit. The drafts of two recommendations on the role of non-executive directors and on directors' remuneration have recently been submitted to consultation.

The take-over directive is best forgotten. The Commission's strictures on this unseemly compromise, introducing an *à la carte* regime for Member Countries, are entirely justified: "The result is a disappointing *de minimis* optional outcome [which] does not underpin a level playing field and is a retrograde step in terms of economic reform" (Commission (2004b)).

In spite of this lapse, and notwithstanding specific objections to some of the directives, the implementation of the legislative program launched in 1999 was a remarkable achievement, both politically, as Parliament and Council were led to give unprecedented priority to the issue of European financial integration, and in substance, as the new legislation has provided some necessary conditions for convergence and competition. It will be readily admitted, however, that. there is still a long way to go: what are then the next policy tasks?

4. What Next?

The FSAP was presented as a grand design, and as such it acquired a momentum of its own. After its completion there may be two opposite temptations, both to be resisted. The first is to launch another ambitious program inaugurating a new season of legislative activism: any kind of a mark-2 action plan, beside receiving little political support[36], would be unnecessary and may prevent a concentration of efforts on other priorities to be pursued, mostly of non-legislative nature. Complacent inaction, while waiting for the new legislation to deliver its benefits, would on the other hand be unwarranted, both because there is at least one major gap to be filled and because it is now time to complement legislation with other initiatives.

The major open issue is the inefficient fragmentation of the European clearing and settlement infrastructure: by raising considerably the cost of cross-border relative to domestic transactions, it is an obstacle to achieving a truly integrated financial system[37]. The Giovannini reports (2001, 2003) list fifteen barriers to greater efficiency. The directive on financial collateral ((2002/47) has partly dealt with the one arising from lack of legal certainty. The Commission's intention to propose a framework directive regarding free access of the users to any chosen system and the authorisation, regulation and supervision of the systems[38] should now represent a priority. Removing most other barriers, however, requires concerted action of market participants: a difficult task, considering the reluctance to abandon entrenched rent positions, but also one where the Commission's initiative may play an important political role.

Whereas the proposed directive on statutory audit is an important complement of the legislation enacted so far, the Company Law Action Plan, launched by the Commission with a recent Communication (COM(2003) 284), is to be viewed with some suspicion, as it may enter a territory where the need for harmonization is less evident and where the borderline between statutory norms and freedom of contract is at times ill defined. Energies and resources had better be saved for other tasks.

The mere size of the European legislation produced in four years is such that its digestion will not be an easy matter. First transposition into

36. As the Irish finance minister Charles McCreevy said at the Commission conference on financial integration (June 2004), "There is little appetite among Member States and industry for a further major programme of EU legislation dealing with the financial services sector at this time."
37. See Giovannini Group (2001) and the Report of the Wise Men Committee (European Commission (2001)).
38. See the Communication (COM(2004) 312)

national laws should not only respect the deadlines, but also be uniformly consistent with the directives. Second, experience will inevitably show instances of legislative gaps or, on the contrary, of unnecessary legislative overkill, requiring in both cases flexible and timely changes. An important part of the Commission's activity should be devoted to monitoring the concrete implementation and the effects of the new legislation [39].

Harmonised legislation is not by itself sufficient to deliver reasonably integrated financial markets. National laws in the financial field are implemented in the end by domestic supervisory authorities, which are also empowered to issue administrative regulations. Inconsistency across different jurisdictions of such regulations and of regulatory practices has often been a practical obstacle to integration. The plea for "a single rulebook", consisting of "a streamlined regulatory framework for financial institutions" (Padoa-Schioppa (2004)) is thus well justified. Does it also imply the establishment of a single European regulator? Apart from any other difficulty, at the moment and probably for a long time to come, the question is purely academic: the delegation of regulatory and enforcement powers to a European agency needs a constitutional basis (Ferrarini (2002)) which is lacking in the Treaty and which has not been provided by the new Constitution. One must therefore seek more pragmatic solutions to approximate that objective.

Following the recommendations of the Lamfalussy report, a Committee of European Securities Regulators (CESR) was established and given a two-fold institutional role: helping the Commission in the drafting of the technical implementing legislation (level 2) and promoting regulatory cooperation (level 3). Two similar committees were recently created for banking and insurance. At level 3 CESR is asked to produce guidelines for national administrative regulations in view of insuring consistent and timely implementation of Community legislation in Member States, to issue joint interpretative recommendations and set common standards, to conduct peer reviews of administrative regulation and regulatory practices in Member States. Though level 3 decisions are not legally binding,

39. This is considered a priority by the Financial Services Committee (2004), which also notes the private sector's reluctance to report failures of implementation and enforcement. See also Securities Expert Group (2004).

there are here the premises for a gradual evolution towards a less fragmented regulatory framework[40]. This evolution will be possible under two conditions: first, the newly insitutionalized regulators' committees should be endowed with adequate resources of their own, which are now lacking; second, their members should be ready to accept an intrusion in their domestic regulatory activities by submitting to their peers' judgement. It is easy to predict that national authorities, anxious as always to preserve their discretionary power, will be reluctant to proceed in this direction[41]. A more precise definition of the committees' tasks and duties may be indispensable, as progress in this area is a necessary complement of legislation in order to achieve greater integration.

5. Conclusions

There has been progress towards European financial integration. The Financial Services Action Plan gave the issue a political momentum that was lacking before. Much has been done, but much remains to be done: another plan is not required, but the political momentum should be maintained. It will not be easy, because the tasks ahead are neither intellectually glamorous nor politically enticing: they often regard more the plumbing of the building, which is essential but which nobody sees, than its visible walls. They are not moreover neutral: as the measures required to further integration often touch the vested interests of several groups and constituencies, there will be strong pressures for leaving things as they are. In this context it is up to the Commission to find the strength to monitor the behaviour of Member States and the concrete application of the new legislation, to win national resistances to regulatory cooperation and to prod market participants into concerted action .

40 Though critical of the Lamfalussy proposal, Hertig and Lee (2003) predict a somewhat similar evolution for CESR, limited however to corporate disclosure issues..

41 It is perhaps telling that the requirement of "peer reviews" is present in the Stockholm Council resolution approving the Lamfalussy proposals, but has disappeared in the CESR chart.

References

Adam, K., T. Jappelli, A.M. Menichini, M. Padula, M. Pagano (2002), *Analyse, Compare and Apply Alternative Indicators and Monitoring Methodologies to Measure the Evolution of Capital Market Integration in the European Union*, Report to the European Commission.

Adjaouté, K. and J.P. Danthine (2003), "European Financial Integration and Equity Returns: A Theory-Based Assessment", in V. Gaspar, Ph. Hartmann, O. Sleijpen eds., *The Tranformation of the European Financial System*, European Central Bank.

Allen F. (2003), Comment to Rajan and Zingales, in V. Gaspar, Ph. Hartmann, O. Sleijpen eds., *The Tranformation of the European Financial System*, European Central Bank.

Allen F. and D. Gale (2000), *Comparing Financial Systems*, MIT Press, Cambridge, Mass..

Baele, L, A Ferrando, P. Hoerdahl, E. Krylova, C. Monnet, "Measuring Financial Integration in the Euro Area", European Central Bank, *Occasional Paper Series*, no. 14/April 2004.

Biais, B. and D. Davydoff (2002), "Internalization, Investor Protection and Market Quality, mimeo.

City of London (2002), "Creating a Single Market for Financial Services"; a discussion paper produced by a working group in the City of London.

Dyck, A. and L. Zingales 2004), "Private Benefits of Control: An International Comparison", Journal of Finance, 59.2.

Economic and Financial Committee (2002), Report by the Economic and Financial Committee on EU Financial Integration, ECFIN/194/02, in European Economy, Economic Papers, 171.

European Central Bank (2003), The integration of Europe's financial markets, Monthly Bulletin, October.

European Commission:

- The "Costs of Non-Europe" in Financial Services". (1999),
- Financial Services: Implementing the Framework for Financial Markets: Action Plan, COM(1999)232 (2001)
- Final Report of the Committee of Wise Men on the Regulation of European Securities Markets. (2004a)
- Financial Integration Monitor: Commission Staff Working Document SEC(2004) 559. (2004b)
- Financial Services: Turning the Corner, Tenth Report (2004c),
- EMU after 5 years, European Economy Special Report. N°.1

Ferrarini, G. (2002), "Pan-European Securities Markets: Policy Issues and Regulatory Responses", Centre for Law and Finance, Working Paper Series, 4.

Financial Services Committee of the European Union (2004), Report on Financial Integration

Giannetti M., L. Guiso, T. Jappelli, M. Padula and M. Pagano (2002), Financial Market Integration,Corporate Financing and Economic Growth: Final Report, European Economy, Economic Papers, 179.

Giovannini Group (2001), "Cross-Border Clearing and Settlement Arrangements in the European Union, European", Economy. Economic Papers, 163. (2003),
– Second Report on EU Clearing and Settlement Arrangements.
Hartmann,Ph., A Maddaloni and S.Manganelli (2003), "The Euro-Area Financial System: Structure, Integration and Policy Initiatives", European Central Bank, Working Paper no.230.
Hellwig, M. (1999), "On the Economics and Politics of Corporate Finance and Corporate Control", in X Vives, ed., *Corporate Governance: Theoretical and empirical perspectives*, Cambridge University Press, Cambridge. (2003)
– "Comment to Rajan and Zingales", in V. Gaspar, Ph. Hartmann, O. Sleijpen, *The Tranformation of the European Financial System*, European Central Bank.
Hertig G. and R. Lee (2003), "Four Predictions about the Future of European Securities Regulation", Mimeo.
International Primary Market Association (2002), "Good Intentions and Flawed Execution: Preliminary Comments on the Proposed Prospectus Directive", mimeo.
La Porta, R,, F. Lopez-de-Silanes, A. Shleifer, R. Vishny (1998), "Law and Finance", Journal of Political Economy, 106. (2000),
– "Investor Protection and Corporate Governance", Journal of Financial Economics, 58.
Lazzari, V. and M. Geranio (2003), "Il mercato delle Initial public offering nell'Europa continentale", in G. Forestieri and v. Lazzari (a cura di), *Il finanziamento delle imprese. Quale futuro?* Bancaria editrice, Roma.
Lee, R. (2002), "A Survey of the Evidence on Fragmentation, Internalisation, and Market Transparency", Oxford Finance Group.
London Economics (2002), "Quantification of the Macro-Economic Impact of Integration of EU Financial Markets: Final Report", mimeo.
Mediobanca (2004), Indagine sui Fondi e Sicav Italiani (1984-2003).
Padoa-Schioppa, T. (2004), "Challenges of Financial Integration in the Post-FSAP Period, Contribution to the High Level Panel at the EC Conference on European Financial Integration".
Pioneer Global Asset Management Research Unit (2002), "Household Wealth in the National Accounts of Europe, the United States and Japan", OECD, OEE, PGAM Research Working Paper no. 1.
Rajan R.G. and L.Zingales (1998), "Financial Dependence and Growth", American Economic Review, 88. (2003),
– "Banks and Markets, the Changing Character of European Finance", in V. Gaspar, Ph. Hartmann, O. Sleijpen eds., *The Tranformation of the European Financial System*, European Central Bank.
Romano, R. (1998), "Empowering Investors: A Market Approach to Securities Regulation", Yale Law Journal, 107.(2001),
– "The Need for Competition in International Securities Regulation", *Theoretical Inquiries in Law*, 2.
Spaventa, L. (2004), "Investor Protection: Theory and Practice", paper prepared for the Conference on Chinese Economy and Security, Beijing.

CHAPTER 13

A Second Central Bank Instrument?

Charles A.E. Goodhart and Boris Hofmann

1. Why Central Banks Need a Second Instrument

There has been a welcome continuing trend of improvement in economic outcomes over recent decades, from the turbulent years of the 1970s, through the cycles of the 1980s (and in the early 1990s), to the recent decade of stable, low inflation and much milder cycles of real output. Some (large?) part of this improvement has been due to beneficial structural changes in the monetary policy framework, with the successful achievement of the euro-zone, and the practical adoption of inflation targeting (IT) as a means of achieving price stability, being key milestones in this successful process. Niels has played a major role in cementing these milestones into place, and the world is better for them.

But there is much work still to do. The decline in volatility in goods and services prices, as measured for example by the HICP, has not been matched by any equivalent decline in the volatility of asset prices. Moreover, the globalisation and liberalisation of banking and financial systems, though highly desirable for long-run trend growth, may nevertheless exacerbate shorter-run asset price booms and busts world-wide. An occasion of real fundamental improvement in the economy may generate rising profits and asset prices, which encourages greater bank lending, which raises asset prices yet further, and so on. Meanwhile improving productivity, appreciating exchange rates and strong tax revenues may help to keep consumer goods prices quiescent, so monetary policy does not automatically offset such an asset price cycle.

However desirable on other grounds, the recent changes to the accounting and regulatory regimes, with the shift to fair (market) values under the International Accounting Standards (IAS) and the adoption of Basel II, will do nothing to check such bank lending/asset price cyclical volatility. Indeed, if some of the more pessimistic prognostications about procyclicality turn out to be justified, such volatility may be exacerbated. In the meantime the sole instrument that Central Banks currently wield, their command over short-term interest rates, is predicated to the maintenance of stability in the consumer price index, and rightly so. Despite proposals to shade interest rate decisions to offset asset price volatility (e.g. Cecchetti et al, 2000), the difficulties of doing so (see Greenspan, 2002, Bernanke and Gertler, 1999) are considerable. Rather than distort the use of the interest rate instrument to try to achieve a second objective, what is needed is a second instrument. The purpose of this second instrument would be to maintain systemic financial stability. This latter objective remains a core purpose of Central Banks, whether or not they also supervise the individual banks, and is complementary to their primary role in achieving price stability, but – at present at least – is a field where Central Banks have few, if any, stabilising instruments at hand, apart from emergency liquidity assistance to help mop up after something goes wrong in the financial system.

2. The Form of a Second Instrument

So, the main problem that we diagnose is a dynamic interaction between bank lending and asset prices, particularly property prices, (see Goodhart and Hofmann, 2003a), leading to asset bubbles and busts. We fear that such (systematic) volatility may be unwittingly exacerbated by the new accounting (IAS) and regulatory measures, (see Goodhart, Hofmann and Segoviano, 2004). The need is to introduce an instrument that will have counter-cyclical characteristics, which could serve to check bank lending during asset price hikes, and vice versa.

The BIS have been advocating such general measures for some time, (Borio, Furfine and Lowe, 2001; Borio and Lowe, 2002; and Borio and White, 2003). In the Conclusions to their 74th Annual Report, (2004), they wrote (p. 143),

"Fortunately, the global economy now appears to be on an upward path, and there is less call for macroeconomic stimulus. We should use this opportunity to reflect on the processes that allowed our armoury of macroeconomic instruments to become so depleted. An obvious point, but not without objections, is that this situation should be addressed directly through more aggressive tightening in good times. In addition, policies to strengthen the financial system, and to encourage more prudent lending behaviour in upturns, might help to mitigate the damage in downturns and reduce the need to resort to aggressive policy easing in the future."

The next question is how do you do this? In an earlier paper, (Goodhart and Hofmann, 2001), we had suggested that, analogously to the method of measuring output gap, we could use deviations of asset prices from a smoothed (Hodrick-Prescott filter) trend to assess the gap between the current asset price and its `fundamental' value. But that got roundly criticised on the grounds of inconsistency with efficient market hypotheses. Borio and Lowe (2002) suggest that the rate of growth of bank lending itself is the key determinant of future asset price movements, but the lags are long and the relationship subject to structural changes in financial intermediation, etc.

Our view now is that a better (perhaps best) approach would be to relate the capital requirement on bank lending to *the rate of change* of asset prices in the relevant sector. Thus the capital adequacy requirement (CAR) on mortgage lending could be related to the rise in housing prices, (relative to HICP inflation), and lending to construction and property companies to the rise in property prices. For manufacturing and services more broadly, the CAR could be related to the rise in equity prices, up when equity prices were appreciating, and vice versa. Similarly, required solvency ratios for life insurance companies would be adjusted countercyclically in response to shifts in equities, bond and property prices.

The purpose of the exercise would be both to build up reserves and to restrain bank lending during asset price booms, so as to release them during asset price depressions. In this respect it has much in common with the current Spanish pre-provisioning policy proposals. The flip-side, however, is that it appears to relax prudential requirements most during bad recessions, just when individual banks and other financial intermediaries are individually at their most fragile. But when the concern of the Central Bank is for the aggregate, systemic state of the system, surely this is the right course.

3. Disintermediation

This proposal that CARs get raised in line with the increase in the relevant asset price (relative to the general increase in the CPI) has quite a lot in common with earlier proposals to vary margin requirements for the purpose of limiting fluctuations in equity prices on the NYSE. Hardouvelis, both when at the FRBNY and subsequently, has advocated this, e.g. 1990, 1992, 1995 and 2002. This was heavily criticised, partly on the argument of inappropriate intervention into private-sector markets, but more so on the grounds that there were so many other ways of speculating on the Stock Exchange that a margin call would distort the pattern of flows without having much, or any, effects on overall trading, or prices.

Similarly it might be argued that state (time) varying CARs would lead to pure disintermediation without much net effect. The extent of disintermediation to other *domestic* lenders would, we would expect, be quite limited. In Europe at least, the CARs are imposed on all credit-extending intermediaries, and so the state (time) variation in CARs would affect them all equally, so there would be no distortion between different forms of mortgage institution.[1] Next, SMEs have no real alternative to banks. Large companies do, and this exercise, which would have the (desired, but probably slight) effect of widening bank spreads in (asset price) booms and lowering them in asset price busts, might induce the bigger companies to raise slightly more of their funds in capital market in booms and slightly less in recessions. But that too might be considered on balance a desirable outcome, with the effect of further dampening asset price fluctuations.

On this view the more serious concern about disintermediation, in respect to this proposal, relates to disintermediation abroad, not domestically. Absent exchange controls, which we are *not* advocating, the most obvious loop-hole is for a bank simply to book domestic currency loans to residents through a foreign subsidiary, financing that through an internal

1. Branches, but not subsidiaries, of foreign banks would not be subject to such time-varying CARs. If, and when, the business of such branches becomes large, the host country often requires that it becomes a subsidiary. Moreover the friction involved in switching between banks will usually outweigh any small pricing differentials that might arise.

transfer of funds. It would probably be necessary to require all domestic currency lending to national residents to be subject to the time-varying CARs, wherever booked. That would, of course, leave the possibility of lending in foreign currency in foreign subsidiaries with the borrower swapping back into domestic currency. Again the frictions involved would probably outweigh the comparative benefit from avoiding such differentials in CARs as might arise between national jurisdictions. Moreover asset price booms and busts, even in spatially fixed and segmented assets such as housing and property, tend to be internationally quite closely correlated, so that differentials between nations in their time-varying CARs would tend to be small.

Overall we doubt whether, unlike the case of margin requirements on stock purchases, the effects of time-varying (state-varying) CARs would be much reduced by systemic disintermediation

4. Empirical Details

Even if the principle of state (time) varying CARs were to be accepted, there would be a mass of detail to work through carefully first. If the variation in CARs were to be based on the rate of change of some benchmark index, what would be the period(s) over which that change would be estimated, what would be the coefficient(s), and how often would the calculation be revised, (e.g. would the massive collapse in equities in October 1987 be reflected in revised (lowered) capital requirements the next day, or on December 31, or when?)? Some categories of bank lending relate fairly obviously to certain asset-price indices, e.g. mortgages to housing prices, property and construction companies to property prices. What do you do with other private sector loans; do you not apply time-varying CARs to them, or do you relate the time-varying CARs to some index of cycles in real output, or of equity prices? If the latter, how far do you seek to disaggregate by sector, if at all?

Next what might be the effect of time-varying CARs on bank behaviour, loan pricing and margins, and hence on borrower responses and bank profitability? There are large unknowns, especially as time (state) varying CARs have never, to our knowledge, been previously introduced. Under these circumstances it would seem sensible to proceed quite cautiously, introducing initially relatively mild cyclical adjustments in required CARs, with, say, a maximum variation of + or – 200 basis points, (i.e. a trough to peak change of at most 400 basis points).

We could do some partial equilibrium counter-factual simulations showing how, for a given, historical pattern of bank credit extension, different methods of varying CARs would have led to a different time path of CARs for each country. Depending on the enthusiasm for this basic idea, we could quite easily do this in subsequent research. A *much* more difficult exercise would be to imbed this into a dynamic general equilibrium model whereby commercial bank and borrower responses would affect total lending, asset price and real output, though in principle this could be done in models of the kind developed by Goodhart, Sunirand and Tsomocos (2003, 2004a and b).

For the purpose of this exercise, however, we have sought to illustrate how our approach might work by examining a mechanism quite closely akin to a time-varying CAR, in the shape of time-varying Loan to Value (LTV) ratios in mortgage lending. Mortgage institutions have introduced, for their own prudential purposes, time-varying LTV ratios, and in a few cases, and a few countries, notably in Hong Kong, e.g. in 1991, these were varied as a result of pressure from the authorities for public policy purposes. So in the next Section we assemble the evidence from prior research studies on the effects of changing LTV ratios on financial markets, and consider how the use of this instrument could be an addition to the authorities' armoury.

5. The Effects of Time-Varying LTVs

Only a few studies have assessed the effect of varying LTVs on credit creation and property prices. Gerlach and Peng (2004) analyse the interaction between bank lending and property prices in Hong Kong. They show that the effect of property prices on bank lending in Hong Kong was significantly reduced after banks started to apply the maximum LTV guideline of the HKMA in 1991. Almeida et al. (2002) assess the effect of cross-country variation in the maximum loan-to-value ratio on the sensitivity of house prices to changes in real income and find that the reaction of house prices to such changes is larger the higher the LTV.

Data on maximum or average LTVs are not readily available. Almeida et al (2002) report maximum LTVs compiled from various sources for a large panel of countries, but the data are only rough estimates and are available only as decennial averages. Thus, as there is not much variation in the data at the individual country level, we have to assess the effect of LTV on bank lending and property prices from an international perspective, based on data for a panel of 16 countries. Following the analysis in Hofmann (2003), we model both aggregate bank lending to the private non-bank sector (bank credit) as a function of GDP, property prices and the short term real interest rate, and also property prices as a function of GDP, bank credit and interest rates[2]. The sample period is first quarter 1985 till fourth quarter 2001.

First, we investigate the long-run link between bank credit, GDP and property prices. Prior unit root tests suggested that real bank lending, real GDP and real property prices are I(1), while the real interest rate appears to be a borderline case between I(1) and (0). We therefore decided to allow only bank credit, GDP and property prices to enter the long-run relationship. We first test for the presence of panel cointegration based on the panel cointegration trace test proposed by Larsson et al. (2001). The test statistic is the standardised average of the N individual Johansen trace test statistics:

$$(1) \qquad \Psi_{LR} = \frac{\sqrt{N}(\overline{LR} - \mu)}{\sqrt{\delta}},$$

where $\overline{LR}$ is the average of the individual trace test statistics and μ and δ are respectively the mean and the variance of the asymptotic distribution of the trace test statistic, which are tabulated in Osterwald-Lenum (1992). Larsson et al. (2001) show that the test statistic has a standard normal distribution. The test is one sided with large positive values of the test statistics suggesting a rejection of the null hypothesis of no cointegration. The 1%, 5% and 10% critical values are 1.96, 1.64 and 1.28 respectively. The test results, which are reported in Table 1, suggest the presence of a single cointegrating relationship.

2. For a detailed description of the data and their sources see Hofmann (2003).

As the next step, we estimate the long-run coefficients linking real bank lending, real GDP and real property prices based on a fixed effects panel dynamic OLS (DOLS) estimator proposed by Kao and Chiang (2000). The results are also reported in Table 1 and suggest that there is a significant positive link between real bank lending and both real GDP and real property prices in the long-run.

Table 1: Panel Cointegration Analysis Results

Panel Cointegration Test			Cointegrating Relationship
$r = 0$	$r \leq 1$	$r \leq 2$	
9.69***	1.14	0.44	C = 1.22Y + 0,26P (0.11) (0,05)

Note: The panel cointegration trace test proposed by Larsson et al. (2001). The 1%, 5% and 10% critical values for the panel cointegration test are respectively 1.96, 1.64 and 1.28. The cointegrating relationship was estimated based on a fixed effects panel dynamic OLS (DOLS) estimator proposed by Kao and Chiang (2000). Standard errors are in parentheses.

In order to assess the effect of LTV on bank credit and property prices we estimate error-correction models (ECMs) for the change in bank credit and the change in property prices. The regressors are the lagged error-correction term, i.e. the deviation of the log of bank credit from the long-run relationship estimated above, four own lags, the current change in real GDP, the lagged change in the short-term real interest rate and the current change in real property prices for the bank credit ECM; and the current change in real bank credit for the property price ECM. In order to prevent simultaneity bias from affecting the estimation, the contemporaneous variables included in each equation were instrumented for using four own lags as instruments. The systems were estimated by pooled fixed effects three-stage least squares in order to account for potential contemporaneous correlation in the errors across equations.

We allowed LTVs to enter both EMCs. We did not find evidence that LTVs had a significant influence on the effect of property prices on credit, as suggested by Gerlach and Peng (2004), nor that LTVs influenced the effect of real GDP on property prices, as suggested by Almeida et al. (2004). What we do find is a strong and highly significant direct effect of

LTVs on credit growth. So we included the current level of the LTV, instrumented by its own four lags, in bank credit ECM. The results are reported in Table 2.

Table 2. Error-Correction Model for Bank Credit and Property Prices

$$\Delta C_t = \underset{(-7.48)}{-0.027}\, ECT_{t-1} + \underset{(6.3)}{0.176}\, \Delta C_{t-1} + \underset{(7.65)}{0.204}\, \Delta C_{t-2} + \underset{(5.28)}{0.143}\, \Delta C_{t-3} + \underset{(2.08)}{0.055}\, \Delta C_{t-4}$$
$$+ \underset{(0.39)}{0.092}\, \Delta Y_t + \underset{(0.21)}{0.0001}\, \Delta r_{t-1} + \underset{(3.04)}{0.154}\, \Delta P_t + \underset{(4.44)}{0.12}\, LTV_t$$

$$\Delta P_t = \underset{(-0.65)}{-0.003}\, ECT_{t-1} + \underset{(9.72)}{0.372}\, \Delta P_{t-1} + \underset{(2.15)}{0.072}\, \Delta P_{t-2} + \underset{(4.07)}{0.131}\, \Delta P_{t-3} - \underset{(-3.60)}{0.101}\, \Delta P_{t-4}$$
$$+ \underset{(1.97)}{0.83}\, \Delta Y_t - \underset{(-4.75)}{0.002}\, \Delta r_{t-1} + \underset{(2.559)}{0.189}\, \Delta C_t$$

Note: T-statistics are in parentheses.

The results suggest that *long-run* causality goes from property prices to bank lending, rather than conversely. The error-correction term in the ECM for bank lending is significantly negative, but insignificant in the property price ECM. Short-run causality appears to go in both directions. The change in real property prices has a significantly positive effect on bank lending, and vice versa. GDP growth and real interest rates appear to matter more for property prices than for bank lending[3].

The LTV has a significantly positive effect on bank lending. This finding suggests that countries with higher maximum LTVs also have experienced faster credit expansion. This result implies, in turn, that variations in the maximum LTV may be used to stabilise bank credit. The average standard deviation of the change in real house prices in our sample of 16 countries is about 5. Since the effect of a change in house prices and of a change in the LTV on credit are not significantly different (see Table 2), appropriate adjustments of the LTV within a band of +/- 10 percentage

3. The finding of bank lending being rather irresponsive to interest rates is consistent with the results of the impulse response analysis in Goodhart and Hofmann (2003b).

points around its mean would already suffice to off-set the effect of 95% percent of the fluctuations of house prices on credit growth. Given an average LTV of 80% in our sample of countries, this would imply a 70-90% band for the variation in the LTV in response to changes in property prices, or in other words that changes in LTV could be used to help to stabilize cyclical fluctuations in credit expansion.

7. Conclusions

Central Banks have two main, core, purposes, to wit the maintenance of price and financial stability. They have one main instrument, the setting of short-term interest rates, which is correctly predicated to the achievement of price stability, inflation targets. Another instrument, emergency lending to banks under pressure, is normally only used *after* financial stability has already come under threat, and, owing to concerns about moral hazard, can only be used sparingly.

So, there is a, currently unfulfilled, need for a second instrument, which could be varied by a Central Bank, to help to maintain financial stability. We suggest that time and state-varying capital adequacy requirements (CARs) could play this role. But in the time available to complete this paper we have not been able to do any empirical research on this front. Instead, we have examined a closely related issue, whether time and state-varying loan to value ratios (LTVs) for mortgage lending could be used to stabilise either the housing market or bank lending to it. Our preliminary results suggest that changes in LTVs do not affect property prices directly, but do have a significant effect on bank lending.

References

Almeida, H., Campello, M. and C. Liu, (2002), "The Financial Accelerator in Household Spending: Evidence from International Housing Markets", mimeo, New York University.

Bank for International Settlements (BIS), (2004), *Annual Report*, No. 74, (Basel: BIS).

Bernanke, B. and M. Gertler, (1999), "Monetary Policy and Asset Price Volatility", in *New Challenges for Monetary Policy*, Federal Reserve Bank of Kansas City, proceedings of the Jackson Hole Conference, August 26-28.

Borio, C., Furfine, C. and P. Lowe, (2001), "Procyclicality of the Financial System and Financial Stability: Issues and Policy Options", in Marrying the Macro and Micro-Prudential Dimensions of Financial Stability, *BIS Papers*, number 1, March, pp 1-57.

Borio, C. and P. Lowe, (2002), "Asset Prices, Financial and Monetary Stability: Exploring the Nexus", paper presented at the BIS conference on "Changes in Risk through Time: Measurement and Policy Options", BIS working papers, number 114, July.

Borio, C. and W.R. White, (2003), "Whither Monetary and Financial Stability? The Implications of Evolving Policy Regimes", in *Monetary Policy and Uncertainty: Adapting to a Changing Economy*, Jackson Hole Symposium, August 2003, (Federal Reserve Bank of Kansas City).

Cecchetti, S., Genberg, H., Lipsky, J. and S. Wadhwani, (2000), *Asset Prices and Central Bank Policy*, Geneva Report on the World Economy 2, CEPR and ICMB.

Gerlach, S. and W. Peng, (2004), "Bank Lending and Property Prices in Hong Kong", forthcoming in Journal of Banking and Finance.

Goodhart, C.A.E. and B. Hofmann, (2001), "Asset Prices, Financial Conditions and the Transmission of Monetary Policy", paper presented at the *Federal Reserve Bank of San Francisco and Stanford Institute for Economic Policy Research* conference on "Asset Prices, Exchange Rates, and Monetary Policy", Stanford University, 2-3 March 2001.

Goodhart, C.A.E. and B. Hofmann, (2003a), "Deflation", paper presented at the ECB Workshop on "Asset Prices and Monetary Policy", 11/12 December at Frankfurt.

Goodhart, C.A.E. and B. Hofmann, (2003b), "Deflation, Credit and Asset Prices", forthcoming in: P. Siklos and R. Burdekin, *The Anatomy of Deflation*, (Cambridge University Press).

Goodhart, C.A.E., Hofmann, B. and M. Segoviano, (2004), "Bank Regulation and Macroeconomic Fluctuations", forthcoming in Oxford Review of Economic Policy, Issue on "European Financial Integration", Vol. 20 (4), Winter.

Goodhart, C.A.E., Sunirand, P. and D.P. Tsomocos, (2003), "A Model to Analyse Financial Fragility", Oxford Financial Research Centre Working Paper No. 2003fe13.

Goodhart, C.A.E., Sunirand, P. and D.P. Tsomocos, (2004a), "A Model to Analyse Financial Fragility: Applications", Journal of Financial Stability (forthcoming).

Goodhart, C.A.E., Sunirand, P. and D.P. Tsomocos, (2004b), "A Risk Assessment Model for Banks", Annals of Finance (forthcoming).

Greenspan, A., (2002), "Economic Volatility", Remarks at the Symposium on *Rethinking Stabilization Policy* of the Federal Reserve Bank of Kansas City at Jackson Hole; Wyoming, (August 30).

Hardouvelis, G.A., (1990), "Margin Requirements, Volatility, and the Transitory Component of Stock Prices", American Economic Review, 80 (4), 736-762, September.

Hardouvelis, G.A. and D. Kim, (1995), "Margin Requirements, Price Fluctuations and Market Participation in Metal Futues", Journal of Money, Credit and Banking, 27 (3), 659-671, August.

Hardouvelis, G.A. and S. Peristiani, (1992), "Margin Requirements, Speculative Trading and Stock Price Fluctuations: the Case of Japan", Quarterly Journal of Economics, 107 (4), 1333-1370, November.

Hardouvelis, G.A. and P. Theodossiou, (2002), "The Asymmetric Relation between Initial Margin Requirements and Stock Market Volatility across Bull and Bear Markets", Review of Financial Studies, 15 (5), 1525-1560.

Hofmann, B. (2003), "Bank Lending and Property Prices: Some International Evidence", HKIMR Working Paper No. 22/2003.

Kao, C. and M. Chiang, (2000), "On the Estimation and Inference of a Cointegrated Regression in Panel Data", *Advances in Econometrics*, 15, 179-222.

Larsson, R., J. Lyhagen and M. Löthgren, (2001), "Likelihood-based Cointegration Tests in Heterogeneous Panels". Econometrics Journal, 4, 109-142.

Osterwald-Lenum, M., (1992), "A Note with Quantiles of the Asymptotic Distribution of the Maximum Likelihood Cointegration Rank Test Statistics", Oxford Bulletin of Economics and Statistics, 54, 461-472.

Part V

The EMU Experience – Perspectives for Other Regions

CHAPTER 14

East Asian Monetary Arrangements: A European Perspective

Tommaso Padoa-Schioppa[1]

East Asia is looking at Europe's experience at a time when Europe is increasingly looking at East Asia. The latter's bearing on Europe is becoming more important, both via bilateral economic relations and via its impact on the global economy. This rising importance is not only due to the increasing participation of the newly industrialised economies in the global economy but also, more recently, to the emergence of China and India on the global scene. At the same time Europe's experience is seen as increasingly relevant for the rapid deepening of regional interdependence in East Asia. In the monetary field, one hears rather frequent allusions to the possibility of having, one day, a single currency in Asia. While the recent pinnacle of Europe's monetary achievement, the introduction of the euro, can be seen as too Europe-specific to be of any practical use in Asia, the much longer evolution of European monetary arrangements and the economic forces behind them may be instructive. Indeed, many of the latter have parallels relevant for Asia.

1. The present article was first submitted for publication in International Finance 2004. I am grateful to Blackwell Publishing Ltd for granting permission to re-publish it in the present book volume.

1. Trade Integration: Similarities and Differences

Trade has been the driving force behind monetary co-operation in Europe, and is likely to be crucial in the case of Asia as well.

Since 1970 the average rate of growth in world trade has been 3.5 times higher than that of world output, leading to an ever-increasing interweaving of economies. This year, trade will again expand significantly faster than the projected rate of world output growth of 4.6 per cent. In 2003, the total value of goods and services trade amounted to about $10 trillion, which is not far away from the total GDP of the United States.

Of the total global trade volume, about one-half is intra-regional, mainly within Europe and East Asia. In the EU-15, about 60 per cent of the countries' external trade remains within the region and in East Asia the share is above 50 per cent (by contrast, in Latin America the share of intra-regional trade over total trade is only around 15 per cent). Distance and common borders are among the most significant explanatory variables in gravity models of international trade. The reasons why they explain much of the regional clustering we observe in global trade include transportation costs, regional similarities in tastes and habits (the so-called home bias in consumption preferences), cultural affinity, and a common history or even language. These very same factors also facilitate the undertaking, by two or more countries within one region, of common policy initiatives aimed to enhance intra-regional trade.

Between regional co-operation, and the expansion of trade there is a clear mutual influence. While a certain degree of prior opening is necessary to initiate regional co-operation, it would be misleading to assess whether two or more countries are appropriate candidates for regional co-operation only on the basis of their current trade integration. Regional co-operation is likely to 'endogenously' foster trade relations and thus also foster economic cohesion in the region.

The experience of most regional arrangements – such as the EU, NAFTA, MERCOSUR and, in Asia, ASEAN – suggests that the instruments to promote regional trade can considerably differ across the world and over time. While the abolition of internal tariffs and quotas leads to a mere free trade area, the setting up of common tariffs and quotas for trade with non-members gives rise to a customs union. The abolition of non-tariff barriers – i.e. the prohibition of any subsidies and regulations that favour domestic producers – identifies, together with the full opening of factor markets, a common market. After over 30 years of efforts the EU became a common market. At the opposite end of the spectrum, NAFTA simply aims at being a free trade area, and MERCOSUR and ASEAN can be classified somewhere in between.

Another crucial distinction is that between regional arrangements that remain intergovernmental and those with common institutions and supranational laws. In the first case, it is quite easy for participants to withdraw from certain commitments, as both Brazil and Argentina did within MERCOSUR. Policy decisions are not binding and need national measures to be implemented. In the second case, there is a superior power, which can establish and enforce the rule on another member or a private party. It can be said that the more ambitious the objective, the greater the need for a degree of supra-nationality.

Europe's very far reaching integration can be traced to a number of factors. After WWII, there was a recognised need for mutual opening of national markets in Western Europe to foster trade and exploit economies of scale. Against this background the Treaty of Rome (1957) explicitly set, for a core group of six countries, the objective of creating a common market based on the free movement of goods, services, labour and capital – the so-called "four freedoms". The process started with the removal of tariffs and quotas, and the creation of a "customs union" (1968).

The Treaty of Rome recognised that other, more opaque barriers hindered exchange, such as non-tariff or regulatory barriers. Such barriers had often been set up for worthy reasons, like the safeguard of worker and consumer health. Hence, the microeconomic regulations underlying them were difficult to remove and could not simply be dismantled. They had to be replaced by common regulations, through an exceedingly vast and slow legislative process.

In 1979, European trade integration received a boost when a court case established the principle of mutual recognition, which prohibits members from closing their domestic market to products lawfully manufactured in other member states. Six years later, concern over the persistence of physical, technical and fiscal barriers led to the Single European Act (an amendment of the Treaty of Rome), which set 1992 as the deadline for the removal of remaining barriers, and the achievement of a unified market.

As more and more countries joined over the years the endeavour of the six founding members, the European Union expanded from 6 to 12 in the 1980s, to 15 in 1995 and to 25 in 2004.

While intra-regional trade grew as a share of total trade among the EU members, the extra-regional trade of the group as a share of GDP also increased significantly over the years, which shows that regional integration does not come at the expense of trade with the rest of the world. Trade creation dominates trade diversion.

Turning to Asia, three peculiarities appear with respect to the pattern followed by Europe. The first is that differences in living standards are considerably larger in East Asia than in the European Union, even when the latter includes the very low income per capita of most of the 10 countries that have just joined it. At the start of the European process in 1960, the GDP per capita of Italy and Luxembourg accounted for, respectively, 80 per cent and around 130 per cent of the simple average of incomes per capita of the six founding countries. By contrast, in North East Asia – i.e. Japan, China, South Korea, Hong Kong and Taiwan – income disparities in the early 1970s ranged from about 25 per cent of the group average in China to 300 per cent in Japan.

A second and related peculiarity concerns the type of integration followed by the two regions. Intra East Asian trade is mainly in intermediate goods, particularly electronics. This contrasts sharply with trade in Europe, which tends to be more in final goods in the same industry, such as motor vehicles, appliances, other consumer durables, food, and machine tools. The pattern followed by East Asia is largely determined by income disparities, and comes closer to the classic model of specialisation and comparative advantage than the one followed by Europe, where living standards are more homogeneous. At the current juncture, despite some lessening of the aforementioned income disparities in the early 1970s – with GDP per capita in Singapore and Hong Kong now accounting for above half that of Japan – the incomes per capita of most other Asian countries are still below 10% of Japan's.

The third peculiarity concerns the method of integration. In Europe the process was strongly driven by politics and was based on the creation and development of a robust institutional framework comparable to that of a state system. This framework implies formal membership, legally binding arrangements, and a legislative and a judiciary power. In Asia, instead, the process has been largely market driven and primarily based on informal, intergovernmental and ad hoc arrangements among governments. Even the contours of the group are rather loose, with a variable composition of participants depending on the subject matter. In a nutshell, contrary to Europe, the development of regional trade in Asia has not waited to be formally enshrined in institutional arrangements to reach a significant magnitude.

Peculiarities make similarities even more striking. Both in Europe and East Asia, the early stage of industrial take off was largely export driven. Japan and the countries that joined it in the 1960s – Singapore, Korea, Taiwan – focused on serving markets external to the region, in particular the United States, in recognition of the lower consumption potential of their neighbours.

Today the whole East Asian region is set on a high growth path. What was among the poorest regions in the world forty years ago has grown on average by over 7 per cent per year since the mid-1980s. GDP per capita in China has multiplied by almost four since 1981. Just as in Europe, intra-regional trade has expanded in parallel with trade openness. From 1982 to the present, the intra-regional trade of the five founding members of ASEAN (Indonesia, Malaysia, the Philippines, Singapore and Thailand) plus Japan, China, Korea, Taiwan and Hong Kong has risen from 35 per cent to above 50 per cent. Trade openness of the region has moved from 30 to 40 per cent.

It is striking that intra-regional trade is so high in spite of the very strong bilateral trade relations of East Asia with the United States. A plan for an ASEAN Free Trade Area was launched in 1992 and, in 2002, six ASEAN countries reduced internal tariffs on most goods to below 5 per cent. The whole ASEAN region is scheduled to become a fully-fledged free trade area in the coming years.

2. Financial Liberalisation and Integration

Turning from trade to finance, the movement of capital and the provision of financial services across frontiers were very often impeded under the early years of the Bretton Woods regime. The two forms of financial repression were used to preserve monetary policy autonomy, to shield the economy from international sources of instability, to protect the domestic financial system, and to preserve the exchange rate from high volatility and large movements.

Over time, as trade expanded, financial repression became less and less sustainable. Indeed, exchanges in goods and services require currency convertibility for their settlement. Convertibility, in turn, allows market participants to exploit trade-related transactions as a way to move capital across borders. Technological and financial innovation do their part in facilitating the circumvention of administrative restrictions.

Moreover, as experience has shown that financial repression could become itself a source of fragility, the safeguard of financial stability was increasingly sought in proper regulation and prudential supervision. The desirability of the free movement of capital to accompany the free movement of trade became gradually almost globally uncontested.

In spite of the above, liberalisation tends in general to proceed much more slowly in the field of finance than in that of trade. In many emerging economies throughout the world capital controls continue to operate, the domestic financial system is protected and the financial transactions of firms and households are subject to restrictions. In China, for instance, while the renminbi became convertible for current account transactions in 1996, and the country has already to a large extent liberalised most transactions related to foreign direct investment, substantial restrictions are maintained on other capital flows. Analogous considerations apply to Asian countries like India and Malaysia.

The expansion of regional trade that started in Europe in the 1950s set in motion powerful forces for financial liberalisation. Indeed the free circulation of capital and the free supply of financial services within the frontiers of the common market were integral parts of the programme established by the Treaty of Rome. The European experience has been one of a full traverse from opening trade, to deregulating financial markets, to freeing the capital account, to increasing monetary co-operation up to the eventual introduction of a single currency.

This traverse, however, was accomplished only very slowly and not without pauses and retreats. Until the end of the 1980s, restrictions on the movement of capital remained in place and continued to be regarded, albeit with decreasing conviction, as a key policy instrument for industrial countries. France and Italy completed the process of liberalisation only in 1990. Spain, Portugal and Ireland made use of temporary restrictions during the 1992 exchange rate crisis. Finally, it was not until 1 January 1994, under a rule in the Maastricht Treaty on European Union, that permanent and/or temporary restrictions on capital movement were entirely lifted.

A final remark on financial opening and liberalisation in Europe is that, unlike for manufacturing and agriculture, the process was carried out in parallel in intra-European relationships and vis-à-vis the outside world.

Looking now at East Asia, a European observer is struck by the fact that, like in Europe, trade integration has proceeded in the region faster than in finance, where, however, it is now underway.

Until 1994, not even Japan, then still the sole East Asian economy belonging to the group of advanced industrial countries, had liberalised the capital account to an extent comparable to that of the other G7 economies. In the course of the 1990s, many other East Asian governments undertook capital flow liberalisation and partial financial market deregulation. The exuberant optimism shown by international financial markets towards the fast-growing region, coupled with fragility in some parts of the financial system, culminated in the crises of 1997-98.

Since the crises, important progress has been made towards limiting vulnerability and strengthening financial systems. This has occurred mainly under the aegis of global initiatives promoted by the G7 and implemented by various international fora (such as the Basel Committee on Banking Supervision or IOSCO) and by the Bretton Woods institutions. As a result of these initiatives there has been good progress in the restructuring of financial systems, as well as in the regulation and prudential supervision of domestic financial sectors.

Yet, with the exceptions of Hong Kong and, to a lesser extent, Japan and Korea, the East Asian countries still have not liberalised their financial systems in the way the EU and the United States have done.

It is well known that when the crisis of the late 1990s erupted, Japan made the proposal to deal with it by creating co-operative arrangements on a regional scale. The idea did not meet the support of the United States and the IMF, and was abandoned. Yet, in recent years regional cooperation among East Asian countries has made some initial steps in the financial field. To help countries that may experience balance of payments difficulties, a system of bilateral swap arrangements has been set up through the so-called Chiang Mai initiative. Efforts to integrate financial markets in the region have also been undertaken. The most relevant are the Asian Bond Fund initiatives I and II of the EMEAP Group of central banks and monetary authorities, and the Asian Bond Market Initiative of the ASEAN+3 group of countries. Such efforts aim to develop regional bond markets.

The intra-regional dialogue is also strengthening through annual meetings of ASEAN+3 Finance Ministers and of EMEAP central bank governors. The ASEAN+3 group of Finance Ministers has initiated several projects designed to improve regional financial co-operation, including the Monitoring of Capital Flows and an Early Warning System. ASEAN has set up working groups to investigate issues related to greater co-operation and to deliver economic studies for deliberation by the regions' politicians. In time, these should assist in the process of addressing weaknesses in some financial systems and in overcoming concerns regarding excessive segmentation of domestic financial systems and divergences in countries' financial structures.

3. Money and Exchange Rates

Trade integration, financial integration, and monetary and exchange rate policies have obvious and far-reaching interrelations. Trade links between countries foster the opening of financial channels, thus pushing towards the gradual liberalisation of the capital account. In turn, the financial sector profoundly interacts with the exchange rate. For example, a perception of financial fragility can lead to a withdrawal of funds not only from an individual financial institution, but also out of the country more generally, thereby putting downward pressure on the exchange rate. In addition, given that the depreciation of a currency may have contagion effects and cross-border repercussions, the financial system of third countries, and thus the exchange rate, could also come under pressure.

Conversely, both trade and financial market integration need to be assisted by an appropriate monetary and exchange rate configuration. Trade and financial transactions are affected by the exchange rate, and exchange rate movements can disturb (or facilitate) the process in a number of ways. The exchange rate may act as a barrier through the transaction costs it imposes or, more importantly, on account of the uncertainty and instability it may generate. It may also act as a channel in the transmission of shocks between countries.

For all these reasons, regional co-operation in the field of exchange rates makes sense and its deepening is entirely consistent with a deepening of real sector interdependence. There emerges a virtuous circle between real sector integration and exchange rate stability. By promoting a more efficient allocation of resources, the expansion of trade and exchange rate stability are likely to jointly support output growth, which, in turn, facilitates the opening-up of markets and the maintenance of a stable exchange rate.

The choice of the exchange rate or monetary regime is not at the complete discretion of governments because it must respect the logic of the so-called "inconsistent quartet". Under this logic, if they opt for free trade and free capital mobility, countries must choose between fixed exchange rates and monetary policy autonomy, since the two are not possible simultaneously. A widely developed regional trade provides a strong case for some degree of exchange rate fix, and the deeper is interdependence, the stronger is such a case. Acknowledging this case implies accepting a concomitant limitation of monetary policy autonomy.

To be fair, all this does not totally exclude combining a degree of regional integration with the maintenance of fluctuation of national currencies. The NAFTA experience illustrates this point. However, as interdependence deepens beyond a free trade area and moves towards a fully-fledged single market, major swings in exchange rates can dramatically shift competitive advantages, alter the rationality of economic calculations, affect profitability and even trigger political tensions. Increasing degrees of interdependence call for increasingly reliable exchange rate stability, which imply greater monetary co-operation and, ultimately, may require a single currency.

In Europe, the quest for exchange rate stability has always been at the heart of co-operative efforts, and its importance has increased in parallel with the deepening of economic interdependence. A single market has been gradually created through the implementation of the free flow of goods, services, capital and workers; the prohibition of subsidies and protectionist regulations; and the enforcement of fundamental laws governing economic activity in supranational courts.

That the 1957 Treaty of Rome only called for a rather loose commitment to treat exchange rate policies "as a matter of common interest" was just an appearance. In reality, such loose commitment had, as a solid backdrop, the strong framework of the Bretton Woods fixed exchange rates regime. True, that system was a global and US-dollar based one, but in practice it played the crucial role of providing exchange rate stability to the European regional co-operative efforts up to the 1970s. Thus, for the first 15 years of its history, European integration proceeded on the basis of a single regime, a regime which presided simultaneously over internal and external, i.e. regional and global, exchange rate relationships.

The transition from a single to a split regime came when the Bretton Woods system collapsed, and was not an easy one. Indeed it took most of the 1970s for Europe to engineer the combination of a "global float with regional peg", that lasted until the adoption of the euro in 1999.

The debate over what sort of European monetary arrangement could replace or complement the one based on the dollar had already begun in the late 1960s, when cracks had started to appear in the edifice of the global fixed exchange rate regime. Then, in the course of the 1970s, Europe de-linked from the dollar and started building its own regional monetary order. Initially it was a small regional peg only involving the currencies of few open countries of limited size – Belgium, Denmark, Luxembourg and the Netherlands – adopting the DM as their anchor (the so-called "snake"). In 1979 this was replaced by the more structured European Monetary System (EMS), in which "large" countries such as France and Italy also took part. By the end of the 1970s, Europe was firmly on a regional peg, while floating vis-à-vis the dollar and the rest of the world.

In the course of the 1980s, also thanks to the exchange rate order provided by the EMS, the integration process took on a new impetus and was extended to the financial field. Inside Europe the conviction gained ground, among both observers and policy makers, that exchange rate instability had to be removed in order to fully reap, and at the same to firm up, the benefits of deepening interdependence. This conviction was strengthened by the "inconsistent quartet" argument, suggesting that the Single Market programme risked being disrupted by exchange rate movements. As the expansion of intra-regional trade was complemented by increasing financial integration and liberalisation, the threat to exchange rate stability grew, and the rationale for pooling monetary sovereignty became increasingly compelling. Eventually the single currency was agreed upon (1991) and implemented (1999).

The euro represents Europe's solution to the "inconsistent quartet". However, the decisive factor in pursuing regional monetary co-operation was undoubtedly a political one, which was not so much based on the technical arguments put forward by economists, as on the political determination to press ahead with the construction of a united Europe. Leaders such as Kohl and Mitterrand espoused the idea of a single currency largely for its strong symbolic appeal. Political will made possible the institutional leap necessary to switch from a system of largely fixed exchange rates to a single currency with a single monetary policy. Monetary union could not have proceeded without this political commitment.

Turning now to East Asia and looking at it through the glasses of the European experience, one sees interesting analogies with problems and challenges Europe was facing in the 1970s. In East Asia, intra-regional trade has gone almost as far as in Europe. Financial liberalisation and opening is at an early stage but progressing, while exchange rate relations are still largely governed by the US dollar.

Indeed most countries in the region strongly refer to an external currency for their exchange rate policy, and this currency is the US dollar. China, Hong Kong and Malaysia are on a tightly pegged regime vis-à-vis the dollar. In the heavily managed floating regimes of Korea, Taiwan, Thailand and Indonesia, the importance of the dollar is on the order of 75 to 95 per cent (see McKinnon and Schnabl, 2003). Even Japan, whose currency is in the league of three key international currencies, has shown a propensity to manage its float much more actively than Europe or the US. Seen in this light, one could say that Asia is still on a sort of dollar standard.

In a way, this situation has a parallel in post World War II Europe. When the Bretton Woods system came to an end, European currencies de-linked from the US dollar, while most Asian currencies maintained their pegs to the dollar, either *de jure* or *de facto*. This has remained the case even after the Asian crisis had revealed the drawbacks of the tight US dollar orientation.

The use of the US dollar as an exchange rate anchor for most of the currencies in the region has served East Asia well in many respects. It has underpinned the expansion of bilateral trade with the United States; it has provided a relatively transparent framework; and it is well understood by financial markets, the business sector, and the public at large. More importantly perhaps, it has provided an orderly exchange rate background to the rapid growth of trade in the region.

At the same time, however, the dollar standard is not without problems. Looking back to the 1990s, the link to the dollar was one of the factors leading to the crises, at the time when a depreciating Japanese yen against a strong US dollar negatively affected the competitiveness of some emerging Asian economies. More recently, while there may have been reasons for the US dollar to depreciate over the past two years, there are fewer reasons, from the point of view of economic fundamentals, why depreciation should have been warranted for East Asia. The region is already, in some parts, dealing with overheating and with rapidly expanding monetary and credit aggregates. Widening current account surpluses and the strong build-up in reserves associated with the exchange rate management are additional sources of potential instability. This explains the increasing calls of the G7 for greater flexibility in Asia's exchange rates.

Although regional monetary co-operation in East Asia is still limited, the Chiang Mai bilateral swap agreements, the Asian Bond Fund, and an increasing network of policy consultations among Asian authorities – to which I referred in the previous section – suggest that a co-operation framework is gradually taking shape.

4. Options for Asia

If the tight US dollar orientation that prevails throughout Asia were to be considered sub-optimal, the question arises as to an alternative exchange rate arrangement for the region. Four categories come to mind: floating for all, a reference to a basket, an intra-Asian exchange rate arrangement, and a single Asian currency.

Without aiming at analysing in detail the appropriateness of any of the four alternatives, a few remarks might be offered on each. First, *floating for all* would imply the adoption of an exchange rate arrangement which is fashionable today and in line with the so-called bipolar view of sustainable regimes. However, while appealing in theory, floating is not easy in practice. Even among the major currency blocks, long periods of independent floating are interrupted by occasional intervention because serious misalignments do occur. Such interventions were not only frequent for the Japanese yen, but even for the euro, the Deutsche Mark and the US dollar. For medium-sized economies, floating is often even less desirable, because the exchange rate may serve as a policy anchor, and markets may be too small to adjust to large changes in capital flows.

Second, *reference to a basket* has some intellectual appeal and is discussed often nowadays. It has the advantage of cushioning the very large exchange rate swings that have been observed between the major currencies. For example, if China had pegged to a basket of major currencies rather than the US dollar alone, the roughly 10 per cent effective depreciation it has experienced since the turn of the millennium would have been attenuated or even avoided altogether. However, baskets are not always easy to manage. They require a liquid foreign exchange market in all reference currencies, and it may be more difficult to manage a banking system for that reason. Baskets have also sometimes proven to be difficult to communicate, because the reference currency established by the basket is not directly quoted in markets or newspapers.

The third option, *an intra-Asian exchange rate arrangement* of the type of the EMS, would be a clear step towards a regional monetary organisation. It would have the advantage of providing an order to intra-regional trade relations, making it independent of the vicissitudes of external currencies. It would also imply a significant commitment of policy makers in the area to co-operation in the field of economic policy. Of course, it would require an assessment of appropriate bilateral exchange rate grids, which are not easy to quantify and to agree with. Moreover, it might involve accepting, de facto, one "leader" in the system, which may be politically and economically arduous. At the time of the first European exchange rate mechanism the policy leader was the Deutsche Mark, but the System was constructed in a symmetrical way .

The fourth option, *a single currency*, would require not only a very advanced degree of economic cohesion, but also strong political support and commitment, as well as the development of common institutions. It would also postulate harmonisation in the legal environment and in financial markets. There are not many experiences of common currencies around the world, and the European experience suggests that a single currency takes decades, not just years, to develop. For this reason, too, it would be surprising if authorities in Asia were to focus today on what can, at best, be the possible endpoint of a monetary co-operation process stretching over decades.

If anything, the European experience suggests the general proposition that consistency of the exchange rate regime with the underlying structural economic relations is key in order to reap the benefits of economic interdependence. It is unlikely that this consideration would imply a monetary union for Asia at the current juncture, but it is plausible that it should imply a closer form of exchange rate co-operation than is the case in Asia today.

5. Conclusion

While defining its own way of pursuing greater regional integration, East Asia shows a keen interest in Europe's experience. In this respect, it may find it useful to focus not only on the very latest, and in a way narrow, steps leading to the introduction of the euro, but also on the wider landscape of trade, monetary and financial co-operation over many decades.

At the risk of oversimplification, the sequence of economic forces and developments that have led Europe can be described as follows. First there was an opening up of the economies to trade after World War II, in an effort to improve allocation ef-ficiency and international integration. Then, the strong regional patterns in trade relations emerged. Thereafter the process was extended to financial integration, including the liberalisation of capital movements and the free provision of financial services cross-border. Europe discovered a need for a single currency at a very advanced stage of its economic interdependence. However, it felt necessary, from an early stage, to create an exchange rate or monetary arrangement consistent with the economic order it was gradually creating. Since the economic order was evolving, the monetary order also needed adjustment.

The increasing importance of economic relations within the East Asian region, and the noticeable advancements in various forms of co-operation, suggest that some regional monetary order may become helpful at some perhaps not too distant point in the future.

Forms of monetary co-operation range from loose consultation among peers to permanent policy co-ordination or even monetary union. The crucial quantum leap along this range is the one between permanent co-ordination and a single monetary policy, because it requires an enormous political, cultural, legal, technical and institutional leap: a leap from an *inter*-national to an *intra*-national (i.e. domestic) dimension. As such, there is still a major difference between the common locking of exchange rates by a number of different countries that still retain monetary sovereignty and the introduction of a single currency, central bank and monetary policy.

The so far prevailing dollar orientation has served the East Asian region well in recent years. However, in the recent past it contributed to the Asian crisis and, looking forward, it may imply an excessively accommodative monetary policy as the dollar depreciates, which might produce overheating and asset price bubbles. The reference to an external currency may not be a steady-state solution, and some adjustments will perhaps be considered at one stage.

In this context, the European experience with regional monetary arrangements may serve as a point of reference as it has allowed for the coexistence of a certain degree of *fixity inside* the region and, since the collapse of Bretton Woods, *flexibility outside* the region. When differentiating between the inside and the outside dimension, the determination of exchange rate may be more complex than simply spanning the space between a fixed and a floating regime. But it also indicates that the available policy options are greater than they may appear at first sight.

References

McKinnon, R. and Schnabl, G. (2003): "The East Asian Dollar Standard, Fear of Floating, and Original Sin", Working Papers 03001, Stanford University, Department of Economics.